Azure Cosmos DB for .NET Developers

by Benjamin Day

https://www.benday.com

May 11, 2026

Table of Contents

Chapter 1 How We Got Here: The Hidden Tax of Relational Development

Before we can talk about Cosmos DB, we need to talk about the world we're coming from. Not because there's anything wrong with it — relational databases are genuinely great technology — but because there's a cost to the relational model that most application developers have been paying for so long they've stopped noticing it. It's like a noise in your house that you only hear when someone visits and says "what's that humming sound?"

This chapter is about making the humming audible. Once you can hear it, the document model isn't just an alternative — it's an answer to a question you didn't know you were asking.

Why Relational Databases Exist

Here's a piece of context that changes how you think about database design: relational databases are an engineering response to expensive storage.

When Edgar Codd published his relational model in 1970, disk storage cost roughly $700,000 per gigabyte (in 2026 dollars). Storing the same piece of data twice wasn't just wasteful — it was genuinely expensive. Normalization — the practice of splitting data into separate tables and eliminating redundancy — wasn't an aesthetic preference. It was an economic necessity. You literally couldn't afford to store a customer's name in both the Customers table and the Orders table.

That economic pressure produced an elegant system. Flat tables. Foreign keys. JOINs to reassemble related data on the fly. Every piece of information stored exactly once. Need the customer's name on an order? Don't store it — JOIN to the Customers table and look it up. A side benefit of this economic constraint is that this design ensures that the data is always consistent because there's only one copy of it.

This is genuinely brilliant engineering for the problem it was solving. And it created a model that's optimized for something most people don't think about: **asking questions you haven't thought of yet.** Because everything is stored separately and connected by keys, you can slice and recombine the data any way you want. "Show me all orders from Texas customers placed in Q3 that included products in the electronics category with an average item price above $50." Relational databases eat that query for breakfast. You couldn't ask that question when you designed the schema, but because the data is normalized and connected by keys, you can ask it now. That's a genuine superpower.

But that superpower comes with a structural consequence that's been shaping our code for decades: **the data in the database doesn't look like the data in your application.** Actually, let me put that a little more precisely: the relational data isn't structured in the same way as the data in your object-oriented application.

How Objects Work

When you're writing C#, you're thinking in terms of objects. An `Order` has a `Customer`. That customer has `Addresses`. You navigate the graph: `order.Customer.Addresses[0].City`. You're walking through relationships like paths through a tree.

Objects have properties that feel natural because they mirror how we think about things:

Identity. This `Order` object IS this order. Two `Order` instances with identical data are still two different objects. You test that with reference equality.

Behavior. Objects do things. `order.CalculateTotal()`. `customer.ValidateAddress()`. The logic lives on (or near) the objects it belongs to.

Navigation. Relationships are direct references. The `Customer` is RIGHT THERE inside the `Order`. You just follow the property.

Hierarchy. Objects naturally form trees. An `Order` contains `LineItems`. Each `LineItem` references a `Product`. The structure is nested, not flat.

This maps well to how we describe business concepts. A customer HAS addresses. An order CONTAINS line items. When your product owner describes the domain, they describe it in terms that map to objects, not tables.

Your domain model — the objects that represent your business — is a living tree. It has shape. It has structure. It branches differently depending on what the business needs. No two domain models look the same because no two businesses are the same. The tree is organic. It's alive.

How Relational Databases Work

Now let's look at the other side.

In the relational world, everything is stored in boxes. Flat, uniform, stackable boxes. A relational database stores data in tables — flat rows, all the same shape. Every customer is a row in the Customers box. Every order is a row in the Orders box. They're not nested inside each other. They sit in separate boxes, connected by label numbers printed on each row.

The properties of relational data are almost the opposite of objects:

No identity, just keys. A row doesn't "know" it's itself. It has a primary key — a label number that identifies it. Two rows with the same key are the same row by definition.

No behavior. Boxes don't do things. They store data and that's it. (Yes, you can put logic in stored procedures, but the boxes themselves are inert.)

No navigation. Want the customer for an order? You don't follow a reference. You JOIN. You ask the database to match rows from the Orders box with rows from the Customers box by comparing their label numbers. That's a fundamentally different operation from `order.Customer` on an object.

Sets, not trees. You're always working with sets of rows. "Give me all orders where the total exceeds $500" — that's a natural question in relational-land. The flatness makes it easy.

Think of a relational database as a warehouse. Rows and rows of uniform, labeled, stackable boxes. Perfectly organized. Easy to search. You can find anything by its label. You can combine boxes from different shelves to answer questions nobody anticipated when the warehouse was built. It's a brilliant system for storage and retrieval.

But it's nothing like a tree.

Both of these models are good at what they're designed for. Trees are great for expressing business logic with hierarchy and behavior. Boxes are great for storing data efficiently and answering ad-hoc questions. The problem is that your application needs both.

The Impedance Mismatch: Trees vs. Boxes

So here's the situation. You've got a beautiful, living domain model in your code — nested, navigable, full of behavior. And you've got a beautiful, organized warehouse in your database — flat, joinable, flexible. And you need them to talk to each other.

But those two things have completely different shapes. The database is always a collection of boxes — flat, uniform, stackable. And the domain model is always shaped like a tree — one root, branches fanning out, sub-branches fanning out from those. `Order` is the root. `LineItems` is a branch. `ShippingAddress` is a branch. `Customer` is a branch with its own `Addresses` sub-branch.

The problem — the whole problem, really — is that you're constantly converting one living tree into a bunch of flat boxes, and a bunch of flat boxes back into one living tree.

To save, you **chop the tree down and pack the pieces into boxes.** You take the `Order` object — this single, living tree with all its branches — and you take it apart. The order header goes into a row in the Orders box. Each line item gets packed into the OrderItems box. The shipping address gets packed into the ShippingInfo box. Label numbers (foreign keys) stitch them together so the warehouse knows which boxes belong to which other boxes. But the tree is gone. It's been pulped, flattened, and packed into storage — turned into boxes.

To read, you **open the boxes and try to reassemble the tree.** You pull out the rows from the Orders box, the OrderItems box, the ShippingInfo box. You match up their label numbers. And then you try to rebuild the tree — nest the line items inside the order, attach the shipping address, reconstruct the living object graph. Every single time.

And here's the thing that makes this metaphor more than a metaphor: **cardboard boxes are made from dead trees.** That's not just a coincidence — it's exactly what's happening in your code. You take a living, structured, meaningful domain object and you kill its structure to make it fit into flat, uniform storage. The tree had shape. It had hierarchy. It had meaning in its branching. The boxes are flat, generic, interchangeable.

And then when you try to rebuild the tree from the boxes? You're doing something that doesn't *quite* work in the real world. You can't bring a tree back to life from cardboard. You can glue the pieces back into roughly the right shape, but something is always at risk of being lost. A branch in the wrong place. A piece that didn't survive the packing. A label that got smudged. Every adapter bug you've ever seen is a box that got mislabeled, or a branch that ended up packed in the wrong box, or a piece that quietly disappeared between the chopping and the reassembly.

This is the **object-relational impedance mismatch**, and it's been frustrating developers for thirty-plus years. It's not because the tools are bad. It's because trees and boxes are fundamentally different shapes. You've got to do a lot of fiddly, essential, tedious work to convert between shapes. If miss something or put something in the wrong place, you could potentially completely change the meaning.

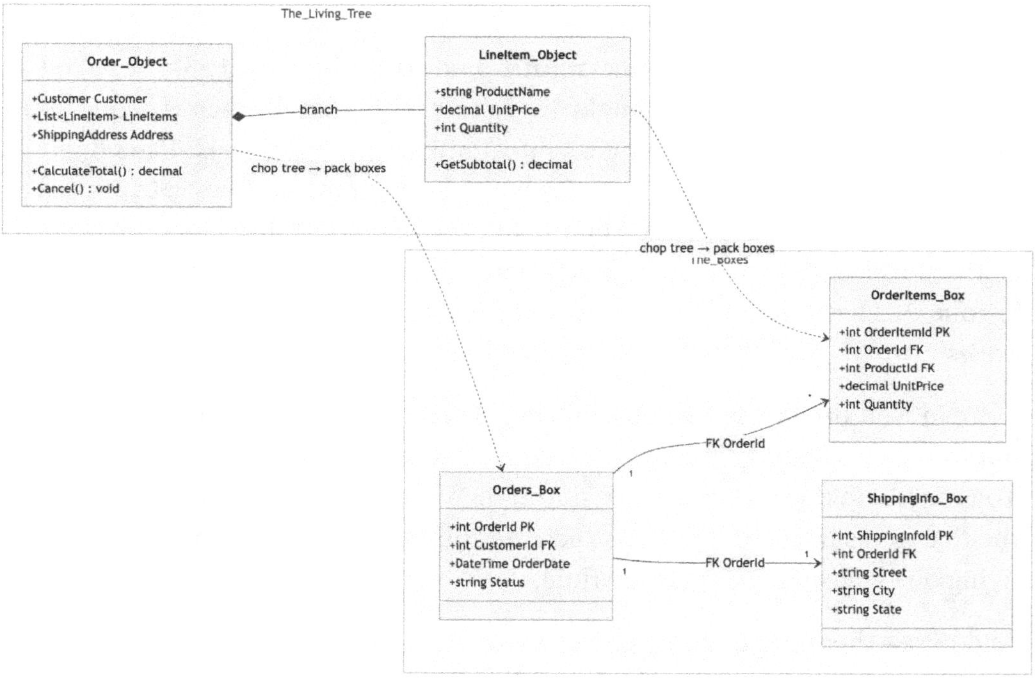

On the left: one living tree. `Order` is the root, `LineItem` is a branch. It's a single, coherent thing. On the right: three separate boxes, connected by label numbers. To save, you chop the tree and pack the pieces into those boxes. To load, you open the boxes and reassemble the tree. Every time.

This isn't a flaw in Entity Framework, SQL Server, or your code. Trees and boxes are just different shapes. The impedance mismatch isn't a bug — it's just what happens when you try to store something alive in something that's flat.

BTW, this translation logic is pretty much *exactly* what EF Core (and other ORMs like NHibernate) are trying to solve. Object-relational mappers (ORM) have a brutally complex problem to solve and they do a surprisingly good job doing it. But it's fundamentally hard and the conversions aren't always clean and elegant.

Your EF Core Entities Are Not Your Domain Objects

This is the point that trips up a lot of developers. And by "trips up" I mean "completely ruins the technical lives of" developers. It sounds like unnecessary ceremony. "Why can't I just use my EF entity classes as my domain model? Why do I need two representations of the same thing?"

Because they aren't the same thing. They have different jobs — and more importantly, they have different shapes. They have different reasons and motivations to change, too — and they don't necessarily even change at the same time.

It probably won't surprise you to find out that I have real preferences for how I want to use EF Core. EF Core is great and I use it all the time. It can do amazing things and has SO MANY features. But just because you can use all those features doesn't mean you should. There are performance concerns and maintainability concerns and understandability concerns and on and on and on.

My preference and recommendation is that you keep your EF Core mappings simple.

An EF Core entity class is shaped like a box. It has an `int Id` because the box needs a label number. It has `virtual ICollection<OrderItem> OrderItems` because EF Core needs navigation properties for lazy loading and JOIN generation. It has foreign key properties, timestamp columns, attributes or fluent configuration that describe the box structure. It's a flat, uniform row in a flat, uniform table — a packing slip for the warehouse.

A domain model class is shaped like a tree. It has the properties and methods that express business rules. `Order.CalculateTotal()`. `Order.CanBeCancelled()`. `Customer.GetDefaultShippingAddress()`. It nests things naturally — the order contains its line items, the customer contains its addresses. It doesn't care about foreign keys or navigation properties or column mappings. It's the living structure your code actually thinks in.

When you try to make one class serve as both the box *and* the tree, it does both jobs poorly:

Your tree gets polluted with box concerns. That `virtual` keyword on your navigation properties isn't a tree concept — it's there for EF Core's change tracker. That `int CustomerId` foreign key property isn't something your tree cares about — it's a label number that tells the warehouse how boxes relate to each other.

Your tree logic has to work around box limitations. You want to model something with value objects or complex hierarchies, but EF Core can't pack it cleanly into boxes. So you compromise the shape of your tree to fit the shape of the boxes. Now the warehouse is dictating how your tree grows.

Your tree becomes coupled to your boxes. Change a column name, and your tree breaks. Add an index, and your box needs a configuration change. The tree and the boxes should be able to evolve independently. When they're the same classes, they can't.

(That problem gets worse and weirder if you try to send your EF Core entities out through your Web API service endpoints...but that's a problem for another day.)

Doing It Right: Hiding EF Core from Your Application

So if your boxes and your trees are separate things, how do you wire it all together? Here's how I structure my applications, and it's a pattern I'm somewhat obsessive about: **EF Core and its boxes should be invisible to every layer except the one that directly talks to the database.**

The service layer shouldn't know EF Core exists. The presentation layer definitely shouldn't know EF Core exists. The domain model shouldn't reference a single EF namespace. EF Core is an implementation detail of data access, and implementation details should be hidden behind interfaces.

Here's what the architecture looks like from the perspective of your application code — the layers that only work with trees:

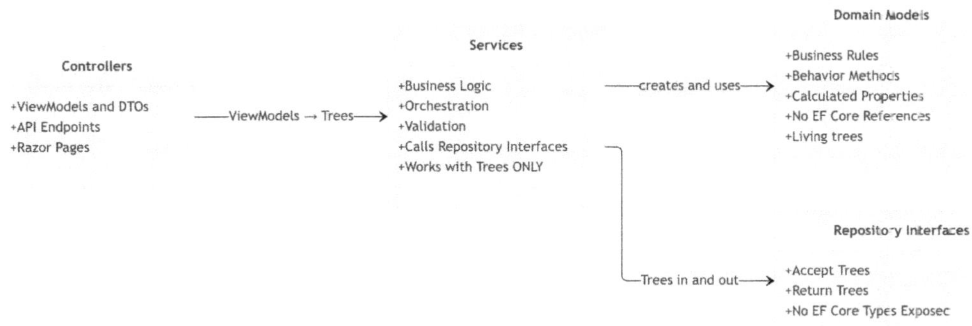

Notice what's *not* in this diagram. No entity classes. No EF Core. No adapters. No boxes anywhere. Everything in this picture works with trees and only trees.

Repository interfaces accept and return trees. Not boxes. The service layer calls `IOrderRepository.GetById(orderId)` and gets back an `Order` tree — a living domain object with all its branches. It calls `IOrderRepository.Save(order)` and passes in an `Order` tree. The service layer never sees a box. It doesn't even know that the boxes exist.

This is the critical design decision: the repository interface is the boundary. Everything above it — controllers, services, domain models — lives in a box-free world. They work with living trees, and the interface promises that trees are all they'll ever need to think about.

But what actually happens behind that interface? Here's where the chopping and reassembly lives:

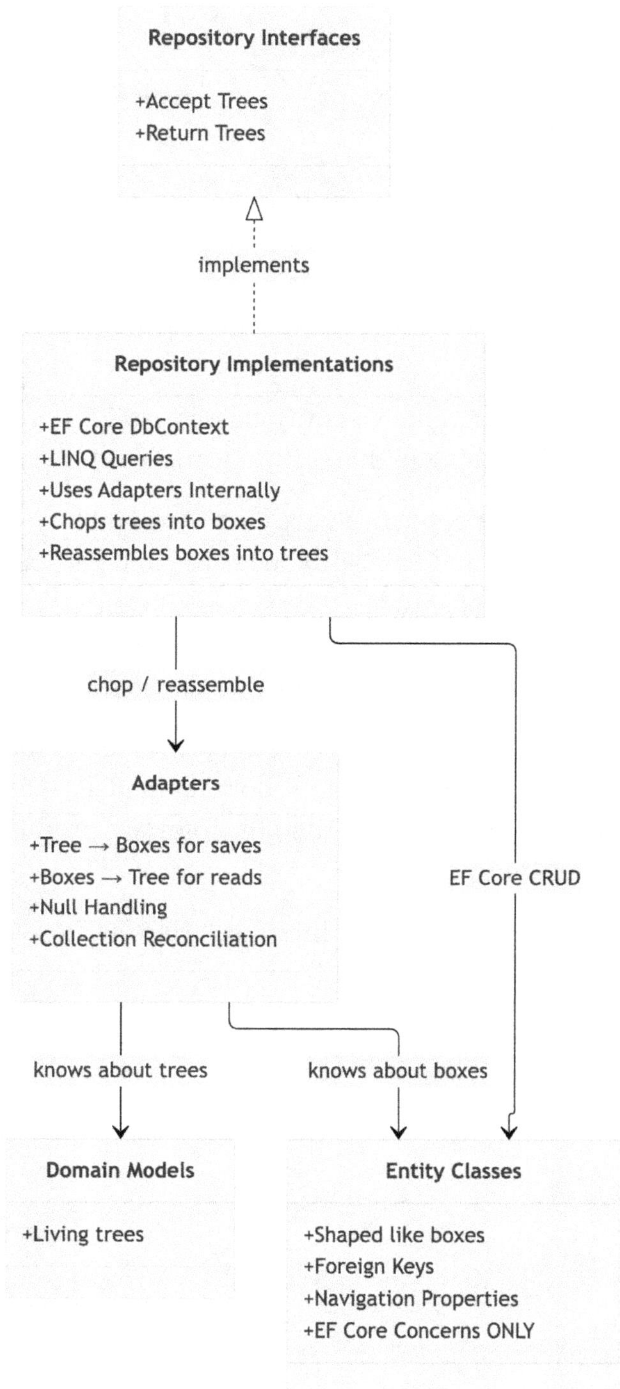

Now the boxes appear. Domain Models shows up again — because it's the shape that crosses the boundary. The adapters are the only code that knows about both shapes.

Repository implementations do the chopping and reassembly internally. The concrete `OrderRepository` takes an adapter and a DbContext via dependency injection. When the service layer calls `Save(order)`, the repository uses the adapter to chop the `Order` tree into `OrderEntity` boxes, then ships those boxes to the warehouse via EF Core. When it loads data, it goes the other direction — pulls `OrderEntity` boxes from the warehouse, uses the adapter to reassemble them into an `Order` tree, returns the living tree.

Adapters are the lumberjack and the arborist. They chop trees into boxes for storage. They reassemble boxes back into trees for use. The adapter class handles the bidirectional conversion — property mapping, null handling, collection reconciliation, type conversion. The adapter is injected into the repository, and nothing else in the system knows it exists.

Boxes are completely hidden. The entity classes live in the data access layer and never escape. No service, no controller, no domain model ever references them. If the warehouse changes — if a box gets a new column, or a column gets renamed, or a table gets restructured — only the boxes and the adapter need to change. Everything else is insulated.

Here's what that looks like with real code, using a Project/ProjectClass example similar to what I use in my own applications. First, the shapes — the tree on the left, the boxes on the right, and the adapter that converts between them:

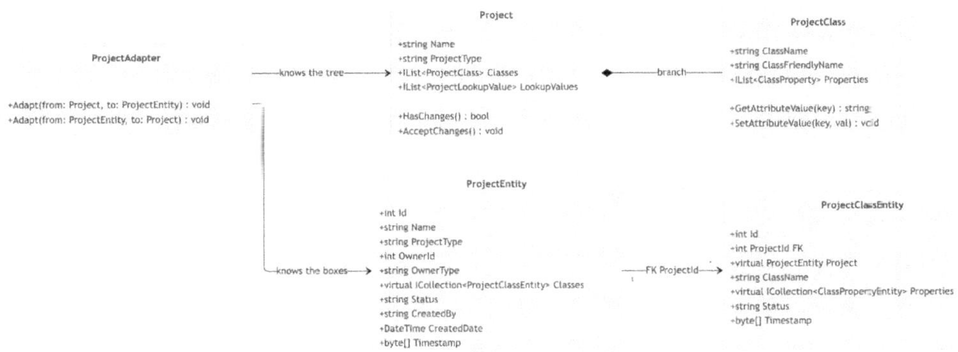

Look at the contrast. On the left, the tree: properties that express what the business cares about — `HasChanges()`, `AcceptChanges()`, child collections that are *branches*. On the right, the boxes: properties that express what the warehouse cares about — `int Id`, `byte[] Timestamp`, `virtual` navigation properties, foreign keys. Same concept. Completely different shapes.

`ProjectAdapter` is the bridge between the two shapes. It has `Adapt()` methods that go in both directions. Tree-to-boxes for saves. Boxes-to-tree for reads. It's the only class that references both the tree types and the box types.

Now here's how the wiring works — who calls what, and who knows about what:

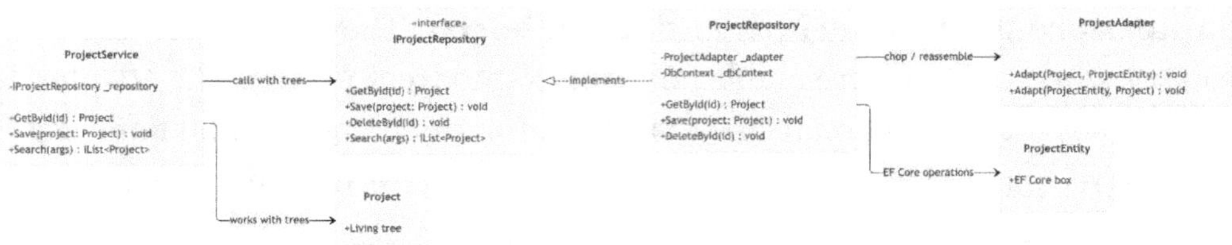

Look at the separation. `ProjectService` works with `Project` trees and calls `IProjectRepository`. That's it. It doesn't know about `ProjectEntity` boxes. It doesn't know about EF Core. It doesn't know about adapters. It calls repository methods that accept and return living trees.

`ProjectRepository` is where the chopping and reassembly happens — and it's the *only* place it happens. It takes a `ProjectAdapter` and a `DbContext` through dependency injection. When the service calls `Save(project)`, the repository uses the adapter to chop the `Project` tree into `ProjectEntity` boxes, then stores the boxes via EF Core. When the service calls `GetById(id)`, the repository pulls `ProjectEntity` boxes from the warehouse, uses the adapter to reassemble them into a `Project` tree, and returns the tree.

Notice what this buys you: if the boxes change — if `ProjectEntity` gets a new column, or a column gets renamed, or a table gets restructured — the only code that changes is the box class and the adapter. The service layer, the tree, the controllers, the tests — none of them change. The warehouse change is absorbed at the boundary where it belongs.

Why the Adapter Layer Is Critical to Unit Test

I want to make a point here that I feel strongly about, because I've seen the damage when teams skip it.

The adapter — the code that chops trees into boxes and reassembles boxes back into trees — is some of the most important code in your system to unit test. Not just "it would be nice." Critical path.

Here's why: the adapter is where the shape changes. And every shape change is a place where something can get lost.

Every property mapping is an assumption. "This branch on the tree maps to this column in the box." "This enum value maps to that string." "This nested collection on the tree maps to these rows in a child box with a foreign key." Each one of those assumptions is a place where bugs hide.

And these bugs are insidious. A mismatched property mapping doesn't throw an exception. It silently packs the wrong data into the wrong box, or silently puts a branch back in the wrong place on the reassembled tree — or completely fails to put the branch there at all. You find out weeks later when someone notices the order total is wrong, or the customer's address isn't updating, or the status field shows "Pending" when it should show "Shipped."

Remember: you're trying to reassemble a living tree from cardboard boxes. The tree that comes back out should match the tree that went in. But the conversion is fundamentally lossy — the tree structure got destroyed during packing, and you're relying on labels and conventions to put it back together. If a label is wrong, or a branch got packed in the wrong box, or a piece was quietly dropped — the reassembled tree looks right until someone leans on the branch that isn't really there.

The adapter layer is also where schema drift becomes visible. Over time, the boxes evolve. A column gets renamed. A new field gets added to a box that the tree doesn't need yet. A tree gains a calculated property that has no column. The adapter absorbs these differences — it's the buffer that lets both shapes change without breaking each other. But if someone adds a branch to the tree and forgets to update the adapter, you get a silent bug. A unit test that verifies "every branch on the tree round-trips correctly through the adapter" catches that the moment someone forgets.

The good news: adapter code is *extremely* unit testable. It's pure shape-conversion logic. No database dependency. No file system dependency. No network calls. Give it a tree, assert you get the right boxes. Give it boxes, assert you get the right tree. Test the edge cases — nulls, empty collections, enum values, default values. These tests are fast, deterministic, and they catch real bugs.

Unit tests don't have dependencies on running systems like SQL Server databases. Integration tests probably do have that dependency. Separating the adapter logic from the EF Core data storage logic means that you can test huge portions of really bug-prone code without having to spin up a database full of data.

Here's the kind of test I'm talking about:

```
[TestMethod]
public void AdaptProjectToEntity_MapsAllProperties()
{
    // Arrange
    var adapter = new ProjectAdapter();
    var tree = CreateSampleProject(); // all branches popu
lated

    var box = new ProjectEntity();

    // Act — chop the tree, pack it into boxes
    adapter.Adapt(tree, box);

    // Assert — did every branch land in the right box?
    Assert.AreEqual(tree.Name, box.Name);
    Assert.AreEqual(tree.ProjectType, box.ProjectType);
    Assert.AreEqual(tree.Classes.Count, box.Classes.Count)
;
    // ... every property verified
}

[TestMethod]
public void AdaptEntityToProject_MapsAllProperties()
{
    // Arrange
```

```
    var adapter = new ProjectAdapter();
    var box = CreateSampleProjectEntity(); // all columns
populated

    var tree = new Project();

    // Act — unpack the boxes, reassemble the tree
    adapter.Adapt(box, tree);

    // Assert — did every box column land on the right bra
nch?
    Assert.AreEqual(box.Name, tree.Name);
    Assert.AreEqual(box.ProjectType, tree.ProjectType);
    Assert.AreEqual(box.Classes.Count, tree.Classes.Count)
;
    // ... every property verified
}
```

No database required. No EF Core. No startup configuration. Just "did the shape conversion work? Did the tree survive the round trip through the boxes?" Run in milliseconds.

I've walked into codebases where the adapter tests were the first tests I wrote — not because they were the most glamorous, but because they were where the most bugs were hiding. Every time I found a bug in production where "the data in the database doesn't match what the UI is showing," the root cause was in the adapter. Every time. Something got lost in the chopping, or something got put on the wrong branch during reassembly.

The Cost of All This

Let me add it up.

To build a well-designed .NET application with EF Core and SQL Server, you need:

Trees — domain model classes that represent your business. They have behavior, rules, and business-shaped hierarchy. They know nothing about boxes.

Boxes — EF entity classes that represent your database. They have foreign keys, navigation properties, and warehouse-shaped structure. They know nothing about trees.

Adapters — classes that chop trees into boxes and reassemble boxes into trees, handling nulls, collections, type conversions, and schema drift. They're the only code that knows about both shapes.

Repository interfaces that accept and return trees. They define what data operations are available without exposing that boxes exist behind the scenes.

Repository implementations that wire up EF Core, use the adapters, and implement the repository interfaces. This is the only code that touches `DbContext` and the warehouse.

Unit tests for the adapters to make sure every branch on the tree maps to the right column in the right box, in both directions, and that nothing gets lost in the conversion.

Integration tests for the repositories to make sure EF Core actually generates the SQL you expect against the real warehouse.

Service layer classes that orchestrate business logic using repository interfaces and trees. They don't know the warehouse exists.

ViewModels or DTOs at the presentation layer — because your trees aren't the right shape for your API responses or your Razor Pages either. (A different kind of shape conversion, but shape conversion all the same.)

That's a lot of infrastructure. And to be clear — it's the *right* infrastructure if you're building a serious application on a relational database. Every layer exists for a reason. Every shape conversion solves a real problem. This is good architecture. I've been building applications this way for years and I believe in it. Everything has a point that connects back to either maintainability or testability or both.

But it's worth pausing to notice how much of that infrastructure exists because of one fundamental fact: **trees and boxes are different shapes.** The impedance mismatch created by the relational model radiates outward into your entire architecture. Every adapter, every mapping, every translation step is a consequence of that core tension.

The boxes exist because the warehouse stores boxes. The trees exist because your code thinks in trees. The adapters exist because someone has to chop and reassemble. The repository interfaces exist to hide the boxes from everything else. The adapter tests exist because things get lost when you chop a living tree into flat boxes and try to reassemble it again. All of that — every line of it — is the cost of working with two different shapes.

And if you stop and think about it for a moment, there's something slightly absurd about the whole enterprise. You take a living tree — your domain model, with its hierarchy and its behavior and its meaning — and you turn it into pulp. You flatten it. You pack it into uniform, stackable boxes and file them in a warehouse. And then the next time someone needs that tree, you pull the boxes back out, open them up, and try to resurrect something living from something dead. You do this hundreds of times a second. You write tests to make sure the reconstruction works. You build entire architectural layers to manage the chopping and reassembly.

You do all of this because fifty-something years ago, disk space cost $700,000 a gigabyte and we couldn't afford to store a tree as a tree.

But what if it didn't have to be this way?

What if the database could store the tree as-is? Living structure intact. Branches in place. No chopping. No boxes. No reassembly. What if your domain objects — with their hierarchy, their nesting, their business-shaped branching — could be the stored documents?

No adapter layer. No entity classes. No warehouse. No impedance mismatch. Just the tree.

That's where Cosmos DB comes in and that's what the next chapter is about.

Chapter 2 Document Thinking: Why Cosmos DB Changes How You Design Software

In the last chapter, we spent a lot of time talking about trees and boxes. Your domain model is a tree — hierarchical, branching, alive with behavior. Your relational database stores boxes — flat, uniform, stackable. Huge portions of your entire architecture exists solely to chop trees into boxes for storage and reassemble boxes back into trees for use.

All because, fifty-something years ago, disk space cost $700,000 a gigabyte and we couldn't afford to store a tree as a tree.

This chapter is about what happens when you can.

But first, I need to talk about the technology that made it possible. And I need to confess something about Star Trek.

JSON: The Transporter Beam for Trees

I'm a Star Trek nerd. (Specifically, a Star Trek: The Next Generation nerd.) And one of the things I've always thought about — because I'm also a nerd-nerd, the kind of nerd who thinks about the engineering behind the fiction — is what the data format would be for the transporter. When Scotty (or O'Brien, if you're a TNG purist) dematerializes someone, the transporter has to encode the complete structure of a living thing into some intermediate format, beam that format somewhere else, and rematerialize the original structure at the other end. The thing that comes out has to be the same thing that went in. Same structure. Same relationships. Same everything.

I think about this because that's what JSON does for object trees.

As someone who's been developing software for close to 30 years, I can say this with confidence: **the invention of JSON has been world-changing.** I know that sounds dramatic for a data format, but it's not an overstatement.

JSON lets you take a tree — a living, branching, hierarchical object — and create a dehydrated representation of it. A text format that captures the full structure: what's nested inside what, which branches contain which sub-branches, the whole shape. You can send that dehydrated representation across a network, write it to a file, store it somewhere. And then at the other end, you rehydrate it — and suddenly you've got a tree again. Same structure. Same nesting. Same shape.

It's a transporter beam for data.

If you got your start in distributed systems when I did — I was doing CORBA in the late '90s, then SOAP, then REST — you know what life was like before JSON. CORBA had IDL and binary protocols. SOAP had XML with schemas and envelopes and namespaces that would make your eyes bleed. Converting objects into a transmittable format and back was a significant engineering problem. Getting it wrong produced exactly the kind of bugs we talked about in the last chapter — something gets lost in the conversion, something ends up in the wrong place, and you find out in production.

JSON changed all of that. It maps naturally to object structures because it IS an object structure. Curly braces for objects. Square brackets for arrays. Nesting for hierarchy. Your C# object serializes to JSON that looks like your object. No schema files. No IDL. No XML namespaces. The tree goes in, the tree comes out.

And there's a reason you see JSON everywhere now. It's not because it's trendy. It's because **JSON lets you skip the tree-to-box conversion entirely.** You don't have to chop the tree into flat pieces to transmit it. You don't have to reassemble it on the other end. The format preserves the shape. The tree survives the trip.

Which brings us to the question that the last chapter was building toward: what if your *database* stored JSON? What if, instead of chopping your tree into boxes and filing them in a warehouse, you could just beam the tree directly into storage — structure intact, branches in place, hierarchy preserved?

Cosmos DB Stores Trees

That's what Azure Cosmos DB does. It stores JSON documents. And a JSON document is a tree.

When you save an `Order` object to Cosmos DB, you don't chop it into an Orders box, an OrderItems box, and a ShippingInfo box. You serialize the entire `Order` tree to JSON — line items nested inside, shipping address nested inside, payment summary nested inside — and store the whole thing as a single document. One tree. One document. No chopping. No boxes.

When you read it back, you don't pull boxes from a warehouse and reassemble a tree. You read one document, deserialize the JSON, and you've got your tree back. Same structure. Same nesting. Same shape. The transporter worked.

No adapter layer to chop and reassemble. No entity classes shaped like boxes. No repository implementations juggling two different shapes. No unit tests verifying that the tree survived the round trip. The tree goes in, the tree comes out. The shape doesn't change.

This is the big insight: **the domain object is the stored document**. Your `Order` class — the one with `CalculateTotal()` and `Cancel()` and nested `LineItems` — serializes to JSON and gets stored directly. The thing you think about in your code is the thing that gets stored in the database. This is one of my favorite things about writing apps that use Cosmos DB.

So you get to skip all that entity stuff and adapt stuff but there is sort of a catch. You need to figure out how you expect to access your documents (aka. your data). In relational databases, you can access your data starting from pretty much any relationship — write your query and get the data in the shape that you need. When you use a document db like Cosmos, you can query from pretty much anywhere in a document's structure but what you end up getting back is the same document.

It's more of a mindset shift than a problem but you need to know where to draw the boundaries around your documents. Which brings us to the most important concept in this entire book.

Aggregate Roots: The Key to Document Design

An aggregate root is a concept from domain-driven design. It sounds fancy but it it's pretty easy to grok. It's also not a new, Cosmos-centric idea either. Even if you're writing applications that store data relationally in SQL Server, you still care about your aggregate roots...they're just relevant a couple layers up the design stack in your Service Layer.

Think about an Order in an e-commerce system. An Order has line items. It has a shipping address. It has a payment summary. These things are all part of the order — they don't make sense on their own. A line item without an order is meaningless. A shipping address floating around without being attached to something is just data noise.

The Order is the **aggregate root**. It's the thing that owns everything inside it. It's the consistency boundary — when you save an Order, you save the whole thing: header, line items, addresses, all of it. When you delete an Order, the line items go with it. They don't have an independent existence.

In a relational system, saving that order might be 10 insert statements and reading that data might take 4 or 5 joins. In Cosmos DB, you save the order and that's it. The query is equally simple — find the matching document and return that document.

Finding the Aggregate Root using Deletes

Here's the key question that'll help you test if you've correctly identified your aggregate roots:

"If you delete the parent, should this other thing disappear too?"

If the answer is yes, it's inside the aggregate. It's part of the tree. It's part of the document.

If the answer is no, it's a separate aggregate. A separate tree. A separate document.

If the answer is maybe, there might be a flaw in your thinking somewhere.

Line items on an order? Delete the order, the line items are gone. They're inside the aggregate. Part of the Order document.

The Customer who placed the order? Delete the order, the customer still exists. The customer is a separate aggregate. A separate document. The order holds a reference to the customer (maybe a customer ID), not the customer itself.

In Cosmos DB, **your aggregate root IS your document.** Everything inside the aggregate boundary gets stored together as a single JSON document. Everything outside it is a separate document with a reference. If you can identify your aggregate roots, you can design your documents. If you can't, then there's some detail you haven't quite nailed yet.

When I was first learning Cosmos DB, I really wish someone had told me this: **document = aggregate root.** It's just such an essential nugget of knowledge and I don't think I saw it in other demos and documentation. Pretty much all of the tutorials I saw started with "here's a JSON document and here's how partition keys work". That's fine but knowing your aggregate roots not only makes your documents make sense but it also makes your application architecture make sense.

What Does It Look Like?

Here's what it looks like when you draw the aggregate boundaries:

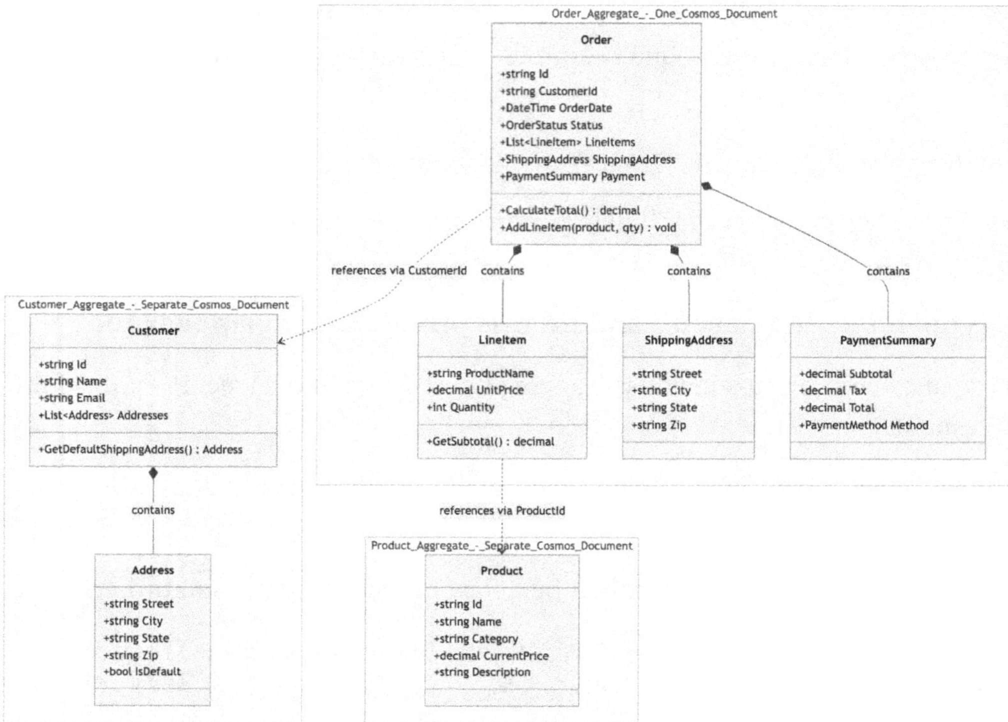

Look at the boundaries. The Order aggregate contains its LineItems, its ShippingAddress, and its PaymentSummary. Delete the order, all of that goes away. **That's one tree. One JSON document in Cosmos DB.**

The Customer aggregate contains its Addresses. Delete the customer, the addresses go away. **That's a separate tree. A separate document.**

The Product aggregate stands alone. Delete a product from the catalog, existing orders that reference it aren't affected — they captured the product name and price at the time of the order.

The dotted lines between aggregates are *references*, not containment. The Order holds a `CustomerId` string — not the Customer object itself. The LineItem holds a `ProductId` and a snapshot of the product name and price — not a live reference to the Product.

Each aggregate root becomes one JSON document. The Order document contains everything inside the Order aggregate boundary. The Customer document contains everything inside the Customer aggregate boundary. They live in the same container (or different containers — a design choice we'll get to later), but they're separate documents. Separate trees.

Denormalization Is a Thing

The aggregate root version of document is the official, definitive copy. To put that in relational database terms, that aggregate root version of the document is the primary key version. But unlike traditional relational database normalization advice that says "thou shalt only have one copy of the data", I frequently break that rule in Cosmos.

I denormalize for convenience, performance, and debugging.

What do I mean by that? I often will copy bits of relevant data from one aggregate root into another aggregate root just so I have it. For example, the `Order` document might end up with a `CustomerName` property or an `Address` property. These become convenience properties that let me display data while avoiding extra calls to Cosmos.

Now I know what you're thinking: if the definitive version of the data changes, what do I do with those convenience values? I don't worry about it. Most of the time, it's actually kind of nice to have the snapshot of what the values were at the time that the document was created.

If I'm worried about those denormalized convenience values getting out of sync, then I'd just skip storing them. Or always get the definitive version and only display that one. Having those extra bits of data in the document can make debugging WAY easier.

Cosmos DB Enforces Your Aggregate Boundaries

Here's the thing that makes aggregate roots and Cosmos DB such a natural fit — and the thing that's fundamentally different from working with EF Core against a relational database.

In the relational world, your aggregate boundaries are a design guideline that you *hope* your team follows. EF Core gives you a `DbSet<T>` for every entity type. You *can* write `context.OrderItems.Where(oi => oi.Quantity > 10)` — reaching directly into order line items without going through the Order.

EF Core doesn't stop you, because enforcing aggregate boundaries isn't its job. The discipline has to come from you.

In Cosmos DB, the aggregate boundaries are *how the data is physically stored.* You can't reach into the line items without loading the Order document, because the line items don't exist independently from the Order. They're nested inside the Order JSON. They don't have their own endpoint, their own query surface, their own independent existence. They exist inside the Order document or they don't exist at all.

You can't accidentally violate an aggregate boundary that Cosmos enforces for you. The storage model and the domain model are the same shape. Less flexibility? Absolutely. More correctness by default? Yah probably. Less object-relational impedance mismatching headaches? Definitely.

Remember what we said in the last chapter about all that infrastructure — the adapters, the entity classes, the repository implementations doing bidirectional shape conversion, the unit tests making sure the tree survived the round trip through the boxes? In Cosmos DB, most of that infrastructure simply isn't needed. The tree goes in, the tree comes out. There's nothing to chop and nothing to reassemble, which means there's nothing to get wrong in the conversion.

So What About EF Core's Cosmos DB Provider?

This is where I'll plant my contrarian flag.

Microsoft ships an EF Core provider for Cosmos DB. You can use `DbContext` and `DbSet<T>` against Cosmos just like you would against SQL Server. I think I understand why they're doing this — one data access library to rule them all. — but I think this is the wrong tool for the job and a distraction.

For Cosmos DB, you just don't need it. It's just extra stuff.

(Disclaimer: I enthusiastically use EF Core for SQL Server and recommend it to my customers.)

I want to be specific about why, because this isn't a knee-jerk take. EF Core is an ORM — an Object-*Relational* Mapper. The "R" is doing important work in that acronym. It exists to bridge the gap between objects and relational schemas. That's its purpose. That's what it's good at. As I said in the last chapter — ORMs have a brutally complex problem to solve, and they do a surprisingly great job.

But Cosmos DB doesn't have relational schemas. It doesn't have tables. It doesn't have foreign keys or JOINs. The gap that EF Core is designed to bridge doesn't exist. There are no boxes for the tree to get chopped into. The tree goes straight into storage as JSON.

So when you use the EF Core Cosmos provider, you're bringing a sophisticated solution to a problem you don't have — and in the process, you're reintroducing complexity that choosing Cosmos DB was supposed to eliminate. You get `DbSet<T>` giving you direct access to every entity type, which re-creates the aggregate boundary problem that Cosmos's document model had naturally solved. You get change tracking overhead that makes no sense when your unit of persistence is a whole document. You get an abstraction layer that hides the things you actually need to understand about Cosmos — partition keys, request units, cross-partition queries — behind a familiar-but-misleading interface.

This isn't EF Core's fault. EF Core is doing exactly what it's designed to do. In this case, it's just a misapplication of a good tool. Think about it in terms of our metaphor: EF Core is a brilliantly engineered tree-chopping-and-box-packing machine. Cosmos DB doesn't use boxes. Bringing EF Core to Cosmos is like hauling a wood chipper to a job site that has a perfectly good storage shed for whole trees. The machine works great — it's just not needed here.

When Cosmos DB Isn't the Answer

I promised honesty, so here it is.

Cosmos DB is the wrong choice when you need complex cross-entity reporting and ad-hoc queries across your entire dataset. "Show me all orders from Q3 where the customer is in Texas and the product category is electronics and the average item price is above $50" — that's a query that relational databases were born for. That's where the boxes-in-a-warehouse model shines. You can combine any box with any other box to answer questions nobody anticipated. That same query in Cosmos DB? Well, it might make your brain hurt. And performance might be "sub-optimal".

It's the wrong choice when your data model is genuinely relational — when the relationships between entities are as important as the entities themselves and you need to traverse those relationships in unpredictable ways.

It's also the wrong choice when your team doesn't have the bandwidth to learn a new mental model. Document thinking isn't harder than relational thinking, but it is *different*, and learning that transition has a cost. If your team is deep in relational expertise and the project doesn't justify the learning curve, that's a perfectly valid reason to stick with what you know.

It's the wrong choice when cost predictability matters more than scalability. Cosmos DB pricing is consumption-based (request units), which is great for elastic workloads but can be surprising for steady-state applications. SQL Server pricing is often more predictable.

None of these are weaknesses of Cosmos DB. They're characteristics of a tool designed for a specific set of problems and different scalability models. The mistake isn't using SQL Server when SQL Server is the right choice — the warehouse full of boxes is great when you need a warehouse full of boxes. The mistake is using Cosmos DB with a relational mental model (trying to cram boxes into a tree database), or using SQL Server when your data is naturally hierarchical and you're going to spend half your architecture chopping and reassembling.

What's Next

So here's where we are. You understand the shapes: trees for your domain, boxes for relational storage, and the cost of converting between them. You understand that JSON is the transporter that lets trees survive a trip to storage and back. You understand that Cosmos DB stores JSON documents — which means it stores trees — and that aggregate roots are the concept that tells you where to draw the document boundaries.

The rest of this book is about building real applications with this mental model. We'll start with the raw SDK — setting up accounts, writing CRUD operations, feeling the friction of doing everything by hand. Then we'll build the abstractions that make it productive, using my Benday.CosmosDb library to encode aggregate root thinking directly into the architecture.

We'll get deep into data modeling — using the "delete the parent" heuristic to make real design decisions about document boundaries, partition keys, and parent-child relationships. We'll talk about query performance and cost, because Cosmos DB will happily let you spend money you didn't need to spend if you don't understand request units and cross-partition queries.

We'll build a complete production application — ASP.NET Core with authentication, authorization, and admin management, all backed by Cosmos DB — to prove that this isn't just theory. And we'll cover the operational reality: Change Feed for event-driven patterns, security and permissions (which are genuinely bizarre and deserve their own chapter), and advanced patterns for teams running Cosmos in production.

But everything starts with the mental model we've built in these first two chapters. Your domain model is a tree. Relational databases store boxes. The impedance mismatch is the cost of converting between them. JSON is the transporter beam that preserves the tree's shape. Cosmos DB stores JSON. Your aggregate root is your document.

No more chopping. No more boxes. Just the tree.

Chapter 3 How Cosmos DB Is Structured: The Four Things You Need to Know

In the first two chapters, we talked about trees and boxes. Your domain model is a tree. Relational databases store boxes. Cosmos DB stores trees — your domain object serialized to JSON, structure intact, no chopping required.

Great. Now let's actually start building something.

But before we write any code, we need to understand how Cosmos DB is organized. There are four concepts you need to know, and one of them — the partition key — is the most important design decision you'll make in any Cosmos application. We're going to spend some time on it because getting it right matters more than almost anything else.

(We're also going to punt on the question of "where do I run this?" for a bit. Cloud? Local emulator? We'll get there in the next chapter. First, let's understand what we're building against.)

The Four Things: Database, Container, Partition Key, Id

Cosmos DB has a nesting structure that's straightforward but important to understand.

Database

A Cosmos DB **database** is the outermost grouping. It's roughly analogous to a database in SQL Server — a logical container for related data. Most applications have one. You might have more if you have genuinely separate workloads that need different throughput configurations, but for most projects, one database is fine.

Not much drama here. Create one, give it a name, move on.

Container

A **container** lives inside a database. This is where your documents actually live. If you're coming from the relational world, a container is the closest analog to maybe a table — but the analogy crumbles almost immediately. A container can hold documents with completely different shapes. Your Order documents and your Customer documents can live in the same container, side by side, with totally different structures. Try that with a SQL Server table.

(How Cosmos tells them apart is through some kind of a discriminator property. That's a topic we'll get to in the data modeling chapter. For now, just know that a container isn't limited to one type of document.)

You need at least one container. I've been pleasantly surprised by how far I can get with just a single container in my apps. But there are definitely reasons why you might want to add more containers and the decision is typically dictated by the access patterns and indexing needs of the data.

(BTW, I'm trying really hard to not get bogged down in the details yet because it gets complicated fast.)

Partition Key

Partition keys are about 90% of the game in Cosmos DB. Get it right and you live an easy life of delight and fulfillment as you endlessly marvel at glory of Cosmos DB's performance and scalability. Get it wrong and you're well and truly hosed. Doomed.

So. Anyway. Partition Keys.

Every container has a **partition key** definition that gets set when you create the container. There are two types of partition keys: single-value and hierarchical. The single-value partition key uses a single property in your documents. Hierarchical uses multiple properties on your documents as the partition key.

Cosmos DB containers are happy to store just about any document (data) as long as it conforms to the partition key. Compare that to relational databases where a table has a fixed schema that's enforced by the database engine. Cosmos DB doesn't enforce much about your data beyond the partition key.

Once you *define* the partition key, all the documents in the container will conform to that definition and that forms the foundation of how Cosmos DB will physically store your data and handle scalability for your container.

I'm going to spend the next few sections on partition keys because they're the fundamental unit of scalability in Cosmos DB. If you understand partition keys, you understand why Cosmos works the way it works.

Detour: Defining 'Identity'

There's a concept in data modeling called **identity**. It describes how you identify individual pieces of data. If we're talking about humans out in real life, we've all got names and that's pretty good at telling the difference between say "Mike Derucki" and "Saul Rosenberg". In C#, identity is governed by the GetHashCode() method that's available on every object. If two objects have the same hash code value, they're the same object. In SQL Server, it's the primary key value for a table.

Identity establishes uniqueness.

Up to this point, I've been deliberately been avoiding abbreviating "Partition Key". The natural abbreviation is "PK" but that also happens to be the common abbreviation for "Primary Key" in relational database land. Cosmos PK != SQL Server PK.

In SQL Server a PK is unique and establishes identity. In Cosmos DB, the PK isn't unique but it's the start of uniqueness — the start of establishing identity.

The `id` Property

Partition keys are only the first part of establishing document identity. The other part is the `id` property. Every document in a container automatically gets an `id` property.

Since "id" is typically though of as the abbreviation for "identity", you'd think that `id` would establish document identity. It doesn't. That `id` value doesn't even have to be unique in the container. (Pro tip: you probably should try to make it unique. More on this later.)

Document identity comes from the combination of the partition key value and the id value.

Every document in Cosmos DB must have an `id` property. It's a string. It uniquely identifies the document *within its partition*. If you try to save a document without an `id` property or with an empty string `id` value, Cosmos DB will automatically populate your document with a Guid value for `id`.

Why Partition Keys Matter More Than Anything Else

I remember about 10-15 years ago, I kept hearing people talk about relational database sharding. "We need to shard the database." "Our sharding strategy needs work." At conferences, in blog posts, in architecture reviews. It was everywhere for a while. I'm pretty sure I even wrote my own sharding engine at some point just to try it out.

Now that I think back on all that sharding chatter, it was the world slowly starting to notice the fundamental scalability limitations of relational databases. When your data lives in tables with foreign keys and JOINs, scaling horizontally ("scaling out") is *hard*. You can scale vertically (bigger server, "scaling up") for a while, but eventually you hit a ceiling of what you're willing to pay or the limits of available hardware. Sharding — splitting data across multiple database instances based on some subset of a key — was the industry's attempt to solve that. And it was painful. Manually managed. Application-level routing. Cross-shard queries and transactions were a nightmare.

What those architects were homing in on, without having the vocabulary for it yet, was the essential design insight that Cosmos DB is built on: **the partition key.**

In Cosmos DB, you can't scale any smaller than the partition key. That's the fundamental unit. Cosmos automatically distributes partitions across physical hardware. When load increases, Cosmos splits and rebalances partitions across more machines. You don't manage shards. You don't configure routing. You chose your partition key when you created the container, and Cosmos handles the rest.

But that also means your partition key choice determines *how* Cosmos can scale your data. If you choose poorly, Cosmos can't help you. If you choose well, Cosmos scales almost invisibly.

All of the performance characteristics, all of the cost behavior, all of the query patterns — they flow from this one decision. The partition key is the most important thing in your Cosmos architecture. Get it right and most other things fall into place. Get it wrong and you'll fight the system forever.

One more thing: the partition key is set when the container is created and **cannot be changed later.** You're stuck with it.

Let's say you've figured out that your partition key config is just plain wrong and you want to change it. The only solution is to create a new container and migrate the data to the new container. It's do-able...but it's kind of a pain. (Guess how I know. Yah. I've messed it up before.)

My Recommended Partition Key for the Chronically Impatient

Before we get in to how you choose, I'm going to give you my TL;DR partition key recommendation.

(Man! You're impatient! Sheesh!)

Here's the recommendation:

- Create a container that uses hierarchical partition keys
- Set the partition key to "/tenantId,/entityType".
    - `tenantId` is the owner of the data (me, you, someone else, etc)
    - `entityType` type is the type of data (Order, Address, Claims, Person, Settings, etc.)

This is what I use all the time and it's served me well.

Now that that's out of the way, let's get into the actual thought process.

Choosing a Partition Key: The Cardinality Sweet Spot

So how do you choose? Let's start with the two extremes, because they illustrate the tradeoff.

Extreme 1: Maximum Uniqueness

You could make your partition key a `Guid.NewGuid().ToString()`. Every single document gets its own unique partition. That's the ultimate in granular scalability and Cosmos can spread your documents across as many physical partitions as it needs.

But it leads to a problem: **cross-partition queries.** If you need to find all orders for a specific customer, and every order has a random GUID as its partition key, Cosmos has to check *every partition* to answer your query. That's called a fan-out query, and it's expensive. It consumes more request units, takes more time, and gets worse as your data grows. Cross-partition queries are not desirable and they get expensive quickly. (More on this later.)

Extreme 2: Everything in One Partition

On the other end, you could set every document's partition key to the same value: `"my_partition_key"`. Now everything is in one partition. Queries are simple — Cosmos knows exactly where to look.

But you've short-circuited Cosmos's ability to scale on your behalf. All your data is on one physical machine. And there's an upper limit — a single logical partition can hold a maximum of 20 GB. Hit that ceiling and you're stuck. You've turned your infinitely scalable document database into a single box that tops out at 20 gigs.

Yah. Not good.

The Middle Ground

What you're aiming for is something in between.

Now, I'm a musician by training. I have a degree in music performance. I did not take a lot of CS courses. So when I tell you that the term we need here is **cardinality**, I want you to know that I find this term unnecessarily fancy. It basically means "uniqueness." How many distinct values does a property have?

Low cardinality = few unique values. Think of a `Status` field with three possible values: "Active", "Inactive", "Pending". That's low cardinality. Low potential for uniqueness.

High cardinality = many unique values. Think of a GUID. That's extremely high cardinality. Every value is unique.

Here's how cardinality maps to your partition key choice:

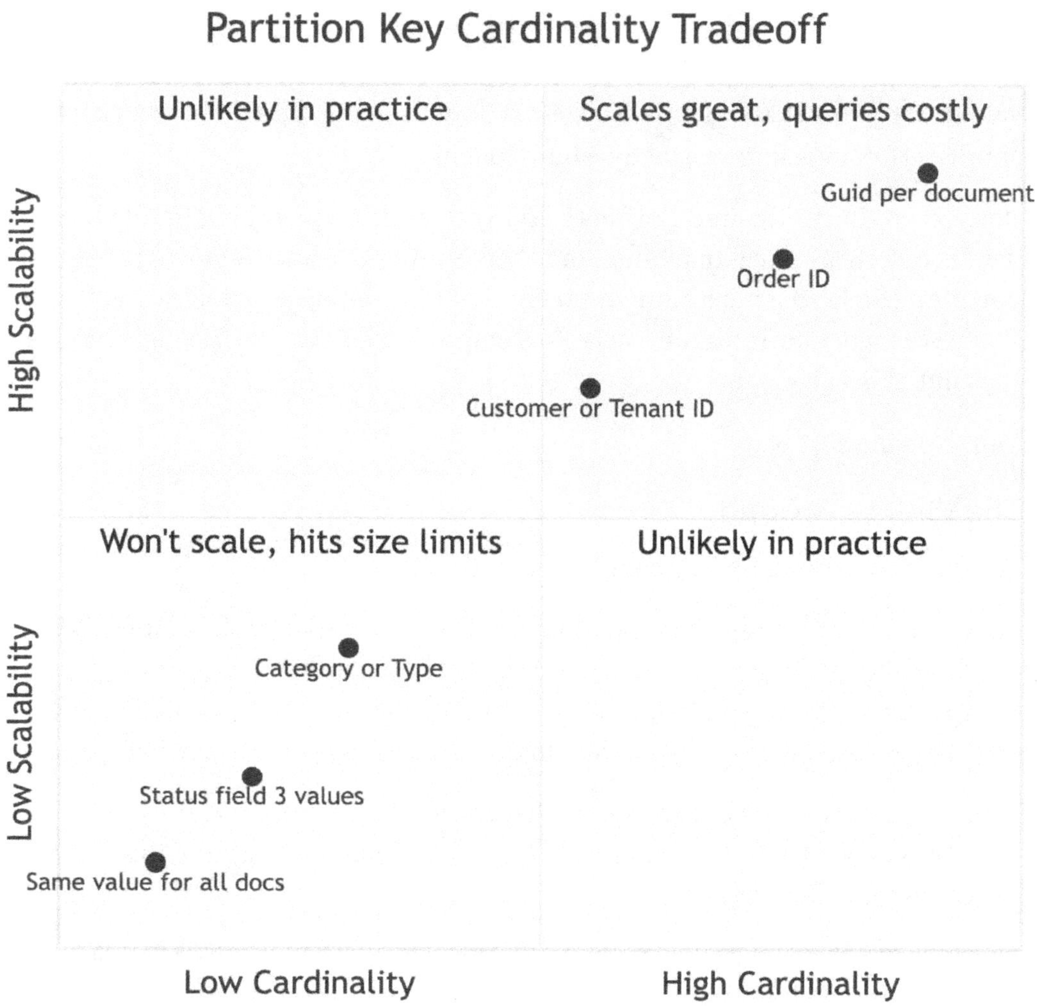

Low cardinality, low scalability: everything jammed into a few partitions. Hits size limits. Bad.

High cardinality, high scalability: everything spread across unique partitions. Scales beautifully. But every query that isn't a point read becomes a cross-partition fan-out. Expensive.

The sweet spot is the middle of that diagonal. You want a partition key with enough cardinality to distribute data well, but that also aligns with how you actually query your data.

The practical heuristic: what do you query by most often? If most of your queries are "get all orders for customer X" or "get all documents for tenant Y," then `customerId` or `tenantId` is probably your partition key. Your most common query runs within a single partition (fast and cheap), and you have enough unique values to distribute data across partitions as you grow.

Don't overthink it. Pick the property that most often appears in your `WHERE` clauses. That's usually your partition key.

A Quick Note on Hierarchical Partition Keys

Cosmos DB also supports **hierarchical partition keys** — partition keys with multiple levels. Instead of a single property like `/customerId`, you can define a key like `/tenantId, /customerId`. This gives you finer-grained distribution while still allowing efficient queries at different levels of the hierarchy.

We'll get deeper into hierarchical partition keys when we talk about data modeling. For now, just know they exist and they're useful when your data has natural grouping levels. (I love hierarchical partition keys.)

Let's See Some Code

Enough concepts. Let's look at some code and store a tree. This whole book assumes that you're writing an application using .NET Core so the natural place to start is with the Microsoft.Azure.Cosmos SDK.

We're going to keep this simple. One domain class, a couple of basic operations. The goal isn't to build a production application — it's to see what the raw SDK looks like and get a feel for some code.

A Simple Domain Model

```
public class Note
{
    public string id { get; set; } = Guid.NewGuid().ToString();
    public string OwnerId { get; set; } = string.Empty;
    public string Title { get; set; } = string.Empty;
    public string Body { get; set; } = string.Empty;
    public DateTime CreatedDate { get; set; } =
                DateTime.UtcNow;
    public List<string> Tags { get; set; } = new();
}
```

A couple of things to notice. The `id` property is lowercase — Cosmos DB requires that specific property name for the document identifier. If you're used to C# conventions, this will bug you...don't worry, we'll fix it later.

The `OwnerId` is going to be our partition key. All of a user's notes will be in the same partition. That means "get all notes for user X" is a single-partition query.

And the `Tags` property is a `List<string>`. In a relational database, tags would be a separate table with a foreign key back to Notes. Here, they're just a list that's nested inside the document. Part of the tree. No boxes needed. Easy.

Connecting, Saving, and Reading

```
using Microsoft.Azure.Cosmos;

// Connect
var client = new CosmosClient(
    "https://localhost:8081",
    // we'll talk about this endpoint next chapter
    "YOUR_KEY_HERE",
    new CosmosClientOptions
    {
        SerializerOptions = new CosmosSerializationOptions
        {
            PropertyNamingPolicy =
                CosmosPropertyNamingPolicy.CamelCase
        }
    }
);

// Get references to database and container
var database = client.GetDatabase("NotesDb");
var container = database.GetContainer("NotesContainer");

// Save a note
var note = new Note
```

```
{
    OwnerId = "user-123",
    Title = "First Cosmos Note",
    Body = "Look ma, no boxes!",
    Tags = new List<string>
         { "cosmos", "getting-started" }
};

var saveResponse = await container.UpsertItemAsync(
    note,
    new PartitionKey(note.OwnerId)
);
Console.WriteLine(
    $"Saved. Cost: {saveResponse.RequestCharge} RUs");

// Read it back
var readResponse = await container.ReadItemAsync<Note>(
    note.id,
    new PartitionKey(note.OwnerId)
);
var loaded = readResponse.Resource;
Console.WriteLine($"Title: {loaded.Title}");
Console.WriteLine(
     $"Tags: {string.Join(", ", loaded.Tags)}");
Console.WriteLine(
     $"Read cost: {readResponse.RequestCharge} RUs");
```

That's a tree going into Cosmos and a tree coming back out. The `Note` object with its nested `Tags` list gets serialized to JSON, stored as a single document, and deserialized back to the same structure. No shredding. No boxes. No adapter layer.

A few things to notice before we move on:

`UpsertItemAsync` creates the document if it doesn't exist, or replaces it if it does (matched by partition key + id). I use upsert rather than create in most situations — it's simpler to reason about.

`new PartitionKey(note.OwnerId)` — you have to manually construct a `PartitionKey` object and pass it with every operation. Every save. Every read. Every query. If you forget it, the SDK won't throw an error. It'll silently do a more expensive operation instead.

`response.RequestCharge` — that's the cost of the operation in Request Units. It's how Cosmos DB bills you. I predict that you'll start getting in the habit of looking at that number.

We'll dig into all of these patterns — and discover what the SDK *doesn't* tell you — in the next chapter when we actually run this code.

What's Next

We've got the mental model: Database → Container → Partition Key → `id`. We understand why the partition key choice is the most important decision in a Cosmos application. We've got cardinality as the framework for making that choice. And we've got some code that saves and reads a document.

But we haven't actually *run* anything yet. In the next chapter, we'll set up a local development environment, execute this code against the Cosmos DB emulator, and then look at what's actually stored in the database. Because what Cosmos stores isn't *quite* what you sent it — there are some extra fields in there, and understanding them matters more than you'd think.

Chapter 4 Running Your Code: The Emulator, System Properties, and SDK Rough Edges

Last chapter we looked at how Cosmos DB is organized — Database, Container, Partition Key, `id` — and we wrote some code to save and read a `Note` document. But we haven't actually run any of it yet.

Let's fix that.

The Emulator: Your Local Cosmos DB

You could create a Cosmos DB account in Azure and run against the cloud, but that (probably) costs money from minute one and means you're making HTTP calls to Azure every time you want to test something during development. Not awful but not ideal.

The better answer is the **Azure Cosmos DB Emulator**. It runs on your machine, implements the same API as the cloud service, and costs nothing. Your code connects to `https://localhost:8081` with a well-known key, and everything works the same as it would against a real Cosmos account. (Disclaimer: the data operations work the same way which is good for development but the performance details are *nothing* like the real thing.)

There are four versions of the Cosmos DB Emulator:

- Windows application
- Windows Docker container
- Linux Docker container
- vNext Linux emulator (preview)

The Windows Version

The Windows-based emulator has been around since 2016 and when it finally arrived, it was kind of big deal. Developers had been asking for it for a long, long time so that they didn't always have to make calls to the real Cosmos DB version in the cloud. It's built to run on Windows only. You can download it from Microsoft's site and it gives you `Microsoft.Azure.Cosmos.Emulator.exe`, which is installed by default at `%ProgramFiles%\Azure Cosmos DB Emulator`.

Ten years on (I'm writing this in 2026), this version of the emulator is showing its age. It's kind of slow to start even on a beast of a dev machine and I find myself frequently wrestling with vague error messages. Once it's up and running, it works well on an x64-based Windows machine. You can run it on Windows ARM64 but it's slower and grumpier.

Windows Docker Container Version

There's a Windows Container version that you can download from `mcr.microsoft.com/cosmosdb/windows/azure-cosmos-emulator`. Rumor has it that this is essentially `Microsoft.Azure.Cosmos.Emulator.exe` wrapped and running in a container. It's unclear whether this is officially still supported or not. It requires running on an x64 processor.

Linux Docker Container Version

There's also an x64-based Linux container version of the emulator. This is where stuff starts to get kinda weird.

I work on an Apple Silicon Macbook about 90% of the time and I *really* wanted to get this version of the emulator running on my machine. No matter what I tried it just wouldn't work but being a total nerd, I just couldn't take "not supported" for an answer. So I cracked open the container image and started looking around. It's been a while since I did this digging but at the time, it appeared to be running in some kind of strange Windows-on-Linux emulator mode.

Essentially an emulator inside of an emulator. Which explains why this version was/is ultra buggy even on x64 hardware and why it just plain refuses to run on ARM or Apple Silicon.

The vNext Emulator

Enter the completely new version of the emulator. The "vNext" emulator is still in preview but it's under active development and it's gotten really good. I use this one all the time. It no longer has the x64 limitations that the previous versions had and happily runs on Docker Desktop via WSL2 on Windows, x64 Linux, Apple Silicon Macs, Windows on ARM, and ARM versions of Linux. I use this version all the time to run integration tests during GitHub Actions builds.

It's tremendous and the setup is easy. Setting it up is basically: install Docker, pull the Docker image, run the container.

What the vNext Emulator Supports (and What It Doesn't)

The vNext emulator is still in preview and under active development. The good news: the stuff you need for day-to-day development is almost all there. The bad news: there are a few gaps that might surprise you.

What works: CRUD operations (create, read, update, delete, patch), batch and bulk APIs, Change Feed, partitioned collections, TTL expiration, queries with filters and projections, JOINs (single and multi-level), ORDER BY, aggregates, range operators, paging, and subdocument queries. That covers the vast majority of what you'll do in application development.

Not yet implemented: Custom index policies, Request Unit reporting, collection performance management, parallel cross-partition queries, and collection feed reads. The RU reporting gap is worth knowing about — you won't get accurate `RequestCharge` values from the emulator, so cost testing needs to happen against a real Cosmos account.

Not planned (ever): Stored procedures, triggers, and UDFs. If your application architecture depends on server-side execution, the vNext emulator can't help you. (My opinion: this is fine. I don't use stored procedures or triggers with Cosmos anyway, and I'd recommend against building dependencies on them. They're not that useful.)

Also worth noting: The .NET SDK doesn't support bulk execution in the emulator, and by default the vNext emulator starts in HTTP mode. The .NET SDK requires HTTPS, so you need to add `--protocol https` when starting the container.

For the full feature matrix, check Microsoft's documentation.

Running the vNext Emulator

If you can't tell by this point, I'll say it directly: I think you should use the vNext emulator.

Install Docker and then use the following commands to run it:

```
# Pull the emulator image
docker pull \
```

```
mcr.microsoft.com/cosmosdb/linux/azure-cosmos-emulator:vnext-preview

# Run it
docker run --name cosmosdb --detach --publish 8081:8081 \
  --publish 1234:1234 \
  -e PROTOCOL=https \
  mcr.microsoft.com/cosmosdb/linux/azure-cosmos-emulator:vnext-preview \
  --protocol https
```

Here's the PowerShell script I actually use to manage the emulator. You can download the startup script here. It handles pulling the latest image, cleaning up stale containers, and starting with the right protocol settings:

```
# PowerShell script to start Azure Cosmos DB Emulator in Docker
# Usage: .\start-cosmos-db-emulator.ps1 [-Remove] [-Pull]

param(
    [switch]$Remove,
    [switch]$Pull
)

if ($Remove) {
    Write-Host "Stopping, killing, and removing any existing 'cosmosd
b' container..."
    docker stop cosmosdb 2>$null
    docker kill cosmosdb 2>$null
    docker rm cosmosdb 2>$null
}

if ($Pull) {
    Write-Host "Pulling the latest Azure Cosmos DB Emulator Docker image..."
    docker pull mcr.microsoft.com/cosmosdb/linux/azure-cosmos-emulator:vnext-
preview
}

# Start the Cosmos DB Emulator container
Write-Host "Starting Azure Cosmos DB Emulator container..."
docker run --name cosmosdb --detach --publish 8081:8081 --publish 123
4:1234 `
  -e PROTOCOL=https `
  mcr.microsoft.com/cosmosdb/linux/azure-cosmos-emulator:vnext-preview `
```

```
  --protocol https

# Show exposed ports
Write-Host "Exposed ports for 'cosmosdb' container:"
docker port cosmosdb

Write-Host
Write-Host "The admin site is available at http://localhost:1234 "
```

Once it's running, open `http://localhost:1234` in your browser for the data explorer — a UI for browsing databases, containers, and documents. The Cosmos DB endpoint itself is at `https://localhost:8081`. We're going to use the data explorer to look at what Cosmos actually stores.

The emulator's endpoint key is a well-known string that Microsoft publishes in their docs. It's not a secret — it's a local emulator, there's nothing to protect.

Creating the Database and Container

Before we can save documents, we need to create the database and container. You can do this through the admin UI but you can also do it using code. Here's the setup code:

```
// Create database if it doesn't exist
var databaseResponse = await client.CreateDatabaseIfNotExistsAsync(
    "NotesDb",
    throughput: 400  // Request Units per second — 400 is the minimum
);
var database = databaseResponse.Database;

// Create container with partition key
var containerProperties = new ContainerProperties
{
    Id = "NotesContainer",
    PartitionKeyPath = "/tenantId"
};

var containerResponse =
    await database.CreateContainerIfNotExistsAsync(
        containerProperties
);
```

```
var container = containerResponse.Container;
```

The `PartitionKeyPath` is a JSON path — `/tenantId` — pointing to the property in your documents that Cosmos will use as the partition key. I'm calling this property `TenantId` because most real-world Cosmos DB applications are multi-tenant — the data for different customers, users, or organizations lives in the same container, and the partition key is what keeps everyone's data separated. We'll get deeper into multi-tenancy in the next chapter, but for now just know that "tenant" means "the boundary of who owns this data." And as we discussed last chapter: the partition key path is set at creation time and can never be changed. (I won't belabor the point again. But I've been burned by it, so I keep mentioning it.)

The `throughput: 400` is provisioned Request Units per second. 400 is the minimum and it's fine for development. We'll talk more about RUs and cost in a later chapter.

Running the Code

Here's the `Note` class from last chapter — a simple domain model we're using to test things out:

```
public class Note
{
    // Yes, I know that 'id' is not using PascalCase
    public string id { get; set; } = Guid.NewGuid().ToString();
    public string TenantId { get; set; } = string.Empty;
    public string Title { get; set; } = string.Empty;
    public string Body { get; set; } = string.Empty;
    public DateTime CreatedDate { get; set; } =
            DateTime.UtcNow;
    public List<string> Tags { get; set; } = new();
}
```

Now let's run the save-and-read code from last chapter:

```
var note = new Note
{
    TenantId = "user-123",
    Title = "First Cosmos Note",
```

```
    Body = "Look ma, no boxes!",
    Tags = new List<string> { "cosmos", "getting-started" }
};

// Save
var saveResponse = await container.UpsertItemAsync(
    note,
    new PartitionKey(note.TenantId)
);
Console.WriteLine($"Saved. Cost: {saveResponse.RequestCharge} RUs");

// Read
var readResponse = await container.ReadItemAsync<Note>(
    note.id,
    new PartitionKey(note.TenantId)
);
Console.WriteLine($"Read. Cost: {readResponse.RequestCharge} RUs");
```

You'll see something like "Saved. Cost: 6.29 RUs" and "Read. Cost: 1 RUs." That point read — fetching a single document by partition key + id — is the cheapest operation in Cosmos. Usually 1 RU.

But now open the data explorer at `http://localhost:1234` and look at what's actually in the database.

What Cosmos DB Actually Stores

Navigate to NotesDb → NotesContainer and click on the document. You'll see something like this:

```
{
    "id": "a1b2c3d4-e5f6-7890-abcd-ef1234567890",
    "tenantId": "user-123",
    "title": "First Cosmos Note",
    "body": "Look ma, no boxes!",
    "createdDate": "2026-03-28T14:30:00.0000000Z",
    "tags": [
        "cosmos",
        "getting-started"
    ],
    "_rid": "KfE0AJkbewcBAAAAAAAAAA==",
    "_self": "dbs/KfE0AA==/colls/KfE0AJkbewc=/docs/KfE0AJkbewcBAAAAAA
```

```
AAAA==/",
    "_etag": "\"00000000-0000-0000-abcd-ef1234567890\"",
    "_attachments": "attachments/",
    "_ts": 1711633800
}
```

Your properties are all there — `tenantId`, `title`, `body`, `tags`. Serialized to camelCase JSON. The tree survived the trip to storage.

But there's a bunch of stuff you didn't put there. Those underscored properties are **system properties** that Cosmos adds to every document automatically. Let's go through them.

The Ones You Can Ignore

`_rid` — an internal resource identifier. Cosmos uses this internally. You won't interact with it (and Microsoft says you shouldn't try.)

`_self` — a URI path to the document. Also internal.

`_attachments` — a legacy feature. Ignore it.

Next, on to the ones that are useful.

`_ts` — The Timestamp

`_ts` is a Unix timestamp (seconds since epoch) representing when the document was last modified. Cosmos updates this automatically on every write. You don't set it, you can't control it, it's always there.

Useful for debugging ("when was this last touched?") and it's the basis for TTL (time-to-live) policies if you ever want documents to auto-expire. But day-to-day, it's mostly a "good to know it's there" thing.

`_etag` — The One That Matters a Lot

This is the important one. I'd go so far as to say that after partition keys, understanding `_etag` is the most practically important thing in this chapter.

`_etag` is a value that changes every time the document is updated. It's Cosmos DB's mechanism for **optimistic concurrency** — and understanding it will save you from a category of bugs that are really hard to diagnose after the fact.

Optimistic concurrency is a method of handling multiple people trying to update the same record and making sure that you aren't stomping on each other's changes.

Here's the scenario. Two users load the same note at the same time. User A changes the title and saves. User B changes the body and saves. Without concurrency protection, User B's save overwrites User A's title change. User A's edit is silently lost. Nobody gets an error. The data is just quietly wrong.

The `_etag` prevents this. The pattern works like this:

1. Read the document. Capture the `_etag` value.
2. Make your changes.
3. Save and pass the `_etag` value along to Cosmos along with a directive that says "only accept this save if the `_etag` hasn't changed."
4. If someone else modified the document in the meantime, the `_etag` will have changed. Cosmos rejects the save with a 412 Precondition Failed.

In code:

```
// Step 1: Read and capture the ETag
var readResponse = await container.ReadItemAsync<Note>(
    noteId,
    new PartitionKey(tenantId)
);
var note = readResponse.Resource;
var etag = readResponse.ETag;

// Step 2: Modify the document
note.Title = "Updated Title";

// Step 3: Save with concurrency check
try
{
    await container.UpsertItemAsync(
        note,
        new PartitionKey(note.TenantId),
        new ItemRequestOptions
        {
```

```
                IfMatchEtag = etag
            }
    );
    Console.WriteLine("Saved successfully.");
}
catch (CosmosException ex) when (ex.StatusCode ==
     System.Net.HttpStatusCode.PreconditionFailed)
{
    Console.WriteLine(
        "Conflict! Someone else modified this document.");
    // Reload, merge changes, retry — your decision
}
```

This works. But look at all the manual plumbing. You have to remember to capture the ETag from the read response. You have to remember to pass it in `ItemRequestOptions` on the write. You have to catch a specific `CosmosException` with a specific HTTP status code.

If you forget any of those steps? You just don't have concurrency protection. Silently. The save succeeds. The other user's changes vanish. And nobody finds out until someone notices the data is wrong, which might be weeks later.

The raw SDK gives you the *mechanism* but not the *safety net*. (Don't worry...I'll show you some code in the next chapter that'll help you out.)

The Silent Cross-Partition Problem

There's another slightly jagged edge I want to show you, and it's the one that costs people extra money in production. (Oh...and potential performance problems, too.)

Let's query for all notes belonging to a user. Here's the right way — specifying the partition key:

```
var query = new QueryDefinition(
    "SELECT * FROM c WHERE c.tenantId = @tenantId"
).WithParameter("@tenantId", "user-123");

var options = new QueryRequestOptions
```

```
{
    PartitionKey = new PartitionKey("user-123")
};

var iterator = container.GetItemQueryIterator<Note>(
     query, requestOptions: options);

var notes = new List<Note>();
double totalRUs = 0;

while (iterator.HasMoreResults)
{
    var batch = await iterator.ReadNextAsync();
    totalRUs += batch.RequestCharge;
    notes.AddRange(batch);
}

Console.WriteLine(
     $"Found {notes.Count} notes. Cost: {totalRUs} RUs");
```

That's a single-partition query. Cosmos goes directly to the "user-123" partition, finds the matching documents, returns them. Fast. Cheap.

Now watch what happens when you leave out the partition key:

```
var options = new QueryRequestOptions
{
    // No PartitionKey specified
};
```

The query still works. Returns the correct results. But now Cosmos fans out to *every partition* in the container to find matching documents. More RUs. More time. Worse as your data grows and you introduce more partition keys and therefore more partitions.

And the SDK says nothing. No warning. No log message. No exception. It silently does the expensive thing and charges you for it.

In the emulator with a handful of documents, you might not even notice the difference. But in production with real data across thousands of partitions, this is the kind of thing that shows up as a surprise on your Azure bill. And nothing in the code tells you it's happening.

Taking Stock

Across these last two chapters, we've gone from concepts to running code. The raw SDK works. You can connect, save, read, query, and handle concurrency. The tree goes in, the tree comes out.

But the developer experience has some real friction:

You construct `PartitionKey` objects manually on every operation. Forget it and the SDK silently does something expensive.

Concurrency control is opt-in and manual. Forget a step and you silently lose data.

Querying requires ceremony. Build a query definition, create request options, get an iterator, loop through pages, accumulate results. A lot of scaffolding for "give me the matching documents."

The SDK doesn't protect you from expensive mistakes. Cross-partition queries look identical to single-partition queries in the code. The only difference shows up in the RU charges.

Nothing connects to the concepts from Chapters 1-2. Where are the aggregate roots? Where's the domain model pattern? The SDK doesn't know about any of that. It doesn't enforce document boundaries. It doesn't know your `Note` class is a domain object. It's just serializing JSON.

Every one of these friction points is a place where the discipline has to come from you. And as I said back in Chapter 1 — discipline doesn't scale as well as we'd like to think it does.

In the next chapter, we'll take every one of these pain points and show what happens when the discipline comes from a utility library instead. When `TenantItemBase` carries its partition key automatically. When the repository builds the right `PartitionKey` for every query without you thinking about it. When cross-partition queries get detected and logged instead of silently executed. When optimistic concurrency is handled by the base class, not by you.

The raw SDK isn't bad. It's just — well — raw. Let's make it better.

Chapter 5 Benday.CosmosDb — The Foundation

At the end of the last chapter, we took stock. We'd written working code against the Cosmos DB SDK, and it was… fine. It worked. But we'd also built up a friction inventory — a list of things that felt harder than they should be.

Here's what was on that list:

5. **Manual partition key construction.** Every read, every write, every query — you're hand-building `PartitionKey` objects. Forget one and you get a cross-partition query instead of a point read. The SDK doesn't warn you.
6. **Opt-in concurrency.** ETags exist, but you have to remember to capture them, remember to pass them back, and remember to catch the specific exception. Forget any step and you silently lose data.
7. **Query ceremony.** Getting a simple list of documents requires `GetItemLinqQueryable`, `ToFeedIterator`, a `while` loop over `ReadNextAsync`, and manual result aggregation. It's not hard. It's just a lot of plumbing for what should be a one-liner.
8. **Silent cross-partition queries.** The same query with and without a partition key returns the same results. One costs 3 RUs. The other costs 30. The SDK says nothing.
9. **No aggregate root awareness.** The SDK doesn't know what your documents represent. It doesn't know that a `Note` and a `Person` are different species of tree in the same container. It doesn't know that `TenantId` is your partition key. Every bit of domain knowledge lives in your head, not in the code.

The raw SDK isn't bad. It's just — well — raw. It gives you mechanisms without guardrails.

This chapter is about adding the guardrails and making these problems fade into the background.

Install a NuGet Package: Benday.CosmosDb

When I first started writing apps that use Cosmos DB, I bumped into all those issues above and started trying to find ways to make them less painful. I wanted nice, standardized things that developers could use that would simply do the right thing. Over time that turned into my Benday.CosmosDb NuGet package. Before we get into the details, let's get the library installed.

```
dotnet add package Benday.CosmosDb
```

The library is open source, MIT licensed, and available on NuGet. The source code is on GitHub at benday-inc/Benday.CosmosDb. (Share and enjoy.)

There's a complete sample application in that repository, too.

The Tree That Stores Itself

Let's start with the biggest item on the friction inventory: no aggregate root awareness.

In Chapter 1, we talked about how domain models are trees — hierarchical, branching structures with identity and behavior. In Chapter 2, we talked about how Cosmos DB stores JSON documents, and JSON documents *are* trees. The whole promise of a document database is that the tree goes straight into storage without being chopped into boxes first.

But when we wrote code with the raw SDK in Chapter 4, that promise didn't quite land. We had a `Note` class, sure. But it was just a POCO (Plain Old C# Object) with some properties. It didn't know what its partition key was. It didn't carry its own concurrency token. It didn't know what kind of document it was in a shared container. All of that knowledge was spread across our application code — in the `PartitionKey` constructors we built by hand, in the `ItemRequestOptions` we remembered (or forgot) to set, in the query filters we wrote to separate notes from other document types.

The `Benday.CosmosDb.DomainModels.TenantItemBase` class fixes this. It's the base class for your domain models in the Benday.CosmosDb library, and it carries everything a document needs to store itself correctly.

Here's what a `Note` class looks like when it inherits from `TenantItemBase`:

```
using Benday.CosmosDb.DomainModels;

public class Note : TenantItemBase
{
    public string Title { get; set; } = string.Empty;
    public string Body { get; set; } = string.Empty;
```

```
    public DateTime CreatedDate { get; set; } =
                DateTime.UtcNow;
    public List<string> Tags { get; set; } = new();
}
```

That's it. That's your domain model. Just your business properties. Everything else — identity, partition key, concurrency, type discrimination — comes from the base class.

Let's look at what `TenantItemBase` gives you.

Id

Every document needs a unique identifier. `TenantItemBase` provides an `Id` property that auto-generates a GUID string. You never have to think about it. If you create a new `Note` and save it, it already has an `Id`. If you want to set your own, you can — but you don't have to.

TenantId and Why Multi-Tenancy Matters

This is the first level of your partition key, and it's worth pausing to talk about why it's called `TenantId` and not something more generic.

Most real-world applications are **multi-tenant**. That just means more than one customer, organization, or user's data lives in the same system. A SaaS product where each company has their own data? Multi-tenant. A note-taking app where each user has their own notes? Multi-tenant. An internal enterprise app where different departments have separate data? Multi-tenant.

The "tenant" is whoever owns the data. Sometimes it's a company. Sometimes it's a user. Sometimes it's a team or a department. Sometimes it's data that's owned by the application itself. The specific meaning depends on your application — but the pattern is the same: you need a boundary that keeps one tenant's data separate from another's.

Cosmos DB is *unusually good* at this. Here's why.

The partition key is Cosmos DB's fundamental unit of performance isolation. All documents with the same partition key live together, get queried together, and scale together. When you make `TenantId` your partition key, you're telling Cosmos: "all of Tenant A's data lives here, all of Tenant B's data lives there." Each tenant gets their own partition, which means their queries don't compete with each other, their data doesn't intermingle, and their performance doesn't degrade as other tenants grow.

In a relational database, you'd typically implement multi-tenancy with a `WHERE TenantId = @tenantId` clause on every query, and you'd rely on discipline (or a query filter) to make sure nobody forgets it. In Cosmos, the partition key enforces it at the storage layer. If your code asks for Tenant A's partition, it physically cannot see Tenant B's documents. The isolation isn't a filter — it's structural.

This is why the library's recommended partition key path is `/tenantId,/entityType` — a hierarchical partition key with two levels. The first level, `TenantId`, gives you tenant isolation. The second level, `EntityType`, gives you type filtering within the tenant. Together, they mean that most of your queries — "give me all Notes for this tenant," "find this Person in this tenant" — hit exactly one partition. No fan-out. No cross-partition costs. Just a direct read from the right place.

And because `TenantId` lives *on the domain model*, it's not something you construct separately when you call the SDK. The document knows where it belongs.

EntityType

This is the second level of your partition key, and it's one of my favorite design decisions in the library. `EntityType` is a read-only property that returns the name of your concrete class. For our `Note` class, `EntityType` automatically returns `"Note"`.

Why does this matter? Because in Cosmos DB, you'll often store multiple types of documents in the same container. Notes, Persons, Comments — they all live together. `EntityType` is how you tell them apart. It's what I call the "species of tree" identifier — your container is a forest, and `EntityType` tells you which species you're looking at.

And because it's computed from the class name via `GetEntityTypeName()`, you can't forget to set it. You can't accidentally set it to the wrong value. It's just correct, every time.

Etag

The ETag property carries the concurrency token from Cosmos DB. When you read a document, the ETag comes back with it. When you save, the library automatically passes it back to Cosmos as an `IfMatchEtag` condition. If someone else modified the document since you read it, the save throws an `OptimisticConcurrencyException`.

Compare that to the raw SDK, where you had to capture the ETag from the response, store it somewhere, and remember to pass it in `ItemRequestOptions`. Here, it's just a property on the object. It round-trips automatically.

The Partition Key Builds Itself

In the raw SDK, every operation required you to construct a `PartitionKey`:

```
// Raw SDK — you build this every time
var partitionKey = new PartitionKey(note.TenantId);

// Or with hierarchical keys:
var partitionKey = new PartitionKeyBuilder()
    .Add(note.TenantId)
    .Add("Note")
    .Build();
```

With the library, the repository constructs the partition key from the item's `TenantId` and `EntityType` properties. You never touch `PartitionKeyBuilder`. The document knows its own partition key because that information is part of its identity.

The default partition key path is `/tenantId,/entityType` — a hierarchical partition key with two levels. The library builds the correct `PartitionKey` object automatically for every read, write, and query.

This is worth pausing on. In the raw SDK, the partition key was something *you* built for *each operation*. With the library, the partition key is something *the document knows about itself*. That's not just fewer lines of code. It's a fundamentally different relationship between your domain model and your storage — and it means an entire category of mistakes (wrong partition key, forgotten partition key, mismatched partition key) simply can't happen.

The Repository: Where the Friction Disappears

The domain model carries the data. The repository handles the operations. Let's look at what changes when you use the library's built-in repository instead of raw `Container` calls.

You Don't Have to Write a Repository Class

With the library's DI registration helper (which we'll cover in detail shortly), you can get a fully functional repository without writing a single repository class:

```
helper.RegisterRepository<Note>();
```

That one line registers `CosmosTenantItemRepository<Note>` as the implementation for `ITenantItemRepository<Note>`. You inject `ITenantItemRepository<Note>` into your code, and you've got save, get by id, get all, delete, paged queries, and bulk operations — all partition-key-aware, all with ETag concurrency, all with RU logging. No custom class. No boilerplate coding required.

In my HonestCheetah application, several entity types use exactly this pattern:

```
CosmosHelper.RegisterRepository<IssueData>();
CosmosHelper.RegisterRepository<GitHubAppInstallationData>();
CosmosHelper.RegisterRepository<GitHubAppTokenData>();
```

Three entity types, three lines, done. Each gets a fully functional repository through `ITenantItemRepository<T>`. They don't have any need for custom queries right now but if they do, I've got a clean spot in my code where I can drop it in.

When You Need Custom Queries

Eventually you'll need queries that go beyond `GetAllAsync` and `GetByIdAsync`. Maybe you need to find notes by tag, or get the most recent notes across all tenants for an admin dashboard. That's when you create a custom repository class:

```
using Benday.CosmosDb.Repositories;
using Microsoft.Azure.Cosmos;
using Microsoft.Extensions.Logging;
using Microsoft.Extensions.Options;
```

```csharp
public class NoteRepository : CosmosTenantItemRepository<Note>
{
    public NoteRepository(
        IOptions<CosmosRepositoryOptions<Note>> options,
        CosmosClient client,
        ILoggerFactory loggerFactory) : base(options, client,
             loggerFactory) { }

    public async Task<List<Note>> GetByTagAsync(
         string tenantId, string tag)
    {
        var context = await GetQueryContextAsync(tenantId);
        var query = context.Queryable.Where(
              n => n.Tags.Contains(tag));
        return await GetResultsAsync(query, "GetByTagAsync",
             context.PartitionKey);
    }
}
```

You still get all the base class operations for free. You're just adding the queries that are specific to your domain. And here's what's nice about the custom query: `GetQueryContextAsync(tenantId)` gives you a LINQ queryable that's already scoped to the right partition. `GetResultsAsync` handles the feed iterator loop, logs the RU cost, and checks for cross-partition queries. You write the `Where` clause. The library handles the plumbing.

The DI registration for a custom repository uses the three-type-parameter overload:

```csharp
// Note = domain model class
// INoteRepository = the repository interface
// NoteRepository = the repository implementation
helper.RegisterRepository<Note, INoteRepository, NoteRepository>();
```

In HonestCheetah, you can see both patterns side by side — simple registrations for entities that only need basic CRUD, and custom repositories for entities that need specialized queries:

```
// Simple — no custom class needed
CosmosHelper.RegisterRepository<IssueData>();
CosmosHelper.RegisterRepository<LinkedGitHubAccount>();

// Custom — entity needs specialized queries
CosmosHelper.RegisterRepository<Project, IProjectRepository,
     CosmosDbProjectRepository>();
CosmosHelper.RegisterRepository<UserData, IUserRepository,
     CosmosDbUserRepository>();
```

Start simple. Add a custom repository when you need one. The library doesn't make you decide up front.

What You Get: The Repository Operations

Whether you're using the built-in `ITenantItemRepository<Note>` or a custom repository class, the operations are the same. In the examples below, `noteRepository` could be either one — the interface gives you everything shown here.

Save

In the raw SDK:

```
// Raw SDK save with concurrency
var response = await container.UpsertItemAsync(
    note,
    new PartitionKey(note.TenantId),
    new ItemRequestOptions { IfMatchEtag = etag }
);
// Don't forget to capture the new ETag
etag = response.ETag;
```

With the library:

```
await noteRepository.SaveAsync(note);
```

One line. The repository builds the partition key from `note.TenantId` and `note.EntityType`. It passes `note.Etag` as the `IfMatchEtag`. After the save, it updates `note.Etag` with the new value from the response. It also syncs the `TimestampUnixStyle` property and logs the RU cost.

If another user modified the document since you read it, you get an `OptimisticConcurrencyException`. Not a raw `CosmosException` with a 412 status code that you have to know to catch — a named exception that tells you exactly what happened.

Get by Id

In the raw SDK, you'd typically do a point read:

```
// Raw SDK point read
var response = await container.ReadItemAsync<Note>(
    noteId,
    new PartitionKey(tenantId)
);
var note = response.Resource;
```

With the library:

```
var note = await noteRepository.GetByIdAsync(tenantId, noteId);
```

The repository does a point read with the correct partition key. One RU, same as the raw SDK. But you didn't have to construct the `PartitionKey` yourself.

Get All (for a Tenant)

```
var notes = await noteRepository.GetAllAsync(tenantId);
```

This queries within the partition — efficient, partition-scoped, ordered by timestamp descending. The query is automatically filtered to documents matching the `Note` entity type.

Delete

```
await noteRepository.DeleteAsync(note);
```

Note that the tenant-scoped delete takes the *item*, not just the id. The repository extracts the partition key from the item itself, so it can do a point delete. Efficient, direct, no cross-partition scan.

Paged Queries

For large result sets:

```
var page = await noteRepository.GetPagedAsync(
    tenantId,
    pageSize: 25
);

// page.Items - the results
// page.ContinuationToken - pass this back for the next page
// page.HasMoreResults - are there more pages?
// page.TotalRequestCharge - how much did this cost?
```

Continuation-token-based pagination, partition-scoped, with RU tracking built in.

Concurrency You Can't Forget

I want to come back to the concurrency story because it's a good example of how the library's design philosophy works.

With the raw SDK, concurrency protection is opt-in. You *can* use ETags, but nothing forces you to. The default behavior — upsert without an ETag check — silently overwrites whatever's there. In Chapter 4, I showed you the code to do it right: capture the ETag, pass it in `ItemRequestOptions`, catch the `CosmosException` with status code 412.

The library inverts this. Concurrency protection is the default because in a production application you're going to need it. Every `SaveAsync` call passes the ETag. If this is a new document (empty ETag), the upsert works as expected. If it's an existing document, the ETag check is automatic. You'd have to go out of your way to *disable* it.

This matters because the most dangerous bugs are the ones that don't throw exceptions. Silently overwriting another user's changes doesn't throw. The save succeeds. The data is wrong. Nobody knows until someone notices the problem, and by then you've lost the information you need to diagnose it.

The library makes the safe thing the easy thing.

The Library Yells When You Do Something Expensive

Remember the silent cross-partition problem from Chapter 4? Same query, same results, wildly different cost — and the SDK says nothing?

The library fixes this in two ways.

Cross-Partition Detection

Every time the library executes a query, it inspects the Cosmos DB diagnostics for signs of a cross-partition operation. If it detects one, it logs a warning to ILogger:

```
*** WARNING ***: Cross-partition query detected
```

It doesn't throw an exception — sometimes cross-partition queries are intentional. But it makes sure you *know*. The raw SDK gives you silence. The library gives you a heads-up.

RU Logging

Every operation — point reads, upserts, queries — logs its Request Unit cost. You'll see entries like:

```
Request Charge (SaveAsync): 6.29
Request Charge (GetByIdAsync): 1.0
Total request charge (GetAllAsync): 12.47
```

This isn't just nice-to-have. It's how you catch performance problems before they become billing problems. When you see a query that should cost 3 RUs costing 30, you know something's wrong. When you see costs creeping up over time, you can investigate before your Azure bill surprises you.

The repository also exposes RU information in `PagedResults<T>.TotalRequestCharge`, so you can surface cost data to your own monitoring.

The [Obsolete] Markers: Guardrails Against the Wrong Pattern

There's one more thing the library does that I want to call out, and it came from a real production incident (that I introduced myself).

The library has two layers of methods. The base `CosmosRepository<T>` class has methods like `GetByIdAsync(string id)` and `DeleteAsync(string id)` that take just an id — no tenant, no partition key. These work, but they do cross-partition queries to find the item first. They're expensive.

The `CosmosTenantItemRepository<T>` class adds tenant-scoped versions: `GetByIdAsync(string tenantId, string id)` and `DeleteAsync(T item)`. These use partition keys directly. They're efficient.

A few months ago, I found some AI-generated code that was calling the non-partition-key version of `GetByIdAsync`. The code worked. The tests passed. But performance in production was bizarre — reads that should have been 1 RU were costing 15-20 RUs. The AI had picked the simpler method signature because it looked right, and nothing in the code told it otherwise.

So I added `[Obsolete]` attributes to the non-partition-key methods. Now the compiler itself tells you — and your AI coding assistant — to use the partition-aware versions. The cross-partition methods still exist for cases where you genuinely need them, but you have to consciously acknowledge the warning by adding a `#pragma warning disable` directive.

Guardrails aren't just for humans anymore.

Wiring It Up

So far we've looked at the domain model and the repository. Let's talk about how you actually configure all of this in an application.

Configuration using the Emulator

If you're running locally against the Cosmos DB emulator, all you need in your `appsettings.json` is this:

```
{
  "CosmosConfiguration": {
    "UseEmulator": true
  }
}
```

This sets a whole bunch of defaults for you for the database name, container name, partition key, etc. The idea is to get you up and running quickly against the emulator. If you want to start customizing some of the values like database name or container name, just add those values into the config along with `UseEmulator`.

```
{
  "CosmosConfiguration": {
```

```
    "UseEmulator": true,
    "DatabaseName": "NotesDb",
    "ContainerName": "NotesContainer"
  }
}
```

Loading the config is one line:

```
var cosmosConfig = builder.Configuration.GetCosmosConfig();
```

Configuration in Detail

So that's the simple, emulator-focused config stuff. What about moving towards production? What else can you configure?

```
{
  "CosmosConfiguration": {
    "Endpoint": "https://localhost:8081",
    "AccountKey": "your-key-here",
    "DatabaseName": "NotesDb",
    "ContainerName": "NotesContainer",
    "PartitionKey": "/tenantId,/entityType",
    "CreateStructures": true,
    "DatabaseThroughput": 400,
    "UseGatewayMode": true,
    "UseHierarchicalPartitionKey": true,
    "AllowBulkExecution": true,
    "UseDefaultAzureCredential": false
  }
}
```

A few things to notice here. `CreateStructures: true` tells the library to create the database and container if they don't exist — handy for development against the emulator. `UseGatewayMode: true` is required as of April 2026 for the vNext emulator (you'll typically set this to `false` in production). And `UseHierarchicalPartitionKey: true` enables the two-level partition key path we've been talking about.

Let's say our application is an ASP.NET app running in an Azure App Service. The best practice for security reasons is to use Azure managed identity for authentication. You'd set the App Service to have managed identity turned on and then you'll grant permissions to that identity in Cosmos DB. (I just yada yada'd past a ton of detail. More on permissions later.)

For a production application, the cosmos config in my `appsettings.json` typically looks something like this:

```
{
  "CosmosConfiguration":
  {
      "Endpoint": "https://mycosmosdb.documents.azure.com:443/"
,
      "DatabaseName": "MyDatabase",
      "ContainerName": "MyContainer",
      "CreateStructures": false,
      "UseDefaultAzureCredential": true
  }
}
```

What's nice about this is that it doesn't have any secrets stored in it (like AccountKey) so I can stuff this into Git if I want to.

DI Registration with CosmosRegistrationHelper

You've already seen `RegisterRepository<Note>()` in the examples above. Here's the full picture of how it fits into application startup:

```
var builder = WebApplication.CreateBuilder(args);

// GetCosmosConfig() is an extension method that reads the conf
ig
var cosmosConfig = builder.Configuration.GetCosmosConfig();

// pass the DI services collection and the cosmos config to the
helper
var helper = new CosmosRegistrationHelper(builder.Services,
      cosmosConfig);
```

```
// Simple entities - no custom repository class needed
helper.RegisterRepository<Note>();
helper.RegisterRepository<Tag>();

// Entity with a custom repository
helper.RegisterRepository<Project, IProjectRepository,
      ProjectRepository>();

// Entity that needs a service layer, too
helper.RegisterRepositoryAndService<Note>();
```

When you create the `CosmosRegistrationHelper`, it configures a singleton `CosmosClient` from your `CosmosConfig`. Each `RegisterRepository` call configures the `CosmosRepositoryOptions<T>` for that entity type and registers the repository as transient.

`RegisterRepositoryAndService<Note>()` does everything `RegisterRepository` does plus registers `TenantItemService<Note>` as the implementation for `ITenantItemService<Note>`. The service layer is intentionally thin — it passes through to the repository. We'll talk about why you'd want that layer in a later chapter when we get into application architecture.

Per-Entity Container Overrides

Here's something that comes up in real applications: you might want different entity types in different containers. Maybe your main entities live in the default container but your webhook log entries need their own container with a completely different partition key.

The three-type-parameter registration method accepts optional overrides:

```
helper.RegisterRepository<
    WebhookLogEntry,
    IWebhookLogRepository, WebhookLogRepository>(
        containerName: "raw-webhooks",
        partitionKey: "/partitionKey"
    );
```

Any parameter you don't specify falls back to the defaults from your `CosmosConfig`. This means you can have one configuration section for the common case and override only what's different per entity type.

Non-ASP.NET Scenarios: CosmosConfigBuilder

Not building a web app? The `CosmosConfigBuilder` provides a fluent API for building configuration in console apps, Azure Functions, or test projects:

```
var config = new CosmosConfigBuilder()
    .ForEmulator()   // preset for local emulator
    .WithDatabase("NotesDb")
    .WithContainer("NotesContainer")
    .UseHierarchicalPartitionKeys()
    .WithCreateStructures()
    .Build();
```

`ForEmulator()` sets the endpoint, account key, and gateway mode for the Cosmos Linux emulator. `Build()` validates that all required fields are set and returns a `CosmosConfig`.

Side by Side: Before and After

Let's put it all together. Here's what the same operations look like in the raw SDK versus the library. This is the code from Chapter 4, reimagined.

Defining a Domain Model

Raw SDK:

```
public class Note
{
    public string id { get; set; } = Guid.NewGuid().ToString();
    public string TenantId { get; set; } = string.Empty;
    public string Title { get; set; } = string.Empty;
    public string Body { get; set; } = string.Empty;
    public DateTime CreatedDate { get; set; } =
         DateTime.UtcNow;
    public List<string> Tags { get; set; } = new();
}
```

Benday.CosmosDb:

```
public class Note : TenantItemBase
{
    public string Title { get; set; } = string.Empty;
    public string Body { get; set; } = string.Empty;
    public DateTime CreatedDate { get; set; } =
         DateTime.UtcNow;
    public List<string> Tags { get; set; } = new();
}
```

The `id` property with its awkward lowercase name is gone. The `TenantId` that you had to declare and manage yourself is handled by the base class. What's left is just your business data. (The tree, not the plumbing.)

Saving a Document

Raw SDK:

```
var partitionKey = new PartitionKeyBuilder()
    .Add(note.TenantId)
    .Add("Note")
    .Build();


try
{
    var response = await container.UpsertItemAsync(
        note, partitionKey,
        new ItemRequestOptions { IfMatchEtag = etag }
    );
    etag = response.ETag;
    Console.WriteLine(
        $"Saved. Cost: {response.RequestCharge} RUs");
}
catch (CosmosException ex)
    when (ex.StatusCode ==
        System.Net.HttpStatusCode.PreconditionFailed)
```

```
{
    Console.WriteLine("Conflict detected.");
}
```

Benday.CosmosDb:

```
try
{
    await noteRepository.SaveAsync(note);
}
catch (OptimisticConcurrencyException)
{
    Console.WriteLine("Conflict detected.");
}
```

Partition key construction: gone. ETag management: gone. RU logging: automatic. The save is one line. The exception is named.

Reading a Document

Raw SDK:

```
var response = await container.ReadItemAsync<Note>(
    noteId,
    new PartitionKey(tenantId)
);
var note = response.Resource;
Console.WriteLine($"Read. Cost: {response.RequestCharge} RUs");
```

Benday.CosmosDb:

```
var note = await noteRepository.GetByIdAsync(tenantId, noteId);
```

Querying Documents

Raw SDK:

```
var queryable = container.GetItemLinqQueryable<Note>(
    requestOptions: new QueryRequestOptions
    {
        PartitionKey = new PartitionKey(tenantId)
```

```
    }
);

var query = queryable
    .Where(n => n.TenantId == tenantId)
    .OrderByDescending(n => n.CreatedDate)
    .ToFeedIterator();

var results = new List<Note>();
while (query.HasMoreResults)
{
    var response = await query.ReadNextAsync();
    results.AddRange(response);
}
```

Benday.CosmosDb:

```
var notes = await noteRepository.GetAllAsync(tenantId);
```

Twelve lines to one. And the one line automatically scopes to the partition, filters by entity type, orders by timestamp, logs the RU cost, and checks for cross-partition queries.

What the Library Actually Did

Let's go back to that friction inventory from Chapter 4 and check things off.

Manual partition key construction. ☑ Gone. The document carries its own `TenantId` and `EntityType`. The repository builds the partition key automatically.

Opt-in concurrency. ☑ Inverted. Concurrency is now the default. ETags round-trip on the domain model. The library throws `OptimisticConcurrencyException` on conflicts.

Query ceremony. ☑ Collapsed. `GetAllAsync(tenantId)` replaces a dozen lines of LINQ-to-feed-iterator plumbing.

Silent cross-partition queries. ☑ The library detects them and logs warnings. The `[Obsolete]` markers nudge you (and your AI coding assistant) toward partition-aware methods.

No aggregate root awareness. ☑ `TenantItemBase` *is* an aggregate root implementation. It carries identity, partition key, concurrency token, and type discrimination. The repository manages one entity type per instance. The type system encodes what used to live only in your head.

But here's the thing I want you to take away from this chapter. The library didn't just reduce the amount of code you write — although it did that. It changed *where the knowledge lives*.

In the raw SDK, the knowledge of how to correctly save a document was spread across your application: the right partition key constructor here, the right ETag handling there, the right query filter somewhere else. Every time you wrote a new operation, you had to remember all of it. And the SDK was perfectly happy to let you forget.

With the library, that knowledge is encoded in the base classes and the repository. `TenantItemBase` knows what it is. The repository knows how to store it correctly. You can focus on what the document *means* to your application instead of how to convince the SDK to handle it properly.

In Chapter 1, I said that the promise of a document database is that the tree goes straight into storage. With the raw SDK, that promise came with a lot of fine print. With the library, the fine print is handled for you.

The tree stores itself.

Next up: Chapter 6, where we get into the really important stuff — partition key strategy and data modeling. How do you decide what goes in a document? When is something its own aggregate root versus a nested object? What happens when entities need to reference each other across document boundaries? That's where the "species of tree" concept from this chapter becomes a design framework.

Chapter 6 Cosmos DB Partition Keys & Data Modeling

In Chapter 5, we introduced `TenantItemBase` and the repository pattern, and I mentioned that `EntityType` is the "species of tree" identifier — the thing that tells you what kind of document you're looking at in a shared container. I also said that `TenantItemBase` is an aggregate root implementation.

But we didn't really dig into what any of that means for how you *design* your data. We used a single `Note` class and moved on. Real applications aren't that simple. Real applications have Persons who have Notes. Notes that have Comments. Lookup tables that provide picklist values. Entities that reference each other, nest inside each other, and sometimes need to exist independently of each other.

This is the chapter where the conceptual vocabulary from Chapters 1 and 2 becomes a practical design framework. By the end of it, you should be able to look at your own domain model and know exactly how to map it into Cosmos DB documents.

One Question That Solves Most of It

When people ask how they should model data in Cosmos DB, I typically start with the following question:

"If you delete the parent, should this disappear too?"

That's it. That one question tells you more about your document structure than any number of blog posts about partition key cardinality or denormalization strategies.

If the answer is **"yes, absolutely"** — the data belongs *inside* the parent document. It's a nested object. An Address on a Person. A line item on an Order. Tags on a Note. These things have no independent existence. They're part of the tree.

If the answer is **"no, it should survive on its own"** — the data is its own document. Its own aggregate root. A Person and a Note might be related, but deleting the Person shouldn't destroy their Notes. (Maybe the Notes get reassigned, maybe they become orphaned, but they don't vanish.) These are separate trees in the same forest.

If the answer is **"it's complicated"** — congratulations, you've found a real design decision. And that ambiguity is actually useful information. It's telling you something about your domain that you need to think through before you write any code.

Let's work through each of these.

Aggregate Roots

The Aggregate Root design pattern is one of those things that doesn't get nearly enough recognition. And to be honest, I feel like a broken record sometimes talking about aggregate root, aggregate root, aggregate root, aggregate root, ad infinitum. In my mind, identifying your system's aggregate roots is *the key* that unlocks good design whether you're storing data in a relational database, document database, or some flat-file storage system you rolled yourself.

The idea isn't new — it's been around for a while — but it feels almost completely unknown to most developers.

An Aggregate Root is the entry point for your data access operations. In an application of any complexity, you'll probably have more than one. It's not unusual to have a half-dozen, dozen or more. The content management system for my website/blog has:

- Page
- BlogEntry
- Menu
- Contact

Let's look at the Menu class because it's fairly simple. My content management system (CMS) can have multiple menu definitions but the default is "main menu". `Menu` extends from `TenantItemBase` and that means it has its own identity — it's an aggregate root.

```
namespace Benday.Cms.Api.DomainModels;

public class Menu : TenantItemBase
{
    public string Name { get; set; } = string.Empty;
```

```
    public List<MenuItem> Items { get; set; } = new();
}
```

But the `Menu` has a collection of `MenuItem` objects and those make up the links that are part of the `Menu`. The `MenuItem` class doesn't have any identity. There's no `MenuItem.Id` property because you'd never get a `MenuItem` on its own. There's no point. You'd never care about a `MenuItem` unless you were doing something related to a `Menu`.

```
public class MenuItem
{
    public string Title { get; set; } = string.Empty;
    public string Url { get; set; } = string.Empty;
    public bool OpenInNewTab { get; set; }
}
```

This means that I'll want a Repository for `Menu` that will at a minimum handle all my CRUD operations for that class.

Aggregate roots don't just organize your data — *they organize your entire application*. Each aggregate root gets a repository. Each repository can get a service layer on top of it. The service layer is where your business logic lives — validation, operations, authorization. The repositories know how to talk to Cosmos. The services know what the business rules are. Everything hides behind interfaces so it's loosely coupled, testable, and maintainable. We'll build this architecture out later in the book when we put a real application together. For now, know that the aggregate root decisions you make in this chapter ripple all the way up and down through your application design.

"Yes, Delete It" — Nested Objects

The simplest case. Some data only makes sense in the context of its parent. It has no identity of its own. You'd never query for it independently. It exists to describe or extend the parent.

Think about a shipping address on an order. You'd probably never say "give me address #47" without knowing which order it belongs to. You might ask to see all orders in Texas though. The difference is subtle but your "where" clause is going after data in the order's address in order to show the orders — you're using the address but what you actually care about is the order.

The address is part of the order. If the order goes away, the address goes with it.

In Cosmos DB, this is just… a property on your document. No special pattern needed.

```
public class Order : TenantItemBase
{
    public string CustomerId { get; set; } = string.Empty;
    public DateTime OrderDate { get; set; } =
        DateTime.UtcNow;
    public Address ShippingAddress { get; set; } = new();
    public Address BillingAddress { get; set; } = new();
    public List<LineItem> Items { get; set; } = new();
    public decimal Total { get; set; }
}

public class Address
{
    public string Street { get; set; } = string.Empty;
    public string City { get; set; } = string.Empty;
    public string State { get; set; } = string.Empty;
    public string PostalCode { get; set; } = string.Empty;
}

public class LineItem
{
    public string ProductId { get; set; } = string.Empty;
    public string ProductName { get; set; } = string.Empty
;
    public int Quantity { get; set; }
    public decimal UnitPrice { get; set; }
}
```

`Address` and `LineItem` don't inherit from `TenantItemBase`. They don't have their own `Id` and they don't have any *use* for an id. They don't have their own

`EntityType`. They're just classes — nested objects that get serialized as part of the Order document's JSON tree.

This is the document database promise at its most direct. In a relational database, this Order would be spread across three or four tables: `Orders`, `Addresses`, `OrderLineItems`, maybe `OrderAddresses` if you're really normalized. You'd need JOINs to reconstruct the Order for display. You'd need transactions to keep the tables consistent. That's a lot of inserts, updates, and joins.

In Cosmos, the Order is one document. One read. One write. The tree stays intact.

The heuristic is simple: if the data has no independent identity and no reason to exist outside its parent, nest it.

"No, It Survives" — Separate Aggregate Roots

Now consider the relationship between a Person and their Notes. If you delete a Person from the system, should all their Notes vanish? Maybe. But maybe not. Maybe those Notes contain institutional knowledge that should be preserved. Maybe they get reassigned to another person. Maybe the business rule is "archive the person but keep the notes."

When the answer to "should this disappear?" is no — or even "maybe not" — you're looking at separate aggregate roots. Separate documents. Separate trees.

In the Benday.CosmosDb library, this means both entities inherit from `TenantItemBase`:

```
public class Person : TenantItemBase
{
    public string FirstName { get; set; } = string.Empty;
    public string LastName { get; set; } = string.Empty;
    public string Email { get; set; } = string.Empty;
}

public class Note : TenantItemBase
{
    public string Title { get; set; } = string.Empty;
```

```
    public string Body { get; set; } = string.Empty;
    public DateTime CreatedDate { get; set; } =
        DateTime.UtcNow;
    public List<string> Tags { get; set; } = new();
}
```

Each has its own `Id`. Each has its own `EntityType` (automatically set to `"Person"` and `"Note"`). Each gets its own repository. Each is independently queryable, independently saveable, independently deletable.

They can live in the same container, and typically they will. The `EntityType` property — the second level of the hierarchical partition key — is what keeps them distinct. When you call `noteRepository.GetAllAsync(tenantId)`, the query is automatically scoped to documents where `EntityType == "Note"`. The Person documents are right there in the same partition, but the repository doesn't see them. Different species of tree in the same forest.

The Container Is a Forest

This is the "species of tree" concept I introduced in Chapter 5, and it's worth expanding on here because it's central to how you think about Cosmos DB containers.

In a relational database, each table holds one type of thing. The `Person` table holds person records. The `Note` table holds notes. You know what you're getting because the table name tells you. And the database engine prohibits you from trying to store a `Note` in the person table. That's schema validation and enforcement.

In Cosmos DB, a container holds *documents*. Those documents can be anything. A single container can hold Person documents, Note documents, Comment documents, and LookupValue documents all mixed together. The container is a forest, and the different document types are different species of tree.

`EntityType` is the species label. It's what makes this work. Without it, you'd have to inspect each document to figure out what it is. With it, the repository can filter by type automatically, and the hierarchical partition key `/tenantId,/entityType` means that queries for "all Notes belonging to tenant X" hit exactly one partition. No scanning through Person documents to find the Notes. No cross-partition fan-out.

This is why my library defaults to a shared container with `EntityType` as the second partition key level. It gives you the organizational clarity of separate tables with the performance characteristics of co-located data. Most of the time, this is what you want.

(There are exceptions — we'll talk about when you'd put an entity type in its own container later in this chapter.)

"It's Complicated" — The Parented Pattern

Now here's where it gets interesting. What about Comments on a Note?

If you delete a Note, should its Comments disappear? Almost certainly yes. A Comment without its parent Note is meaningless. It's a response to something that no longer exists.

But Comments aren't quite like line items on an Order. A Comment has its own identity — you might need to edit a specific comment, delete a specific comment, query for "all comments by this user." It has its own lifecycle even though it exists in the context of a parent.

So it fails the "just nest it" test (it has independent identity) but it also fails the "separate aggregate root" test (it shouldn't survive deletion of its parent). It's somewhere in between.

This is what the `ParentedItemBase` class is for.

ParentedItemBase

`Benday.CosmosDb.ParentedItemBase` inherits from `TenantItemBase` and adds two properties that help us to handle these bridging relationships:

```
public abstract class ParentedItemBase : TenantItemBase, I
ParentedItem
{
    public string ParentId { get; set; } = string.Empty;
    public abstract string ParentEntityType { get; set; }
}
```

`ParentId` is the `Id` of the parent document. `ParentEntityType` is the `EntityType` of the parent — which species of tree is the parent. `ParentEntityType` is abstract, which means your concrete class *must* implement it. You can't forget to specify what kind of parent this entity belongs to.

Something that I want to point out here about data enforcement. In a relational database, you'd probably use a foreign key constraint to define, validate, and enforce this relationship. Cosmos DB doesn't do that kind of enforcement — but that doesn't mean that you don't have to worry about it. Those data validation concerns just hop up a tier or two in the application and become part of the C# code instead of the relational database schemas.

> ***Snarky aside on data validation***
>
> *As a halfway serious snarky aside... I kinda think we developers have gotten lazy about data validation because we know/think that the RDBMS will do it for us and therefore save us from our mistakes. That ends up putting your data validation logic in the data storage implementation, and I think that's just architecturally weird.*
>
> *It might have worked fine when you had simple, two-tier client-server applications, but in complex service-oriented systems at scale?*
>
> *Your data validation tends to happen way too late, and that causes you to write a lot of complex exception handling.*

Here's what a Comment class looks like:

```
public class Comment : ParentedItemBase
{
    public string AuthorName { get; set; } = string.Empty;
    public string Body { get; set; } = string.Empty;
    public DateTime CreatedDate { get; set; } =
         DateTime.UtcNow;

    public override string ParentEntityType
    {
        get => nameof(Note);
        set { } // Required by interface, but the value is fixed
```

```
    }
}
```

A Comment is its own document in the container. It has its own `Id`, its own `EntityType` (`"Comment"`), its own `Etag`. But it also knows who its parent is (`ParentId`) and what kind of parent it has (`ParentEntityType` returns `"Note"`).

This gives you the best of both worlds. Comments are independently queryable and editable — they're real documents. But the parent relationship is explicit in the data model, so you can find all comments for a note, and when you delete a note, you know exactly which comments to clean up.

Querying by Parent

The library provides `CosmosDbParentedItemRepository<T>` (or you use `IParentedItemRepository<T>` through DI) which adds a key method:

```
var comments = await commentRepository.GetAllByParentIdAsy
nc(
    tenantId,
    noteId,
    "Note"  // optional: filter by parent entity type
);
```

This queries within the tenant partition for all Comment documents whose `ParentId` matches the specified note. Efficient, partition-scoped, and type-aware.

Registration follows the same pattern from Chapter 5:

```
// Simple — no custom repository class needed
helper.RegisterParentedRepository<Comment>();

// With a custom repository
helper.RegisterParentedRepository<Comment,
    ICommentRepository, CommentRepository>();

// With a service layer too
helper.RegisterParentedRepositoryAndService<Comment>();
```

When to Use ParentedItemBase vs. Nesting

It's important to remember that the maximum size of a document in Cosmos DB is 2MB. Two megabytes. On the one hand, you can fit an awful lot of text into 2MB. On the other hand, there's a lot of stuff that's bigger than 2MB. 2MB is comfortable size constraint but it's not huge and you have to plan for it.

That said, here's my rule of thumb:

Nest it (plain property on the parent) when the child data has no independent identity, you'll never query for it outside the context of its parent, and the collection is small and bounded. Addresses on an Order. Tags on a Note. Phone numbers on a Person.

Make it a parented item (ParentedItemBase) when the child has its own identity, you need to query or edit it independently, the collection could grow large and eventually bump up against that 2MB limit, or the child has its own lifecycle (creation, modification, deletion at different times than the parent). Comments on a Note. Attachments on a ticket. Activity log entries on a project.

Make it a separate aggregate root (TenantItemBase) when the entity should survive the deletion of whatever it's currently associated with, when the relationship might change, or when it's referenced by multiple parents. A Person associated with multiple Projects. A Tag definition used across many Notes. Lookup values shared by the whole application.

But then again maybe you solve the delete problem by not solving it. In the Notes and Comments scenario, maybe it's easier to just nest the data but don't actually delete the Notes or Comments — do a **soft delete** instead. Add a boolean property to the document called `IsDeleted` and set it to true and just hide the record. If you need to get at the comments, the data is all still there.

There are options.

Denormalization: When Copying Data Is the Right Answer

If you've spent your career in relational databases, you've probably internalized a rule: **THOU SHALT NOT DUPLICATE DATA!** You know the drill and the buzzwords. Normalize. Single source of truth. If a customer's name appears in the Orders table and the Customers table, you've done something wrong.

In Cosmos DB, that rule doesn't apply the same way. In fact, strategic denormalization is often the *right* design choice.

Here's why. In a relational database, JOINs are cheap. Retrieving a customer name from a related table during an order query costs almost nothing. So you normalize — store the name once, JOIN when you need it. (Plus, storage space used to be expensive and every byte was precious.)

In Cosmos DB, there are no JOINs across documents. (Cosmos has a `JOIN` keyword, but it operates within a single document — joining across nested arrays, not across separate documents.) If your Order document needs to display the customer's name, you have two choices: make a separate read to the Customer document (that's another RU and another round trip), or store the customer's name directly on the Order.

Storing it on the Order is denormalization, and it's often the better choice. Here's when:

Denormalize when the data is a snapshot. An Order should record the customer's name *at the time the order was placed.* If the customer changes their name later, the Order should still show the original name. The denormalized copy isn't duplicate data — it's a historical record. The snapshot IS the point.

Denormalize when you need the data for display. If every time you display a list of Comments, you need to show the author's name, storing that name on the Comment saves you from making a separate Person read for every comment in the list. At scale, those extra reads add up fast — both in RUs and in latency.

Denormalize when the source data changes rarely. If a product's name changes once a year, the cost of updating the denormalized copies once a year is far less than the cost of JOINing to the product table thousands of times a day.

Don't denormalize when the data changes frequently and consistency matters immediately. If a user changes their email address and every document in the system needs to reflect that change in real-time, denormalization creates a consistency problem. In those cases, either accept the extra reads or use the Change Feed (Chapter 8) to propagate updates asynchronously.

A Person is a standalone aggregate root. It has its own identity, its own lifecycle, and no parent. Deleting a Person doesn't cascade to anything else in the system. It's registered with a custom repository because the app needs Person-specific queries:

```
helper.RegisterRepository<Person, IPersonRepository, Perso
nRepository>();
```

Note — An Aggregate Root That's Also a Parent

```
public class Note : TenantItemBase
{
    public string Title { get; set; } = string.Empty;
    public string Body { get; set; } = string.Empty;
    public DateTime CreatedDate { get; set; } =
        DateTime.UtcNow;
    public List<string> Tags { get; set; } = new();
}
```

A Note is also a standalone aggregate root — `TenantItemBase`, not `ParentedItemBase`. But it's also a parent: Comments reference it via `ParentId`.

Note that `Tags` is a nested list — simple strings with no independent identity. They pass the "nest it" test: no one queries for a tag outside the context of its note. (If you needed a global tag directory, *that* would be a separate aggregate root.)

Comment — A Parented Item

```
public class Comment : ParentedItemBase
{
    public string AuthorName { get; set; } = string.Empty;
    public string Body { get; set; } = string.Empty;
    public DateTime CreatedDate { get; set; } =
        DateTime.UtcNow;

    public override string ParentEntityType
    {
```

```
            get => nameof(Note);
            set { }
        }
    }
```

A Comment has its own document, its own identity, its own `EntityType`. But it belongs to a Note. If the Note is deleted, the Comments should be cleaned up. The `ParentId` links it back to its parent Note. `ParentEntityType` returns `"Note"` — the species of tree that's the parent.

`AuthorName` is denormalized. The Comment stores the author's name at creation time rather than referencing a Person by ID and requiring a separate read. If the author changes their display name later, existing Comments retain the name that was current when the comment was written. The snapshot is the point.

LookupValue — An Aggregate Root in a Separate Container

```
public class LookupValue : TenantItemBase
{
    public string LookupType { get; set; } = string.Empty;
    public string LookupKey { get; set; } = string.Empty;
    public string LookupValue { get; set; } = string.Empty
;
    public int DisplayOrder { get; set; }
}
```

LookupValues are reference data — the values that populate dropdown lists. Status values, categories, priorities. They're aggregate roots (each has independent identity), but they often live in a separate container because they have different access patterns than the core business data. They're read frequently, written rarely, and might benefit from different throughput settings.

```
helper.RegisterRepository<LookupValue>(
    containerName: "LookupContainer"
);
```

BTW, I'm not saying you *should* do it this way, but you *could*. Creating a separate container costs you more money in Azure spend. Want to keep your costs as low as possible? Maybe you stick to a single container.

The Patterns at a Glance

Entity	Base Class	Pattern	Container
Person	`TenantItemBase`	Aggregate root	Default
Note	`TenantItemBase`	Aggregate root (also a parent)	Default
Comment	`ParentedItemBase`	Parented item (belongs to Note)	Default
LookupValue	`TenantItemBase`	Aggregate root	Separate

Four entity types. Three patterns (aggregate root, parented item, separate container). One coherent application.

Designing Your Own Domain

You've now seen the full toolkit. Here's the process I use when modeling a new domain for Cosmos DB:

Start with your entities. List the things your application manages. Don't think about storage yet — just the domain objects.

Apply the delete question to each relationship. For every "X has Y" relationship, ask: if you delete X, should Y disappear? That answer determines whether Y is nested, parented, or independent.

Identify your aggregate roots. These are the entities that have independent identity and independent lifecycle. They inherit from `TenantItemBase`. Each gets its own repository.

Identify your parented items. These are entities with independent identity that exist in the context of a parent. They inherit from `ParentedItemBase`. Each knows its parent's ID and entity type.

Nest everything else. Data that has no independent identity and no reason to exist outside its parent is just a property. A class, a list, a nested object. No base class. No repository.

Default to one container. Put everything in a shared container with `/tenantId,/entityType` unless you have a specific reason not to. High-volume writes, different partition keys, different TTL policies — those are reasons. "It feels cleaner" is not.

Denormalize deliberately. For each cross-document reference, ask: will I need this data every time I read this document? Is the data a snapshot that should be preserved? If yes, denormalize it. If the data changes frequently and consistency matters immediately, don't.

Most applications I've built follow this pattern, and the modeling decisions become almost mechanical once you've internalized the delete question. The hard part isn't the pattern — it's being honest about your domain. The delete question forces that honesty.

Next up: Chapter 7, where we talk about the thing everyone actually cares about — money. Request Units, query cost, indexing policies, and how to stop your Cosmos DB bill from surprising you. The RU logging and cross-partition detection from Chapter 5 become essential tools.

Chapter 7 Cosmos DB Query Performance & Cost

There's a well-worn adage in software development that goes something like this: only optimize performance for the problems you *know* you have. Why is this interesting? Because preemptively optimizing your code for performance problems that you don't officially know that you have usually is a waste of time – or wrong – and almost always adds weird complexity.

Now why am I bringing this up? Because it's one of those things that drives me crazy. It drives me crazy to see developers fixing non-existent performance problems. But it launches me into space when they do it on received wisdom about some vague rumor about some best practice that some buddy's sister's neighbor heard someone say on a plane about what sometimes might cause blah blah blah issue.

Wasting time and adding complexity on a performance problem that they don't actually know they have based on a hypothetical understanding of how something works.

So now let's pivot this to software development with Cosmos DB.

Cosmos follows a fairly common cloud service pattern where they bill you for a combination of usage, effort, and storage. Cosmos is amazingly fast even when you do stuff in your code that performs terribly. That means that Cosmos can often just absorb your logic's inefficient operations and still give you great performance.

But there's a catch.

You might end up with a big ol' bill. Basically, it's a new kind of performance problem where the cloud systems you're relying on, do the *right things* for real-time performance that end up costing you *money*.

Those systems are making a good decision, too – why be artificially slow if you don't have to be?

This chapter is all about showing you real numbers so that you know how to optimize for efficiency and cost at the same time.

What Was My Process?

Throughout this book, I've been dropping hints. In Chapter 3, you saw `response.RequestCharge` for the first time. In Chapter 4, I showed you how cross-partition queries silently cost more. In Chapter 5, I showed you my library's RU logging and cross-partition detection. I kept saying "we'll talk about cost later."

We've gotten to that part. Now has become later.

In order to develop this chapter, I built a test harness, ran it against a real Cosmos DB account in Azure, and measured the `RequestCharge` on every operation — inserts, reads, updates, deletes, queries, bulk operations, etc. My goal was to try to think of all the things that might make a difference and then measure it. I also ran the same tests against the local emulator. (Yah. Uhhh...don't pay attention to the `RequestCharge` numbers from the emulator. Seriously.)

I was legit surprised by what was and wasn't important.

But before the numbers make sense, you need to understand how Cosmos charges you — because the billing model changes what the numbers mean.

How Cosmos DB Charges You

Cosmos DB costs break down into three components: throughput (Request Units), storage, and data egress. Throughput is where most of your money goes, and it's where most of your optimization opportunities are.

Request Units: The Currency of Cosmos

A Request Unit is Cosmos DB's way of normalizing compute cost. Instead of tracking CPU, memory, and I/O separately, Cosmos rolls them all into a single number. Every operation — every read, write, query, and delete — consumes some number of RUs, and that number is deterministic. The same operation on the same data costs the same RUs every time.

The baseline: a point read of a 1 KB document (that's a `ReadItemAsync` with partition key + id) costs 1 RU. Everything else is measured relative to that. A write costs more than a read. A larger document costs more than a smaller one. A query costs more than a point read. But the 1 RU point read is your anchor.

> ***The RU, the Metric System, and Water***
>
> *Ok. So I'm an American. We use "freedom units" (or whatever they're actually called) to measure stuff rather than the Metric System. Inches, feet, yards, miles, degrees in Fahrenheit — all that stuff. It's a mess. It's based on nothing coherent.*
>
> *The metric system makes so much more sense. A milliliter is a cubic centimeter. A milliliter of water weighs a gram. Everything in the metric system grows out of that. It's all based on some basic measurements of water.*
>
> *In Cosmos DB, the RU is the water. A point read of a 1 KB document by partition key and id costs 1 RU. All the other operations are calculated relative to that. It makes sense...just like the metric system.*

Storage

You pay for the data you store — currently about $0.25 per GB per month for most regions. This includes your documents, your indexes, and your backups. For most applications, storage cost is small relative to throughput cost. But it's worth knowing that indexes take up space too, which we'll come back to when we talk about indexing policies.

Data Egress

Data leaving Azure or moving between regions costs money. Data coming in is free. For single-region applications, egress is usually negligible. For multi-region setups, it adds up.

> ***A note on geo-replication and cost***
>
> *This is getting a little into the weeds for this chapter, but Cosmos DB has geo-replication options for distributing your data across Azure regions. And guess what — they all feed into cost, too. From a developer point of view, you don't exactly have to worry about it — it's more of an Azure portal configuration kind of thing. But if your application has front-ends in multiple regions for performance or redundancy/failover, then it's probably something you'll want to look into for Cosmos, too. The short version: every region you replicate to increases your throughput bill. We'll cover geo-replication in more detail in Chapter 11.*

Serverless vs. Provisioned vs. Autoscale

Before the RU numbers mean anything, you need to understand how you're being billed for them. Cosmos DB has three throughput modes, and each one changes the math.

Provisioned (Manual)

You reserve a specific number of Request Units per second (RU/s) — say, 400 — and you're billed by the hour for whatever your peak was during that hour. If you provision 400 RU/s and your application uses 200 RU/s, you pay for 400. If it spikes to 600, you get throttled — Cosmos returns HTTP 429 (Too Many Requests) and your application has to retry.

400 RU/s is the minimum, and it's what we've been using throughout this book. It's fine for development and low-traffic applications. For production, you'll typically provision higher and adjust based on monitoring.

So this provisioned model has an upside and downside. The upside: predictable cost. The downside: you're guessing. Over-provision and you waste money. Under-provision and you get throttled.

BTW, getting throttled isn't necessarily bad as long as you and your application planned for it and handle it gracefully.

Autoscale

You set a maximum RU/s — say, 4,000 — and Cosmos automatically scales between 10% of your max (400) and your max (4,000) based on actual demand. You're billed for the peak RU/s used in each hour.

This is often the sweet spot for production workloads with variable traffic. You don't waste money during quiet periods, and you don't get throttled during spikes. The cost per RU is slightly higher than manual provisioned, but the waste reduction usually more than compensates.

Serverless

No provisioning at all. You pay per RU consumed, period. No reservations, no 429 throttling (within reason), no capacity planning.

Serverless is great for development, testing, proof-of-concept projects, and low-traffic applications. It's also good for workloads with very spiky, unpredictable traffic — the kind where provisioned throughput would mean either constant throttling or massive over-provisioning.

The per-RU cost is higher than provisioned, so at sustained high throughput, serverless gets expensive. But for many applications — especially early in their lifecycle — it's the simplest and cheapest option.

The Free Tier

New Cosmos DB accounts are eligible for a free tier: 1,000 RU/s of provisioned throughput and 25 GB of storage per month, at no cost. One free-tier account per Azure subscription. If you're learning or prototyping, this is the way to start with real, actual, running-in-Azure Cosmos DB.

The Local Emulator

Remember, there's also always the local emulator. That's totally free. And you don't have to create an Azure Subscription. But it's not the real, actual, running in-Azure version of Cosmos DB. The RU numbers from the emulator are almost hilariously unhelpful so if you care about trying to prove out your RUU (request unit usage) that's when it's time to sign up.

For the rest of the chapter, I just want you to remember that I'm going to stop reminding you that the emulator exists because those RU numbers aren't helpful for usage profiling. Ok? Good. And that pretty much wraps it up for the emulator.

Which One Should You Pick?

For development and learning: serverless or the free tier. Zero capacity planning, zero waste.

For production with variable traffic: autoscale. Let Cosmos handle the scaling.

For production with predictable, steady traffic: manual provisioned. You know your baseline, you set it, you monitor it.

You can change modes later, so don't overthink it at the start. Get your application working first, then optimize the billing model based on actual usage patterns.

What Operations Actually Cost: The Numbers

Okay. Let's look at real numbers. Everything that follows comes from a test harness I built and ran against a real Cosmos DB account in Azure East US 2. Not the emulator — a real account with real RU reporting. Additionally, I spun up a Windows 11 virtual machine in East US 2 and ran the tests from that VM so that I could remove/minimize network latency as much as possible.

I tested six document types across a range of sizes and property counts:

Doc Type	Size	Properties	Description
SmallDoc	220 B	5	Tiny — id, tenantId, entityType, title, date
MediumDoc	1.3 KB	22	Moderate — core properties plus 15 strings, tags, address
WideDoc	1.8 KB	100	Same size as MediumDoc but 100 short properties
LargeDoc	27 KB	18	Nested objects, lists of objects, long text
BlobDoc	1.5 MB	4	One giant text property, minimal indexing surface
WideBlobDoc	1.5 MB	503	Same size as BlobDoc but 500+ short properties

Two containers: one with Cosmos's default indexing policy (index everything), one with a custom policy that only indexes the four properties I actually query on.

CRUD Costs — Default Indexing

Operation	Small Doc	Medium Doc	Wide Doc	Large Doc	Blob Doc	Wide Blob Doc
Insert	7.43	18.86	**44.95**	55.24	1,252	1,443
Point Read	1.00	1.05	1.05	2.19	291.80	292.18

Operation	Small Doc	Medium Doc	Wide Doc	Large Doc	Blob Doc	Wide Blob Doc
Upsert	10.29	12.95	12.95	22.86	2,500	2,537
Replace	10.67	13.33	13.33	23.24	2,500	2,537
Delete	6.29	6.29	6.29	6.29	6.29	6.29

A few things jump out.

Point reads are cheap and proportional to size. SmallDoc is 1 RU. LargeDoc at 27 KB is 2.19 RUs. Even BlobDoc at 1.5 MB is about 292 RUs — expensive in absolute terms, but proportional to the massive payload. If you're designing for cost, keep your frequently-read documents small.

Deletes are always 6.29 RUs. This surprised me. Whether the document is 220 bytes or 1.5 megabytes, the delete costs exactly 6.29 RUs. The delete operation apparently has a fixed cost regardless of document size.

Upsert and Replace cost the same. I expected Replace (`ReplaceItemAsync`) to be cheaper than Upsert (`UpsertItemAsync`) since Upsert has to check whether the document exists first. But the numbers are nearly identical — 10.29 vs 10.67 for SmallDoc, dead even at 2,500 for BlobDoc. The existence check apparently costs almost nothing. It seems like there's no cost reason to prefer one over the other.

Writes cost more than inserts for WideDoc. Look at WideDoc: the insert costs 44.95 RUs, but the upsert and replace cost only 12.95 and 13.33. That seems backwards until you realize that the insert is creating 100 new index entries from scratch, while the upsert/replace is updating existing index entries. Index updates are apparently cheaper than index creation.

But the most interesting finding is in the insert column.

The Property Count Bombshell

Look at MediumDoc and WideDoc. MediumDoc is 1.3 KB with 22 properties. WideDoc is 1.8 KB with 100 properties. Almost the same size — within 500 bytes of each other.

But the insert cost? MediumDoc: 18.86 RUs. WideDoc: **44.95 RUs.** More than double.

The only meaningful difference is the number of properties. Same basic size, same partition key, same container — but WideDoc has 78 more properties, and each one gets indexed under the default policy.

This is the indexing tax. Every property in your document that gets indexed costs you RUs on each write. More properties means more index entries means more write cost. Document size matters, but property count matters *independently of size.*

This has real implications for document design. If you're storing documents with lots of small properties — configuration objects, metadata dictionaries, denormalized records with many fields — the default indexing policy is silently inflating your write costs.

The Fix: Custom Indexing

The default indexing policy is to index everything. So what happens when you stop indexing *everything*?

I created a second container with a custom indexing policy that only indexes the four properties that participate in actual queries: `tenantId`, `entityType`, `title`, and `createdDate`. Everything else is excluded. Then I ran the same inserts.

Doc Type	Props	Default Index	Custom Index	Savings
SmallDoc	5	7.43	7.05	5%
MediumDoc	22	18.86	8.38	**56%**
WideDoc	100	44.95	8.38	**81%**
LargeDoc	18	55.24	13.33	**76%**
BlobDoc	4	1,252	1,251	~0%
WideBlobDoc	503	1,443	1,251	**13%**

WideDoc drops from 44.95 to 8.38 RUs — an 81% reduction in write cost.

And here's the kicker: with custom indexing, MediumDoc and WideDoc now cost *exactly the same* to insert: 8.38 RUs. Remove the indexing overhead, and the cost is driven by payload size, not property count. Those extra 78 properties were pure indexing tax.

BlobDoc barely changes — 1,252 to 1,251. It only has 4 properties, so there's almost nothing to index. The cost is purely payload. But WideBlobDoc (same size, 503 properties) drops from 1,443 to 1,251 — the 13% difference is entirely indexing overhead.

How to Customize Your Indexing Policy

Cosmos DB indexes everything by default. The default policy looks like this:

```
{
    "indexingMode": "consistent",
    "automatic": true,
    "includedPaths": [
        { "path": "/*" }
    ],
    "excludedPaths": [
        { "path": "/\"_etag\"/?" }
    ]
}
```

The /* wildcard means every property on every document gets indexed. To customize, you flip the approach: exclude everything, then include only what you need.

```
{
    "indexingMode": "consistent",
    "automatic": true,
    "includedPaths": [
        { "path": "/tenantId/*" },
        { "path": "/entityType/*" },
        { "path": "/title/*" },
        { "path": "/createdDate/*" }
    ],
    "excludedPaths": [
        { "path": "/*" }
```

```
    ]
}
```

A few important details here:

`id` and `_ts` are always indexed regardless of your policy. You can't turn them off, and you don't need to include them explicitly.

The partition key is NOT automatically indexed. This one is subtle and important. If you're using hierarchical partition keys (`/tenantId,/entityType`), you should include those paths in your indexing policy. Otherwise, queries filtering on the partition key hierarchy can force full scans, costing more RUs.

You can change the policy at any time without downtime. Cosmos transforms the index in the background using your provisioned RUs at lower priority than your application's operations. Your reads and writes continue normally during the transformation.

The tradeoff is real. If you exclude a property from the index and then query on it, Cosmos falls back to a full scan within the partition — which costs more RUs than an indexed query. The key is knowing your query patterns. *Index what you query on. Exclude everything else.* In Chapter 11, we'll look at how the library's diagnostics can tell you which indexes your queries actually used — and which ones Cosmos wishes you had.

Read cost is not affected by indexing policy. Indexing is a write-time cost. The savings show up on inserts and upserts. Reads and point reads cost the same regardless of your indexing configuration.

The Patch API: Not the Savings You'd Expect

Cosmos DB has a Patch API (`PatchItemAsync`) that lets you update individual properties on a document without reading and replacing the whole thing. On paper, this sounds like it *should* be dramatically cheaper for large documents — why send 1.5 MB back to Cosmos when you're only changing the title?

I tested single-property and multi-property patches across all document sizes.

Doc Type	Size	Upsert	Replace	Patch (1 prop)	Patch (3 props)
SmallDoc	220 B	10.29	10.67	10.79	11.80
MediumDoc	1.3 KB	12.95	13.33	13.49	13.57
WideDoc	1.8 KB	12.95	13.33	13.49	14.57
LargeDoc	27 KB	22.86	23.24	23.52	24.85
BlobDoc	1.5 MB	2,500	2,500	2,532	2,596
WideBlob Doc	1.5 MB	2,537	2,537	2,568	2,632

Patch costs the same or *slightly more* than Upsert and Replace across every document size. Patching one property on a 1.5 MB BlobDoc costs 2,532 RUs — versus 2,500 for replacing the entire document. Cosmos appears to charge based on the document size, not the amount of data you're changing.

I honestly did not see this coming. I expected Patch would be dramatically cheaper for large documents. It isn't. The Patch API is a convenience for avoiding read-modify-write cycles, but it's not a cost optimization. I suppose you could make an argument that avoiding the 'read' saves you some RUs but by itself, Patch isn't moving the RU needle.

Why This Matters for Application Design

Let's say for a moment that I hypothetically ran these tests and found that the patch operations saved a ton of RUs versus Upsert. (To make sure I'm 100% clear: the data shows the opposite.)

Why would this matter? Why *does* this matter? The answer is: complexity.

The reason is that then you, might be tempted to add change-detection logic to your application — track which properties changed, issue targeted Patch calls instead of full Upserts, optimize away unnecessary full-document writes.

Next if you care about change detection, that starts to point you towards using EF Core to help with your Cosmos traffic. Which would make sense because EF Core has a built-in change tracker so it knows which properties are "dirty". Therefore, EF Core would be a natural technology for detecting individual property changes and issuing targeted patch operations.

But back to what the numbers say. The numbers say: don't bother. The RU cost is the same.

If you rolled your own change detection logic, the complexity is non-trivial. If you used EF Core, then that adds an additional dependency in your app and almost certainly more code.

Everything you write has to be maintained. It's code inventory and feature inventory that you have to worry about.

As a software architect, I've got to say that I'm seriously relieved to find that there's _no reason _to add this complexity to your apps. Just Upsert the whole document and keep your code simple. The end.

BTW, If you're using my `Benday.CosmosDb` library, `SaveAsync` does the right thing and calls Upsert.

Point Read vs. Query: Use the Right Tool

Here's a mistake that I've made myself. It's sneaky: thinking that you're doing an efficient point read when in fact you're running a query. I made this mistake enough that I actually added `[Obsolete]` markers to certain methods in my library to give me a compiler warning if I was doing something sub-optimal.

I tested three ways to retrieve a single SmallDoc:

Approach	RU Cost
`ReadItemAsync` (partition key + id)	1.00
Query `WHERE id = @id` (with partition key)	3.02
Query `WHERE title = @title` (with partition key)	3.02

A point read costs 1 RU. That's the basis of the whole RU system. A query that returns the exact same single document costs 3.02 RUs — three times more expensive. And it doesn't matter whether you're querying by `id` or by `title`; the query machinery itself has a baseline cost that exceeds the point read.

The lesson is simple: if you have the partition key and the id, use `ReadItemAsync`. Always. Don't use a query to fetch something you can point-read. Otherwise, you're throwing away 2 RUs every time.

This is why the library's `CosmosTenantItemRepository<T>` has `GetByIdAsync(string tenantId, string id)` as the primary method, and the parameterless `GetByIdAsync(string id)` (which runs a cross-partition query) is marked `[Obsolete]`. It's not really obsolete but I didn't want anyone (or me) to use the inefficient version without warning. The API nudges you — and your AI coding assistant — toward the efficient path. And if you actually need the inefficient path — and you might — then it's there for you.

Query Cost Scales with Results

What about queries that return multiple documents? Does cost scale linearly with the result set?

Query	Docs Returned	RU Cost
SELECT TOP 5	5	3.04
SELECT TOP 50	50	4.36
SELECT * (all 500)	500	17.57

Cost grows with the result set, but not linearly. There's a baseline query cost (~3 RUs) that dominates at low result counts. At higher counts, each additional document adds only a small incremental cost — maybe a few hundredths of an RU per document.

The practical lesson: pagination matters. If you only need 50 results, don't fetch 500 and filter in memory. Use `TOP`, use continuation tokens, use `GetPagedAsync` from the library. Every document you fetch that you don't need is a fraction of an RU wasted — and fractions add up at scale.

> ***The Heat-Death of the Universe vs. Wasted RUs***
>
> *The heat-death of the universe is the inevitable time in the far, far, far, distant future where all the usable energy in the universe has been spent. Everything reaches the same temperature. Nothing can happen anymore because there are no energy differences left to drive anything.*
>
> *My point though is that the heat-death of the universe is not imminent.*

> *So I just wrote a moment ago that those wasted fractions of RUs add up to something meaningful at scale. And now I'm going to undermine my point about wasted RUs.*
>
> *If you're running at the scale of Amazon or Facebook or Azure DevOps Services, those wasted RUs will add up to meaningful waste.*
>
> *But if you're not running at that scale or anything close to that scale, maybe you should just write the code that's easy to write, easy to maintain, and easy to understand. Sure, there's waste...but at the scale of your application, it'll take until the heat-death of the universe for it to amount to anything measurable. So don't worry about it.*

Projection: Does SELECT * Waste Money?

In SQL Server, selecting only the columns you need is a well-established best practice. Is the same true in Cosmos?

Query	Docs	RU Cost
SmallDoc SELECT *	50	4.36
SmallDoc SELECT id, title, date	50	4.56
LargeDoc SELECT *	50	20.29
LargeDoc SELECT id, title	50	6.84

For small documents, projection actually costs *slightly more* — 4.56 vs. 4.36. The projection machinery has overhead, and when the documents are already small, that overhead exceeds the savings.

For large documents, the story is completely different. SELECT * on 50 LargeDocs costs 20.29 RUs. Projecting just `id` and `title` drops it to 6.84 — a 66% savings.

So the rule isn't "always use projection." It's "use projection when your documents are large and you don't need every property." For small documents, don't bother — the overhead isn't worth it. And if you're not running at huge scale, then you might not ever see the difference even with a higher RU cost. (see "The Heat-Death of the Universe vs. Wasted RUs" discussion above)

Server-Side COUNT vs. Fetch-and-Count

Here's another common mistake: fetching all the documents and counting them in C# when all you need is the count. Let's say that you want to know how many orders were placed in Massachusetts in the last 24 hours. You don't care about the orders themselves — only the count.

There are two ways to count them:

- Server-side count
- C# count in memory using Length or Count() from System.Linq

Approach	SmallDoc (500 docs)	LargeDoc (50 docs)
Server-side `SELECT VALUE COUNT(1)`	3.09	3.09
Client-side fetch all + `.Count()`	17.57	20.29
Savings	**5.7x**	**6.6x**

A server-side COUNT in Cosmos costs about 3 RUs regardless of document size. Why would that be the case? Well, the answer is that doing a server-side count doesn't need to fetch any data. It just counts the matching records.

The other approach isn't any different than retrieving the data as if you were going to display it in a list or a grid. Cosmos finds the matching records and then retrieves the data. Cosmos is done at this point but there's more work to do in your app because that data needs to be transferred over wire and then deserialized into objects and something like `IEnumerable<T>`.

The LargeDoc comparison makes this especially clear: the server-side count costs the same 3.09 RUs whether the documents are 220 bytes or 27 KB. The client-side cost jumps from 17.57 to 20.29 because you're transferring bigger documents.

The lesson: if you just need a count, use `SELECT VALUE COUNT(1)` in your query. Don't use LINQ's `.Count()` on a result set you fetched from Cosmos — you've already paid for the full fetch by the time you count.

> ***How does LINQ work? How does LINQ's Count() method work?***
>
> *Nerd alert! It's important to know how LINQ actually works. Everything is based on* `IEnumerable` *or* `IEnumerable<T>`*. It's all riding on top of the Iterator Pattern. (That's also how* `foreach` *works.)*
>
> *All those handy methods in LINQ like Where(), Select(), OrderBy(), etc. — they're all looking at your data in some form of IEnumerable. Notice that I'm saying* `IEnumerable<T>` *and not something like* `List<T>`*. That dependency on an interface instead of a concrete implementation allows a TON of flexibility and also a lot of performance optimization.*
>
> *One thing that you'll see if you look at EF Core or the Cosmos DB SDK for .NET is that there's an interface called* `IQueryable`*.* `IQueryable` *implements* `IEnumerable` *by the way and this lets .NET define a potential query against a datastore and only run that query when the data is actually needed.*
>
> *If you build an IQueryable LINQ query against Cosmos and stick it in a variable called* `myQuery` *but then never run it, then you've used no RUs.*
>
> *But then take that same* `IQueryable` *instance and call* `myQuery.Count()`*. Now, a smart* `IQueryable` *provider might translate that into a server-side COUNT — it never fetches the rows. But depending on the provider and how you've built the query, it might just fetch everything and count client-side. And if you call* `myQuery.ToList()` *first and then check* `.Count`*, you've definitely fetched everything — and you're paying for the full data transfer.*
>
> *If you want the data AND you want the count, you might actually be running the Cosmos query* ***twice*** *— or worse, fetching everything twice.*

The Cross-Partition Surprise

A cross-partition query is a query that doesn't use a partition key value and therefore causes Cosmos to look at all the partitions in your container.

I've been telling you throughout this book that cross-partition queries are expensive. So I tested it. And the results are — well — somewhat hard to come by. Surprising and confusing, too.

This data is nuts.

Query	Docs	RU	Cross-Partition Detected?
With partition key	500	17.57	No
Without partition key	500	15.70	No
All tenants, no PK	1,002	29.28	No

The query *without* a partition key cost 15.70 RUs — actually *less* than the 17.57 with a partition key. And none of the queries were flagged as cross-partition.

What's going on? The answer is that I don't know for sure but I've got a guess. My guess is all of our test data was fitting into a single physical partition in Cosmos.

Let's remember that there's a difference between "logically partitioned" and "physically partitioned" in Cosmos DB. Logically partitioned means that our data is stored in a way that describes a usable partitioning scheme. Physically partitioned means that Cosmos has moved that partition's data onto a separate node inside of Cosmos.

Just because data *can be* physically partitioned doesn't mean that Cosmos DB will *always* physically partition your data. Cosmos DB waits until it figures out that the data volume warrants physically rearranging your data.

Considering our test data, with only a thousand or so documents totaling a few megabytes, there's not much to fan out onto physical partitions. So even though we might have had a whole bunch of local partitions, our data all lived in one physical partition. Therefore, we ran queries and didn't see any warnings about cross-partition queries.

Cross-partition queries are only expensive when there are actually multiple physical partitions to query — and that only happens when your data grows large enough for Cosmos to split.

But you need to plan ahead! You need to think about your logical partitioning scheme ahead of time because you can't change the partition key config for a container. So this is one of those rare places where you kinda have to optimize for a performance problem you don't actually know you have.

Why This Matters

This is actually a really important finding for this book. Here's what it means in practice:

You can't feel the cross-partition pain during development. Your test data is too small for Cosmos to split across physical partitions. Every query hits one partition no matter what. The RU difference between a good query and a bad query is negligible.

The cross-partition detection in the library won't fire during development either. The library checks the diagnostics for signs of multi-partition fan-out. If there's only one physical partition, there's nothing to detect.

By the time cross-partition queries become expensive, you're in production. You've got real data, real traffic, and real money on the line. The query patterns that were "fine" in development are suddenly costing 10x or 50x more than they should.

This is why the library's guardrails exist. The partition-key-aware methods, the `[Obsolete]` markers, the cross-partition detection — they're there because you can't test for this problem. You have to *design for it* from the beginning, trusting that the pain will materialize later if you don't.

I verified this by checking the raw Cosmos diagnostics. Every query, regardless of whether it specified a partition key, hit `PartitionKeyRangeId: "0"` — a single partition key range. Even with 1,000+ documents across 100+ different `tenantId` values, Cosmos kept everything in one physical partition.

Bulk Operations: Speed, Not Savings

Is there an RU discount for inserting documents in bulk versus one at a time?

Approach	Total RU	Per Doc	Time	Throttled
Individual inserts	743.00	7.43	3,263 ms	0
TransactionalBatch	742.86	7.43	136 ms	0
Bulk execution	743.00	7.43	2,221 ms	30

No. The per-document RU cost is virtually identical across all three approaches — about 7.43 RUs per SmallDoc. Cosmos charges for the work regardless of how you submit it.

But the time difference is dramatic. TransactionalBatch finished in 136 milliseconds — one network round trip for 100 documents. Individual inserts took over 3 seconds — 100 round trips. That's a 24x speedup.

Bulk execution (firing all requests concurrently with `Task.WhenAll` using the `AllowBulkExecution` client option) hit 30 throttled requests at our 400 RU/s provisioned throughput. It's fast in theory, but at low throughput, you'll spend most of your time retrying after 429s.

The lesson: **batch for speed, not for cost savings.** `TransactionalBatch` is the clear winner for throughput when all items share a partition key. Just remember that all items in a batch must share the same partition key and the total batch size must stay under 2 MB.

The 2 MB Limit: What the Error Looks Like

Speaking of 2 MB — in Chapter 6, I mentioned the maximum document size. Let's see what actually happens when you exceed it.

I created a document at 2,150,539 bytes — just over the 2 MB line — and tried to save it.

Real Cosmos account: `CosmosException` with HTTP status code **413 (RequestEntityTooLarge)** and the message "Request size is too large." Clear, immediate, no ambiguity.

The emulator? **Status 200. Document saved successfully.** The emulator accepted a document that the real service rejects. More on that next.

The Emulator ~~Lies to You~~ Can't Count

I ran every single test against both the real Cosmos account and the vNext emulator. I mentioned back in Chapter 4 that the emulator doesn't report accurate RU values. Now let me show you what that actually looks like and exactly how inaccurate it is.

Operation	Doc Type	Real RU	Emulator RU
Insert	SmallDoc	7.43	1.00
Insert	WideDoc	44.95	1.00
Insert	BlobDoc	1,252	1.00
Point Read	SmallDoc	1.00	1.00
Point Read	BlobDoc	291.80	1.00
Patch (1 prop)	BlobDoc	2,532	1.00
Query (500 docs)	SmallDoc	17.57	1.00
COUNT (500 docs)	SmallDoc	3.09	1.00
Batch (100 docs)	SmallDoc	742.86	1.00

Every. Single. Operation. 1.00 RU.

Insert a 220-byte document? 1 RU. Insert a 1.5 megabyte document? 1 RU. Patch a single property on a 1.5 MB document? 1 RU. Query 500 documents? 1 RU. Batch insert 100 documents? 1 RU. The emulator reports 1.00 for everything regardless of document size, operation type, or complexity.

And it's not just RU reporting. The emulator also: - Accepted our 2.1 MB over-limit document (real account: 413 error) - Never detected cross-partition queries (although that's understandable at small data volumes) - Reported 0.00 total RUs for bulk execution of 100 documents

The emulator is great for development. It's fast, it's free, it runs on my Mac, it runs on Windows and Linux, and the CRUD operations work correctly. But it cannot tell you what your operations actually cost, and it won't enforce all the limits that the real service does.

For cost estimation, for performance testing, and for validating document size limits — you need a real Azure account. Full stop.

Container Throughput Decisions

In Chapter 6, we talked about when to put entity types in separate containers. Now you can see the cost dimension of that decision.

When multiple entity types share a container, they share throughput. If your webhook event processor suddenly hammers 300 RU/s of writes, that leaves only 100 RU/s for your user-facing queries (at 400 RU/s provisioned). Your users see latency spikes or 429 errors because a background process consumed the budget.

A separate container with its own provisioned throughput isolates the blast radius. The webhook container can throttle without affecting user-facing operations. But separate containers mean separate provisioned throughput, which means a higher minimum spend — each container needs at least 400 RU/s (or use serverless).

Shared throughput at the database level is a middle ground. You provision throughput on the database (minimum 400 RU/s), and all containers in that database share it. Cosmos distributes the RUs across containers automatically. This is cheaper than per-container provisioning but gives you less isolation.

The right choice depends on your traffic patterns. If all your entity types have similar, steady traffic — shared throughput or a single container is fine. If one entity type is bursty and could starve the others — give it its own container and its own throughput.

Practical Cost Checklist

Here's a checklist for thinking about and planning Cosmos DB cost:

Customize your indexing policy. If your documents have more than a handful of properties, don't index everything. Only index the properties you filter and sort on. The write savings can be 50-80% for wide documents.

Use point reads when you have the id. `ReadItemAsync` costs 1 RU. A query returning the same document costs 3 RUs. Always point-read when you can.

Don't bother with Patch for cost savings. The Patch API costs the same as Upsert. It's a convenience for avoiding read-modify-write cycles, not a cost optimization. Just Upsert the whole document and keep your code simple.

Use server-side COUNT, not fetch-and-count. `SELECT VALUE COUNT(1)` costs ~3 RUs regardless of document size. Fetching all documents and counting client-side costs 6-7x more because you're paying for data transfer.

Use projection for large documents. SELECT * on small documents is fine. On large documents, projecting only the properties you need can save 60% or more on query cost.

Paginate your queries. Don't fetch 500 documents when you need 50. Use `TOP`, continuation tokens, or `GetPagedAsync`.

Design for partition isolation. Cross-partition queries are cheap during development because everything fits in one physical partition. They get expensive at scale. Use partition-key-aware queries from the start.

Batch for speed, not cost. TransactionalBatch is 24x faster than individual inserts. The per-document RU cost is the same, but the latency improvement is dramatic.

Don't trust the emulator for cost or limits. Use it for development. Use a real Azure account for cost estimation and performance testing. The emulator reports 1.00 RU for everything and accepts documents over 2 MB.

Start with serverless or free tier. Don't provision throughput until you understand your traffic patterns. You can always switch to provisioned later.

Monitor with my library's RU logging. The `RequestCharge` on every operation tells you exactly what you're spending. Watch for operations that cost more than you expect — that's where the optimization opportunities hide.

Next up: Chapter 8, where we talk about the Change Feed — the feature that makes Cosmos DB more than just a database. Event-driven patterns, the boilerplate nobody warns you about, and an Azure Functions cold-start trick that saves you money.

Chapter 8 Cosmos DB Change Feed & Event Patterns

When I was learning Cosmos DB, I kept hearing about this "Change Feed" thing. People seemed really excited about it. Blog posts. Conference talks. Microsoft's own documentation devoted significant real estate to it.

But for the longest time, I really never understood why it was all that interesting.

Probably because I was thinking about it wrong. I was thinking it was analogous to SQL Server triggers — a mechanism for knowing when data changed. And honestly, as someone who's been writing enterprise applications for a couple of decades, there have definitely been some times where I was darned glad that I had an audit trail — audit tables — corresponding to my primary tables in my SQL schema. Audit trails are valuable. I'm not dismissing them.

But triggers? Auditing? That's… fine. It's not *exciting*. And I just didn't understand why anyone would get that excited about knowing when data changed. I mean, wouldn't that just be some kind of application tier concern? My app wrote the data. My app already knows what happened. Why does the database need to tell me something I just did?

It took me a while to realize that I was asking the wrong question. Instead of asking "why would I want to know when data changed?", the question is better put as "why would *someone else* want to know?"

The Code That Writes Probably Isn't the Code That Responds

Here's the shift in thinking that made the Change Feed click for me.

When you write a document to Cosmos, *your* code knows that happened. But what if the code that *responds* to that change isn't your code? What if it's a different application? A different deployment? A different team's responsibility? What if it doesn't even have to be running at the same time as your write?

As a developer and an application architect, I want to keep integrations *between* apps as clean as possible. I really don't want to know much about other apps because I'll have a tendency to — well, let me put it a different way — the needs of those other apps tend to leak into my app like a water leak in a boat. Here's me. There's you. We have boundaries. The blood-brain barrier.

And then the really selfish reason: if your app goes down, I don't want you taking me down with you.

Think about it in SQL Server terms for a second. You've got a trigger that writes an audit record. If the audit table's disk is full, or the audit trigger throws an exception, or there's a deadlock in the audit logic — your primary INSERT fails. The whole transaction rolls back. Your user's operation fails because of something entirely unrelated to the primary function of your application. That's not great for resilience. That's not great for graceful failure handling.

Synchronous coupling means shared fate. When everything runs in the same transaction, everything fails together.

The Change Feed is a tool for breaking that coupling. The write to Cosmos succeeds on its own terms. Some other process, somewhere else, at some other time, picks up the change and does whatever it needs to do with it. If that other process is down, your write still succeeded. If that other app is running kind of slow, your write was still fast. If it crashes halfway through processing, your write is fine and the Change Feed still has the event waiting for when the processor comes back.

You don't even have to *think* about it. That's the difference. That's why people get excited.

What the Change Feed Actually Is

Let's get concrete. Every time you create or update a document in a Cosmos DB container, that change is recorded in the container's Change Feed. It's an ordered, persistent log of changes — ordered within each logical partition key, with each change appearing exactly once.

The Change Feed gives you a way to *read* that log. You set up a processor (or an Azure Function trigger) that monitors the container, and whenever new changes appear, your code runs.

A few important mechanical details:

Creates and updates, not deletes. In the default "latest version" mode, the Change Feed captures creates and updates but *not* deletes. If you delete a document, that deletion doesn't appear in the feed. If you need to react to deletions, you have two options: use soft deletes (set a `deleted` property to `true` and optionally set a TTL for auto-cleanup later), or use the newer "all versions and deletes" mode which captures everything including deletes and intermediate updates.

Latest version only. In the default mode, if a document is updated three times in quick succession, the Change Feed shows it once — with the final state after the third update. You don't see the intermediate versions. If you need every intermediate version, that's the "all versions and deletes" mode.

Ordered per partition key. Changes within the same partition key are guaranteed to arrive in order. Changes across different partition keys have no ordering guarantee. For most applications, this is fine — events for the same tenant or the same entity arrive in sequence, which is what matters.

Persistent. Unlike a message queue where messages expire, the Change Feed in latest version mode retains changes as long as the document exists in the container. You can replay from the beginning if you need to.

The persistence feature has a side benefit. Since it doesn't disappear, it allows the same item in the Change Feed to be used as a trigger for multiple processors or systems. If you're using a message in something like an Azure Storage Queue, once the message is dequeued (read), no one else can see that message.

The SQL Server Trigger Analogy (and Where It Breaks Down)

If you're coming from SQL Server, the Change Feed is *conceptually* similar to triggers — something changes in the database, code runs in response.

But there's a crucial difference: SQL Server triggers are synchronous. The trigger runs inside your exact same transaction as your INSERT, UPDATE, or DELETE. The caller waits while the trigger runs. If the trigger fails, the transaction rolls back.

The Change Feed is asynchronous. Your write completes immediately and returns to the caller. The processing happens later — or not at all, if nobody's listening. The processing could happen within milliseconds, seconds, minutes, hours, or days. If the processor fails, the original write is fine.

This is a *feature*, not a limitation. It means a slow or failing consumer can't slow down or break your writes. It means you can deploy, restart, or rewrite the consumer without affecting the writer. It means the writer and the consumer have different lifecycles, different failure modes, and different scaling characteristics.

Why Async Processing Matters (Even in Small Apps)

You might be thinking that this async processing model is overkill for your app. "I'm not building a distributed system. I don't need event-driven architecture. I just have a web app." I get it. It adds complexity. It breaks your single application into something that looks a little more like two applications. More stuff to deploy. More stuff to break.

I appreciate and respect that thinking. That mindset has a healthy fear of the unknown: "I don't quite know how to do this async thing and it could be a bottomless pit of complexity and bugs." But implementing asynchronous processing in an app is pretty easy to do.

Once I wrapped my head around it, I've been *surprised* by how often I want to use async processing even in small-ish apps. Especially in web apps. There are all kinds of things that you *could* process on the same thread/request in an ASP.NET app — sending notification emails, generating PDFs, syncing data to an external system, updating search indexes, writing detailed audit logs, data parsing & processing — but every one of those adds latency to the user's request. It might scale just fine. But users get snippy when the app starts to "feel slow."

Moving that work out of band — write the primary data, queue up the side effects, respond to the user — makes your app *feel* faster even when the total work is the same. Your end user doesn't think about performance the same way that a developer would. They don't care that saving a record takes 1ms followed by 3 seconds to send an email. Instead, they see it as "the Save button took 3 seconds to respond" followed by "your app is slow".

The Chocolate and Peanut Butter

And now I'm going to start talking about Azure Functions. (I'll bet you didn't see that coming.)

The async processing pattern and Azure Functions running in Consumption Plan mode are the chocolate and peanut butter of this world. The rassam and rice. The champagne and pizza. (Seriously...if you haven't tried a dry sparkling wine with greasy, salty pizza, you really should give it a try.)

Azure Functions has a whole bunch of ways to run them and one of those ways is called "Consumption Plan". Azure Functions run in Consumption Plan mode are dirt cheap. You pay per execution. Your Change Feed processor runs for 200 milliseconds to process a webhook event and then goes back to sleep. You're paying for 200 milliseconds of compute. Compare that to running a dedicated background worker in an App Service that's alive 24/7 whether there's work to do or not.

This combination is amazing for handling out-of-band processing work. Especially when speed of processing isn't a hard requirement. If "processed within a few seconds" is just as good as "processed immediately", you can save a TON of money by running on a Consumption Plan.

Keep Your Stuff Separated

As The Offspring said in their 1994 classic "Come Out and Play": *You've gotta keep em separated.* Prescient words of distributed software wisdom from the pre-internet era. (Yes, I *am* GenX. How could you tell?)

Keeping things separated and isolated is another reason why the async pattern matters. It's about keeping things separated in Azure for uptime and reliability.

If you're running your background processing on the same App Service as your web app, you've created shared fate again. If a deployment from your Azure DevOps or GitHub Actions pipeline makes something a liiiiiittttllleee bit slow or unstable on that App Service Plan, you're at risk of *everything* falling apart. It might not be for a long time — maybe just a minute or less — but Murphy's Law says that that's the moment that your biggest customer loses their changes. Your users see errors because your background PDF generation hogged the CPU. Or your background processing stalls because your web traffic spiked and consumed all the available threads.

Keeping the web app, the webhook receiver, and the background processor in separate Azure resources means they succeed and fail independently. Each one can be deployed independently. Each one can scale independently. The blast radius of any single problem is contained.

> ***Public Service Announcement: App Services vs. App Service Plans***
>
> *If you use Azure App Services, make sure you're 100% clear on the difference between an "App Service" and an "App Service Plan." An App Service is your application — your web app, your API. An App Service Plan is the underlying compute resource — the VM(s) that host your App Services.*
>
> *The App Service Plan is the thing that you pay for and the thing that you scale. Multiple App Services can happily share a single App Service Plan. But if you need to scale one App Service, you're actually going to be scaling the PLAN and therefore scaling all the other App Services running on that plan.*
>
> *The gotcha: if you put your web app and your background worker on the same App Service Plan, they share CPU, memory, and deployment slots. They're on the same VM. You haven't actually separated anything — you've just put two processes in the same blast radius. If the Plan goes down, the app services on that plan go down.*
>
> *That's not good or bad. But it's absolutely essential that you know that that's how it works.*
>
> *This has cost me money. And I've seen it cost at least a handful of customers extra money, too where they over-provision plans and pay way more than they need. It's a common misunderstanding and an easy mistake to make.*
>
> *Make sure you know which plan each of your services is running on.*

Honest Cheetah: The Change Feed in Production

Let me show you how this all comes together in a real application. My app, Honest Cheetah (https://www.honestcheetah.com), is a delivery intelligence tool that integrates with GitHub Project & Issues. GitHub sends webhook events — issue changes, project updates, status transitions — and Honest Cheetah processes them into flow metrics like cycle time and throughput and lets the user forecast when work is likely to get done. (BTW, it's free and there's also a version for Azure DevOps that's also free. There's also a demo mode, if you just want to try it out.)

Those webhook events from GitHub are the lifeblood of Honest Cheetah (HC). If HC misses a webhook event, the project management data might get weird. GitHub has some amount of retry logic but if my webhook receiver endpoint is down for a minute or two, GitHub is probably going to give up on that message. Also, if my receiver endpoint doesn't return an HTTP 200 (success) fast enough, it'll mark that message as failed and potentially try to deliver it again.

Stability and uptime of that webhook receiver endpoint is *crucial.*

The Architecture

The architecture for Honest Cheetah for GitHub has three pieces:

1. The Webhook Receiver (Azure Function — Consumption Plan)

GitHub POSTs a webhook event. The receiver validates the message signature for validity (is this a legitimate message from GitHub?), extracts a few metadata fields from the payload, wraps the raw JSON into a `RawWebhookEvent` document with a 1-hour TTL, and writes it to a `raw-webhooks` container in Cosmos DB.

That's it. Super simple and minimalist. It doesn't parse the event. It doesn't update any domain data. It doesn't call any services. It just validates that it actually came from GitHub, captures the raw data, and tells GitHub that "we got it" as fast as possible.

Why? Because the webhook receiver needs to be *up*. If it's down, I miss events from GitHub. GitHub will retry a few times, but if my endpoint is consistently slow or unavailable, I lose data. So I kept it bare bones — minimal dependencies, minimal reasons to fail. Validate auth, grab the raw payload, store it, respond. Sort out any problems later.

In the Git repo for Honest Cheetah, the webhook receiver code is kept in a separate folder and there are almost no or literally no dependencies to anything else in the HC app. This means that the GitHub Actions continuous deployment pipeline almost never needs to run. That means that the receiver almost never gets updated and has just about zero downtime for deployments.

2. The Change Feed Processor (Azure Function — Consumption Plan)

A second Azure Function monitors the `raw-webhooks` container via a Cosmos DB Change Feed trigger. When new raw webhook events appear in the change feed, the processor picks them up and does the actual work: deserializing payloads, routing by event type (issue events, project events, installation events), calling domain services to update `ProjectIssue` records in HC with status change history, and writing processed data to the main `Data` container in Cosmos.

This is where all the complexity lives. Domain logic, service dependencies, error handling. If this Function crashes or needs to be redeployed, the raw events are sitting safely in Cosmos waiting. When the processor comes back, it picks up from where it left off.

If this part of the HC application is down, it's not great...but it's also not that big of a deal. If this goes down for a while, some data in the UI might not get refreshed from GitHub...but overall the app is still running. When when the change feed processor comes back up, it'll catch up on the backlog pretty quickly.

3. The Web Application (ASP.NET Core — App Service)

This is the user interface portion of the app. It's what the user sees and interacts with.

The main Honest Cheetah web app reads from the `Data` container to display dashboards, metrics, and reports. It doesn't know anything about webhooks or raw events. It just reads processed data.

Once again, there's that moat — the failure protection boundary — around this part of the app. If the webhook receiver goes down or the change feed processor goes down, the data in the UI gets a little stale but we're still up. This reliability goes in the other direction, too. If the web app goes down, it doesn't nuke the change feed processor or the receiver.

Three separate deployments. Three separate scaling profiles. Three separate failure domains.

The Transient Buffer Pattern

The `raw-webhooks` container deserves special attention. It has a 1-hour time to live (TTL) on every document. Raw webhook payloads arrive, sit in the container long enough for the Change Feed processor to pick them up, and then Cosmos automatically deletes them.

This means the raw container never grows. It's a transient buffer — basically a queue that happens to be a Cosmos container. The Change Feed is what makes it work as a queue: writes go in one side, the processor reads from the other side via the feed.

The 1-hour TTL is generous — the processor typically picks up events within seconds. But the buffer gives you breathing room. If the processor is down for maintenance or experiencing issues, you've got an hour of events safely stored before they start expiring. (I could make this TTL longer if I wanted.)

The Flow Diagram

Here's how the pieces connect:

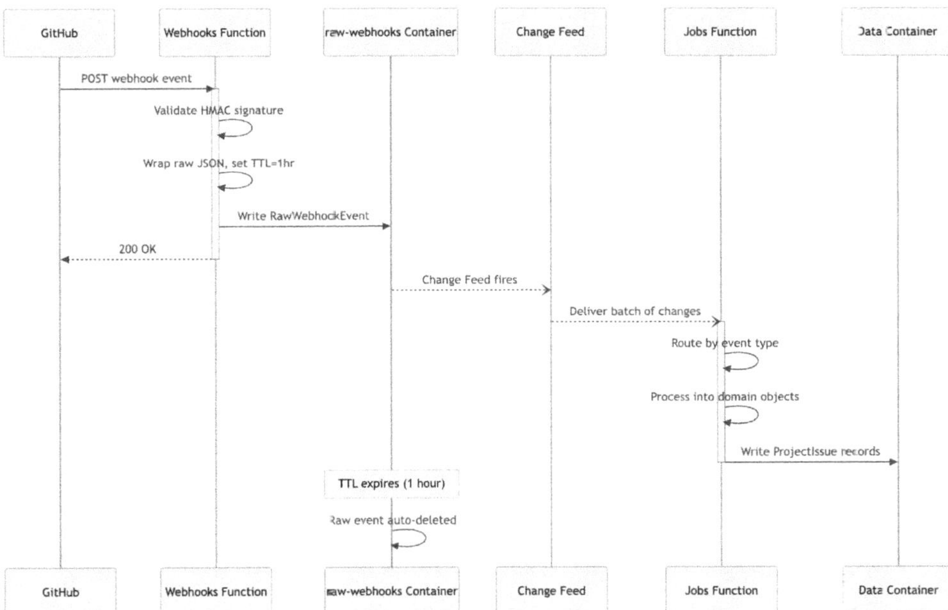

The KeepWarm Trick

There's a practical problem with Consumption Plan Azure Functions: cold starts. If a Function hasn't run in a while, Azure deallocates it. The next time it needs to run, there's a warmup delay while Azure spins up a new instance, loads your code, initializes your dependencies. That delay is unpredictable — could be a second, could be ten seconds, could be longer.

For Honest Cheetah, this is a real problem. GitHub webhook traffic comes in 24/7, but it's bursty. There's no reasonable, logical, predictable downtime. If I didn't have a mitigation strategy, the Azure Function would probably get shut down at least a handful of times per week or per day. That would almost certainly cause dropped or delayed message processing because the warmup time for Consumption Plan Functions can be wickedly unpredictable.

The fix is dead-simple: a timer trigger that fires every 5 minutes and does nothing.

```
[Function("KeepWarm")]
public void Run([TimerTrigger("0 */5 * * * *")] TimerInfo myTimer)
{
    _logger.LogDebug("KeepWarm triggered at {Timestamp}",
   DateTime.UtcNow);
}
```

That's it. Five lines. The timer fires, the Function logs a debug message, and the Function goes back to waiting. But because it ran, Azure keeps the instance warm. The next time a Change Feed event arrives, there's no cold start delay.

Put one of these in the app that you're deploying to your Consumption Plan Function App and suddenly you're avoiding the cold start problem. You're telling Azure Functions that you are indeed using this, so don't turn me off.

I have this in both of my Function Apps — the webhook receiver and the Change Feed processor. A few pennies a month in execution costs. Zero dropped messages from cold starts.

If your Consumption Plan Functions process time-sensitive events, add a KeepWarm trigger. It's the best ROI of any code you'll write.

How to Set It Up: The Azure Functions Binding

There are two ways to consume the Change Feed in .NET: the Azure Functions Cosmos DB trigger (the easy way) and the SDK's `ChangeFeedProcessor` (the control-freak way). Let's start with the easy way, which is what Honest Cheetah uses.

The Trigger

```
[Function("WebhookProcessor")]
public async Task Run(
    [CosmosDBTrigger(
        databaseName: "%CosmosDatabase%",
        containerName: "%CosmosRawWebhooksContainer%",
```

```
        Connection = "CosmosConnection",
        LeaseContainerName = "leases",
        CreateLeaseContainerIfNotExists = false,
        StartFromBeginning = false)]
    IReadOnlyList<RawWebhookEvent> events)
{
    foreach (var evt in events)
    {
        try
        {
            await ProcessEventAsync(evt);
        }
        catch (Exception ex)
        {
            _logger.LogError(ex,
               "Error processing event {EventId}", evt.Id);
               // Don't rethrow - continue processing
               // other events in the batch
        }
    }
}
```

The [CosmosDBTrigger] attribute tells Azure Functions to monitor a Cosmos container for changes and invoke this method whenever new documents appear. The %...% syntax reads values from app settings and saves you from having to hard-code values into the trigger attributes. Connection references a set of app settings for Cosmos authentication (endpoint, credential, client ID for managed identity).

The Function receives a batch of changed documents — not one at a time. You iterate through the batch and process each one.

The Lease Container

The LeaseContainerName = "leases" points to a separate Cosmos container that tracks the processor's position in the Change Feed. This is the checkpoint system. When your processor finishes a batch, the Azure Functions runtime updates the lease to record how far through the feed you've read. If the processor restarts, it picks up from the last checkpoint, not from the beginning.

You need to create this container yourself (note `CreateLeaseContainerIfNotExists = false` — I prefer explicit control over container creation). A simple container with `/id` as the partition key works. The lease documents are small and managed entirely by the runtime.

> ***Don't delete the lease container.*** *If the lease container is accidentally deleted, the processor loses its checkpoints. Depending on your `StartFromBeginning` setting, it will either start reprocessing from the beginning of the feed (potentially reprocessing millions of documents) or start from "now" and miss everything between the last checkpoint and now. Neither is great. (Yup...I've made this mistake, too.)*

The Producer Side

On the write side, Honest Cheetah uses the `[CosmosDBOutput]` binding to write raw webhook events:

```
[Function("WebhookReceiver")]
[CosmosDBOutput("%CosmosDatabase%", "%CosmosContainer%",
    Connection = "CosmosConnection")]
public async Task<object> Run(
    [HttpTrigger(AuthorizationLevel.Anonymous, "post",
        Route = "github/webhook")] HttpRequest req)
{
    // Validate HMAC signature
    // Extract metadata from payload
    // Return a RawWebhookEvent object —
    // the binding writes it to Cosmos
}
```

The `[CosmosDBOutput]` binding writes the returned object to Cosmos automatically. You don't even call a repository or a `CosmosClient` — you just return the document and the binding handles the write. About as thin as a webhook receiver can get.

Configuration

Both Function Apps use managed identity for Cosmos DB authentication — no connection strings. The app settings look like:

```
CosmosConnection__accountEndpoint = https://your-account.docume
nts.azure.com:443/
CosmosConnection__credential = managedidentity
CosmosConnection__clientId = <your-managed-identity-client-id>
```

The `__accountEndpoint`, `__credential`, and `__clientId` suffixes are the Azure Functions convention for configuring Cosmos connections via managed identity. None of these are secrets — they're endpoint URLs and identity references, not keys or passwords. Whether to commit them to Git is a team decision, but there's nothing here that would grant access on its own.

How to Set It Up: The SDK's ChangeFeedProcessor

If you're not using Azure Functions — maybe your processor runs inside an ASP.NET Core app or a background worker service or even a command line app — you'll use the SDK's `ChangeFeedProcessor` directly. This gives you more control but requires more setup code.

```
Container monitoredContainer = cosmosClient
    .GetDatabase("MyDatabase")
    .GetContainer("my-container");

Container leaseContainer = cosmosClient
    .GetDatabase("MyDatabase")
    .GetContainer("leases");

ChangeFeedProcessor processor = monitoredContainer
    .GetChangeFeedProcessorBuilder<MyDocument>(
        processorName: "myProcessor",
        onChangesDelegate: HandleChangesAsync)
    .WithInstanceName("instance-1")
    .WithLeaseContainer(leaseContainer)
    .WithStartFromBeginning()
    .Build();
```

```
await processor.StartAsync();

// Later, on shutdown:
await processor.StopAsync();
```

The handler delegate:

```
static async Task HandleChangesAsync(
    ChangeFeedProcessorContext context,
    IReadOnlyCollection<MyDocument> changes,
    CancellationToken cancellationToken)
{
    foreach (var doc in changes)
    {
        // Process each changed document
    }
}
```

This approach requires you to manage the processor lifecycle yourself — starting it when your app starts, stopping it gracefully on shutdown. You also need to handle the lease container creation, instance naming (important if you're running multiple instances for scale), and error handling within the delegate.

The Azure Functions binding does all of this for you. For most applications, the binding is the right choice. Use the SDK directly when you need fine-grained control over polling intervals, batch sizes, error handling strategies, or when you're running in a host that isn't Azure Functions.

The Gotchas Nobody Warns You About

The Change Feed is powerful, but there are a few sharp edges. Here's what I've learned from running it in production.

Swallowed Errors = Silent Data Loss

Look at the error handling in my processor code:

```
foreach (var evt in events)
{
    try
    {
        await ProcessEventAsync(evt);
    }
    catch (Exception ex)
    {
        _logger.LogError(ex, "Error processing event {EventId}"
,
              evt.Id);
        // Don't rethrow — continue processing other events
    }
}
```

If `ProcessEventAsync` throws, the exception is caught, logged, and swallowed. The loop continues to the next event. When the batch completes, the Change Feed checkpoint advances past the failed event.

That failed event is gone. It won't be retried. It exists in the logs, but it's not in a dead-letter queue. There's no built-in mechanism to replay it.

Why do I do it this way? Because the alternative is worse. If you rethrow the exception, the entire batch fails. The checkpoint doesn't advance. The Change Feed delivers the *same batch* again. If the first event in the batch is the one that's broken, you're stuck in an infinite retry loop — the poisoned event blocks everything behind it.

So you have a choice: swallow errors and accept that individual events can fail silently, or rethrow and risk a single bad event blocking your entire pipeline. Neither option is great.

The right long-term answer is a dead-letter pattern — catch the error, write the failed event to a separate dead-letter container, and continue processing. Then build monitoring and a replay mechanism for the dead-letter container. I'll be honest: Honest Cheetah doesn't have this yet. It's on the list.

In-Memory Idempotency Is Fragile

Honest Cheetah's processor uses a `static ConcurrentDictionary` to track which events it's already processed, preventing duplicate processing if the same event somehow arrives twice. This works fine… until the Function App restarts. On a cold start, that dictionary is empty. If the checkpoint didn't advance before the restart, events could be reprocessed.

The Change Feed guarantees "at least once" delivery. If your processing needs to be idempotent — and it almost always should be — you need durable idempotency tracking, not an in-memory dictionary. That means checking a database or a distributed cache before processing each event.

Latest Version Mode Has Blind Spots

The default Change Feed mode ("latest version") has two significant limitations:

No intermediate updates. If a document is updated three times rapidly, you see the final state, not the journey. If your processing logic cares about the sequence of changes (state machine transitions, audit trails), you either need to encode that history in the document itself or switch to "all versions and deletes" mode.

No deletes. Deleting a document doesn't generate a Change Feed event in latest version mode. The most common workaround is soft deletes — instead of deleting, set a `deleted` property to `true` (which *is* an update and *does* appear in the feed), then set a TTL on the document so Cosmos cleans it up automatically later.

For Honest Cheetah, neither of these are a concern because I'm always reacting to a message that GitHub sends me. I'm not using the change feed to handle changes made to the core data of HC itself.

The Lease Container Is a Single Point of…Confusion

The lease container is just a regular Cosmos container with lease documents managed by the runtime. But if something goes wrong with it — accidental deletion, corruption, misconfigured partition key — your Change Feed processor loses its place. Depending on your `StartFromBeginning` setting, you'll either reprocess everything or skip to "now" and lose everything in between.

Treat the lease container like you'd treat any other production data. Don't delete it. Back up your understanding of what's in it. And set

`CreateLeaseContainerIfNotExists = false` so you're making explicit choices about container creation.

Other Things You Can Do with the Change Feed

Webhook processing is my use case, but the Change Feed enables several other patterns worth knowing about.

Cache invalidation and search index sync. When a document changes in Cosmos, a Change Feed processor updates a Redis cache or an Azure AI Search index. Your read path hits the cache/index (fast and cheap), while the write path goes to Cosmos (durable and consistent). The Change Feed keeps them in sync — eventually. This is a classic CQRS-adjacent pattern.

Denormalization propagation. Remember Chapter 6's discussion of denormalization? If a Person's name is copied into their Note documents for performance, and the Person changes their name, a Change Feed processor can propagate that change to all the denormalized copies. This is how you keep denormalized data from going stale without rebuilding everything on every write.

Materialized views. A Change Feed processor that reads raw operational data and maintains pre-computed summaries — leaderboards, dashboards, aggregated metrics. Honest Cheetah's flow metrics (throughput, cycle time) are essentially materialized views built from raw webhook events.

Event sourcing. If you model all changes as append-only writes (never update, never delete), the Change Feed becomes your event log. You can replay events from the beginning to rebuild state, build multiple materialized views from the same event stream, or integrate with external systems. This is a deep architectural pattern that's beyond the scope of this chapter, but the Change Feed makes it possible in Cosmos.

Data tiering. Move "cold" data from your primary Cosmos container to cheaper storage (Azure Blob Storage, Table Storage) based on age or access patterns. A Change Feed processor watches for documents that meet your archival criteria and copies them to cold storage.

Eventual Consistency: A Philosophy

Let me close with something that might seem like a detour but isn't.

SQL Server and relational databases are built around ACID transactions. Atomicity, Consistency, Isolation, Durability. It all worked or it all didn't work. If anything goes wrong, everything rolls back. The system is never in an inconsistent state — or at least, it tries very hard not to be.

The Change Feed and the async processing patterns in this chapter operate on a different model: eventual consistency. The raw webhook event is written, but it's not processed yet. The user's update is saved, but the search index doesn't reflect it yet. The Person's name changed, but the denormalized copies in their Notes still show the old name. For some period of time — usually milliseconds to seconds, occasionally longer — the system is in an inconsistent state.

And that's okay. It's a deliberate mindset. It's a choice for reliability and scaling.

If I were going to get a tattoo about my philosophy of life, it might very well be "eventual consistency." A belief that bad things can happen — that things can NOT go my way — that I can lose or make mistakes or whatever, and that I'll be able to handle it. I might not *love it*, but I can handle it.

I find myself quoting Rilke's poem "Already the Ripening Barberries Are Red" and the "believing that there are visions after visions" line a lot. You wouldn't think it, but a random German poet from the early 1900s has stuff to teach us about eventual consistency in our distributed systems 125 years later.

Eventual consistency isn't a compromise. It's a design choice that trades the control-freaky illusion of perfect consistency for real resilience and real decoupling. ACID transactions say "everything succeeds together or fails together." Eventual consistency says "things might be temporarily out of sync, but the system converges to the right state, and in the meantime, nothing is broken — just not yet complete."

The Change Feed is how Cosmos DB gives you the tools to build eventually consistent systems that are resilient, decoupled, and observable. It's not triggers. It's not auditing. It's the infrastructure for building systems that handle imperfection gracefully.

Next up: Chapter 9, where we talk about Security & Permissions — the chapter is about the stuff that makes people angry because the Azure Portal speaks in riddles and whispers to them about what permissions your app actually has.

Chapter 9 Cosmos DB: Security & Permissions

This is Chapter 9 of *Azure Cosmos DB for .NET Developers*. Previous: Chapter 8: Change Feed & Event Patterns.

I'm a huge fan of Cosmos DB — enough to spend lots and lots of time writing this book. I like writing apps against it and I think it makes so many excellent things possible and easier with application architecture. I use it every day and I've used it in multiple production systems.

So when I say this next bit, hopefully, you'll know that I'm saying the following with a heavy heart filled with regret. Here goes.

Permissions management in Cosmos DB is hard. It's just kind of obtuse. That said, this permissions management jumble isn't unique to just Cosmos DB. SQL Azure and Key Vault definitely wrestle with this, too. I'd bet that a lot of other Azure products also would have similar issues.

It all comes down to a not-exactly-obvious distinction between *defining* resources in Azure and *using* resources in Azure.

Hopefully by the end of this chapter, it'll be less confusing.

Access Keys vs. Azure Managed Identity

After dumping on permissions management in Cosmos DB, I'm going to immediately reverse myself. There is an "easy button" — a way of accessing your Cosmos stuff that makes sense.

Access Keys

The easy way to access Cosmos DB is using **access keys**. You open up the portal and go to the **Keys** section and then all the stuff that you want is right there. It's got your endpoint URL and it's got your access keys. There's even a nicely formatted connection string that you can copy and paste. There are read-write keys and read-only keys, too.

Grab these read-write keys and you're good to go. You can do admin tasks like creating databases and containers and you also do data access so you can read and write data.

What's not to love? It's not as secure as you'd want to be.

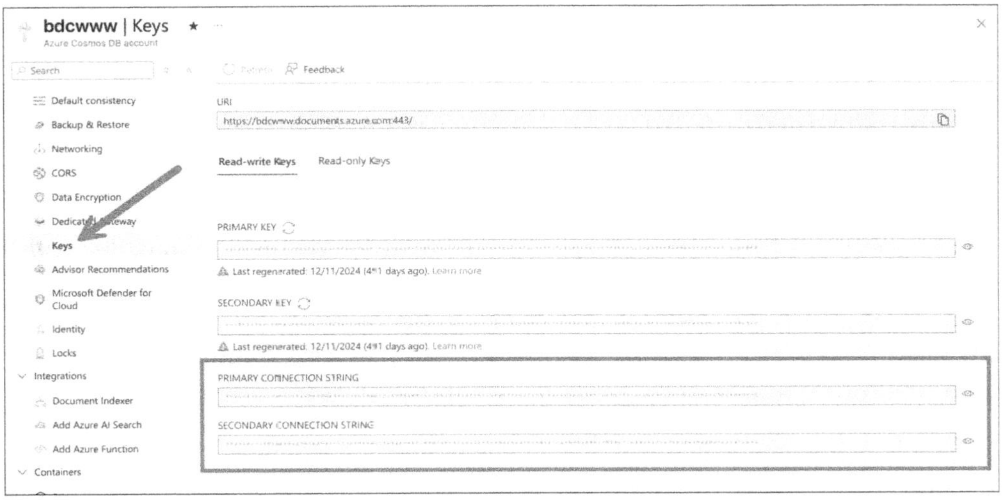

Blast from the Past: On-Prem SQL Server Active Directory Auth

Remember back to the days of writing .NET apps against SQL Server and everything ran inside your data center? No cloud stuff. No Azure stuff. Just apps running on a server that's joined to your Active Directory Domain. Your app probably had a connection string that looked something like this:

```
Server=sqlserver123; Database=billing-prod; Integrated
Security=True;
```

Notice that there's no password in that connection string. Heck! There's not even a *username* in that string. It's because of that `Integrated Security=True` thingy. You probably had to do some admin in Internet Information Server (IIS) to configure your application's App Pool to run as a certain specific user. It was a little bit fiddly but once you did that, you didn't have to worry about passwords anymore. You could grant that app pool user the right permissions in SQL Server and then the security stuff all got handled via Active Directory. No passwords required. You probably even turned off username/password-based auth in SQL Server for even tighter security.

No pasting passwords into app.config or appsettings.json. No clear-text passwords for someone to steal. No passwords anywhere.

Then comes February 2010 and Azure becomes a thing and suddenly we're back to passwords (aka. tokens).

Azure Managed Identity

Fast forward to September of 2017 and Microsoft announces **Azure AD Managed Service Identity**. That ultimately got renamed **Azure Managed Identity**. What Azure Managed Identity does is let you get back to something password-less that looks more like that on-prem passwordless auth to SQL Server. Except this time, the goal is to be able to go passwordless to just about everything Azure to everything else in Azure.

It can get a little fiddly at first but it's the best-practice for Azure security and it puts all that permissions management stuff into Entra. It's unified and passwordless and centrally maintained.

This identity starts by going to the Azure resource that needs the permission. For example, the App Services Web App that runs www.benday.com uses a system managed identity. To set it up, I open the web app in the Azure Portal and went to the **Identity** section, then I set the **Status** to on and clicked save. That does some magic in my Entra tenant for my Azure Subscription and then I get a guid value that describes the object id for my web app.

Once I have that object id guid, I can grant it permissions in Cosmos and then the app runs without using a password.

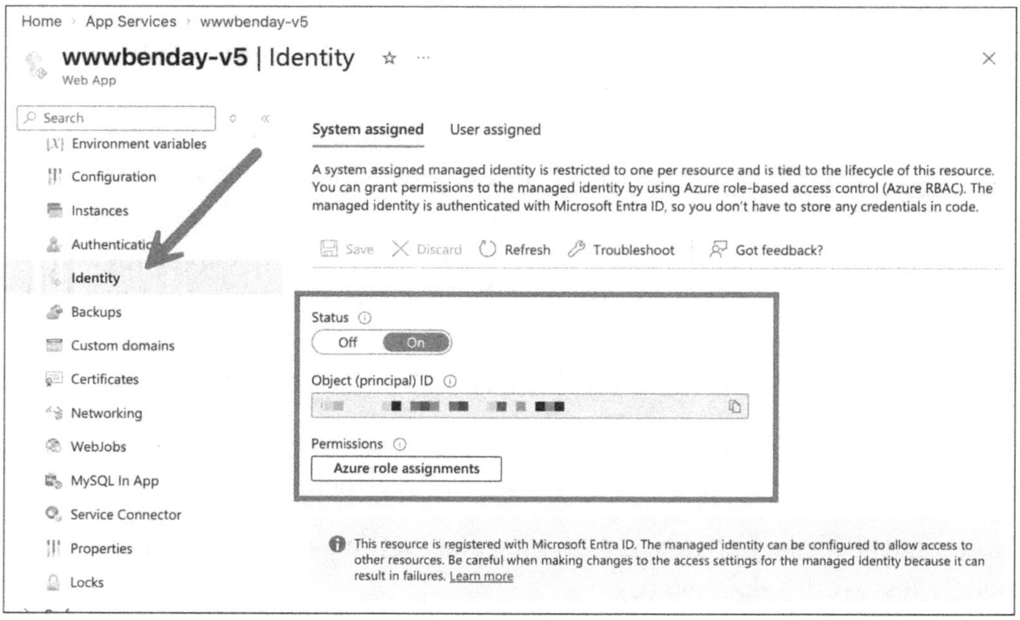

There's also an option to create a **user assigned** identity that works pretty much the same way. It roughly the equivalent of having your IIS app pool run as a specific user. I tend to use the system managed identity but that's more of a personal preference thing.

But anyway, now that I've showed you that **Identity** section on the Azure Portal, go click around in your resources on Azure. Pretty much everything has that Identity section in the admin UI and for production systems, you probably want to AVOID using anything other than Azure Identity.

Best practice: no access tokens and no passwords.

What about Key Vault?

Yahhhhhh...I knew that this would have to come up. Key Vault tries to bridge the divide between using passwords/tokens securely and being completely password-free. I think of it as an intermediate form of passwordless auth in Azure.

Let's look at the product launch timeline:

- Azure is announced in 2010
- Azure Key Vault is announced in 2015
- Azure Managed Identity is announced in 2017

Key Vault comes before Identity and gives you a way to store keys, secrets, and certificates in Azure in a way that allows you to control access to those secrets. So a permissions layer over the secret stuff.

There's still a need for Key Vault in a whole bunch of different scenarios. But for the .NET app to Cosmos DB use case, the most straightforward approach is Azure Managed Identity.

The Quest & The Core Problem

To summarize what we've covered so far in this chapter: it all comes down to my strong recommendation that you do auth to Cosmos DB using Azure Identity (Entra ID, etc).

If passwordless auth using Identity is the recommendation, next I'm going to give something to try.

The Quest

You've made it to chapter 9 of this book. You know some things about Cosmos DB. You've written some code. You've tried some stuff on the emulator. At a minimum you've reached the 'mildly dangerous' skill level.

I've got a mission for you. A cosmos quest. Go to the Azure Portal (https://portal.azure.com) and go to an existing Cosmos DB instance. Now I want you to grant a user permissions to read and write data to Cosmos.

Go ahead. Give it a try. I'll wait.

You probably clicked **Access control (IAM)** and then something like **Add role assignment**. Then you went looking for kind of permission with the words *read* or *write* or maybe *contributor* in the name. Sound about right?

And you completely struck out. It's not there.

There are things like **Cosmos DB Account Reader Role** and **DocumentDB Account Contributor** but when you read the description, it's not really what you want — they're all about administration of databases and containers but not reading or writing data *inside* those container. But you try one or two hoping that it'll work and you try to access Cosmos from your app. And your app responds with something like:

```
Request is blocked because principal [your-app-identity] does not hav
e
required RBAC permissions to perform action
[Microsoft.DocumentDB/databaseAccounts/readMetadata] on resource [/].
```

Whatever you did isn't right.

The Core Problem

You tried to grant permissions to an Identity in Cosmos via the Azure Portal and failed...

...or did you?

You didn't fail exactly. You didn't achieve your goal but it wasn't for lack of trying.

You just simply cannot grant data access permissions via the Azure Portal for Cosmos DB.

The End.

The Two Permission Systems

The first thing that is going to sound weird and is going to keep sounding weird for a little while is that Cosmos DB has *two separate permission systems*, and they don't really know about each other.

They are the **control plane** and the **data plane**.

The control plane is the Azure-y resource-y stuff. Creating a Cosmos DB account. Creating a database inside that account. Creating a container inside that database. Changing throughput. Modifying an indexing policy. Setting up a TTL. Configuring a vector indexing policy. Deleting any of those things. If it's a configuration change about the *shape* of your Cosmos resources, it's a control plane operation. These permissions are managed the same way permissions are managed for basically every other Azure resource — through standard Azure RBAC, the stuff the portal's **Access control (IAM)** blade is built for.

The data plane is the stuff your application does within those resources. Read a document. Write a document. Run a query. Listen to the change feed. Bulk import a million records. Anything where you're poking at *the data inside* Cosmos — rather than the *shape of* Cosmos — is a data plane operation. These permissions are managed through a completely separate, Cosmos-specific RBAC system that was added to the product a few years ago.

Here's where it gets weirder. The portal's IAM blade — the one where you assign roles — *only shows you control plane roles*. The data plane roles aren't there. They exist. They're real. They work. They're just not surfaced in the UI that looks like it should be surfacing them.

So when you go to the portal and assign a role to your App Service's managed identity and you pick something that sounds like it might let your app read documents — something like **Cosmos DB Account Reader Role** — what you've actually granted is control plane access. Your identity can now view the account's configuration. It can read the list of databases. It cannot read a single document in those databases. That's a different system entirely.

Your app hits a document read, Cosmos says "do you have data plane permission for that?", the answer comes back "no, but they do have control plane permission," and Cosmos says "that's nice, I don't care, request denied."

This is the first thing to internalize. **Account-level RBAC (what the portal surfaces) is NOT the same thing as data-plane RBAC (what your application needs).** You need both. At the same time. For different purposes. And they're configured separately.

Control Plane vs. Data Plane: The Breakdown

OK, two planes, two systems. What actually lives in each one? The split isn't always obvious from the operation name, so here's the full list.

Operation	Plane	Who grants it
Create, delete, or modify the Cosmos account	Control	Owner / Contributor on the subscription or resource group
Read account keys and connection strings	Control	Contributor on the account (Cosmos DB Operator does **not** grant this)
Create or delete a database	Control	Cosmos DB Operator
Create or delete a container	Control	Cosmos DB Operator
Modify a container's indexing policy	Control	Cosmos DB Operator
Modify a container's vector indexing policy	Control	Cosmos DB Operator
Modify a container's TTL settings	Control	Cosmos DB Operator
Modify throughput (autoscale, manual, RU/s)	Control	Cosmos DB Operator
Modify unique key constraints (at container creation)	Control	Cosmos DB Operator

Operation	Plane	Who grants it
Configure backup policy, failover, network rules	Control	Contributor on the account
Create or remove data-plane role assignments	Control	Contributor on the account
Read a document (point read)	Data	Cosmos DB Built-in Data Reader
Query documents	Data	Cosmos DB Built-in Data Reader
Read the change feed	Data	Cosmos DB Built-in Data Reader
Create, replace, upsert, or patch a document	Data	Cosmos DB Built-in Data Contributor
Delete a document	Data	Cosmos DB Built-in Data Contributor
Bulk operations on documents	Data	Cosmos DB Built-in Data Contributor
Execute a transactional batch	Data	Cosmos DB Built-in Data Contributor
Read account metadata (needed for SDK handshake)	Data	Both built-in data roles include `readMetadata`

Two things jump out at me when I look at this table.

Cosmos DB Operator gives you "schema", not data. That's the whole point of the role. It exists specifically so you can grant "can create and configure containers but cannot read any of the data inside them" to a deployment identity. That's the role you'd give to your CI/CD pipeline. It is not the role your running app should have.

Let's say that again: your app running in production shouldn't have control plane access for security reasons. Unless you've got some kind of exotic situation, the app just simply shouldn't need it. So don't grant it.

Your running app needs one role, not two. If your production App Service has both control plane and data plane rights, you've over-granted. The split exists to enforce the separation — deployment tooling configures the shape, the running app touches the data, and neither can do the other's job by accident. That's the architecture to aim for.

How You Actually Grant Data Plane Access

So if the portal can't do it, what can? There are five paths that work, roughly in the order most people pick them up.

Azure CLI. The everyday tool. `az cosmosdb sql role assignment create` with the account name, resource group, principal ID, and role definition ID. This is what I use for ad-hoc grants during development and it's what most tutorials default to. The canonical command looks like this:

```
az cosmosdb sql role assignment create \
  --account-name <your-cosmos-account-name> \
  --resource-group <your-resource-group> \
  --scope "/" \
  --principal-id <the-object-id-of-the-identity> \
  --role-definition-id 00000000-0000-0000-0000-000000000002
```

That last parameter is the magic GUID. `00000000-0000-0000-0000-000000000002` is Built-in Data Contributor. `00000000-0000-0000-0000-000000000001` is Built-in Data Reader. Those IDs are not typos. They are sequential magic numbers. They look like somebody generated them on a Monday morning. They are, in fact, the actual values you have to paste into role assignment commands. I don't love it either. But once you've seen them a few times you can recognize them — if you spot `0000...0002` in a script, you know somebody is granting Cosmos data plane contributor access.

The `--principal-id` is the thing that gets a little confusing. It is not the user's email address. It is not the App Service's name. It is the **object ID** of the identity in Microsoft Entra ID.

For a user in Entra: `az ad user show --id your.email@example.com --query id -o tsv`

For a managed identity on an App Service: go to the App Service in the portal, click **Identity**, and copy the **Object (principal) ID**. Or, from the command line: `az webapp identity show --name <app-name> --resource-group <rg> --query principalId -o tsv`

Azure PowerShell. `New-AzCosmosDBSqlRoleAssignment` from the `Az.CosmosDB` module. Same semantics as the CLI, different syntax. If your team lives in PowerShell, use this.

Bicep or ARM templates. Declare a `Microsoft.DocumentDB/databaseAccounts/sqlRoleAssignments` resource in your infrastructure code, parented to the Cosmos account. This is the right answer for production — role assignments belong in your IaC alongside the Cosmos account itself, not as imperative CLI commands someone ran once and forgot about.

If you're using a lot of this Infrastructure as Code (IaC) stuff, you might find that this is where you want to use "user assigned" identities rather than "system managed" identities. I find this especially helpful for Bicep but the reason is a little 'in the weeds'. The system managed identity is represented by a guid value that's created when the identity is created for a resource. If you want to reference that object id guid in your Bicep stuff, you often have to do extra stuff to find that guid value. If you do it as a "user assigned" identity, then you declare that identity in Bicep and it becomes an actual, easily referenceable thing. That gives you a certain amount of "compile time" checking.

Terraform. `azurerm_cosmosdb_sql_role_assignment`. Same idea as Bicep, different IaC ecosystem.

Direct REST API. `az rest --method PUT` against the management plane, if you're desperate or scripting in a language that doesn't have Azure tooling. Rarely needed.

The portal is not on that list. (Meh.)

Seeing What's Actually Assigned

Because the portal won't show you data plane role assignments, the CLI is also how you view them. To list every data plane role assignment on an account:

```
az cosmosdb sql role assignment list \
  --account-name <your-cosmos-account-name> \
  --resource-group <your-resource-group>
```

The output includes the principal ID, the scope, and the role definition ID for each assignment. Combine it with `az ad sp show --id <principal-id>` or `az ad user show --id <principal-id>` and you can resolve each GUID back to a human-readable identity.

This is the only way to answer the question "who has data plane access to our production Cosmos?" And it's a question you're going to need to answer eventually — during a security audit, during onboarding a new team member, or during a "why does this deployment keep working when we thought we removed that service principal six months ago" investigation. Bookmark the command. We'll come back to it in Chapter 14 when we cover operational audit patterns in more depth.

Granting Permissions Across Subscriptions

Here's some sand to pour in your gears. A thing that comes up all the time in enterprise-land: Azure Identity permissions across subscriptions.

Let's say you've got a managed identity (or a user, or a service principal) in one subscription, and the Cosmos DB account you want to grant it access to lives in a different subscription. This happens constantly — shared platform services in one subscription, per-team or per-environment application workloads in others, a "platform" subscription with a managed identity that needs data plane access to half a dozen Cosmos accounts scattered across a bunch of other subscriptions.

The Microsoft docs mostly show you `az account set --subscription <sub-id>` and then run your command. That works fine when you're granting permissions within just one subscription. It gets confusing and annoying and buggy real fast when you're granting permissions across several subscriptions in the same script, because every command after the `az account set` is now pointing at the new subscription, and it's easy to lose track of which one you're currently on. (Go ahead. Ask me how I know this is confusing, annoying, and buggy.)

The better approach is to pass `--subscription` directly on each command. That flag is a global parameter — every `az` command accepts it — and it accepts either the subscription name or its GUID. Pass it inline and the command targets that specific subscription without changing your shell's current context. Nothing to forget to reset afterward.

```
az cosmosdb sql role assignment create \
  --subscription <subscription-name-or-id> \
  --account-name <account> \
  --resource-group <rg> \
  --scope "/" \
  --principal-id <object-id-of-the-identity> \
  --role-definition-id 00000000-0000-0000-0000-000000000002
```

One thing that's worth knowing for this scenario: the **principal ID is tenant-scoped, not subscription-scoped**. An object ID in Entra ID is unique across your whole tenant. So you can take a managed identity that lives in Subscription A and grant it data plane access to a Cosmos account in Subscription B, as long as both subscriptions are in the same Entra tenant. The principal ID doesn't change. What changes is the `--subscription` you're targeting with the assignment command — that has to match the subscription where the Cosmos account lives.

This is actually a really common real-world pattern. A shared managed identity in a "platform" subscription that needs data plane access to Cosmos accounts in several "application" subscriptions. The identity is one object. The role assignments live in each Cosmos account's subscription. You'd script it as a loop that calls `az cosmosdb sql role assignment create` with a different `--subscription` each iteration, same `--principal-id` every time. Explicit, scriptable, and you never have to wonder which subscription your shell is pointed at.

It's Messy...So Why Did Microsoft Do It This Way?

Caveat first: I don't work at Microsoft. I don't have a source on the inside telling me what the Cosmos team was thinking. What follows is educated guessing.

I think permissions management in Cosmos DB is confusing. But why did it end up this way? Why was it built this way? Why isn't this more streamlined?

It's the Way that Azure Works

Azure consists of what feels like a nearly endless list of products. These products are available for you to create via the Azure Portal and when you create an instance of one of these products it becomes a **resource**. And resources live in **resource groups**. Azure as an automated system administration and an automated data center admin "tool", is spinning up and billing you for the use of resources.

It's all about resources.

I started using Azure about a year before it was publicly announced. Back in those days it used to be called "Project Red Dog". So that's probably 2009-ish that I first got involved in what would become Azure.

Back then I did TONS of system administration as part of my work as a software architect and DevOps process consultant. Setting up and administering Window Server. Setting up and administering Active Directory Domain Controllers. Installing and configuring SQL Server and SQL Server clusters. Load balancers. Team Foundation Server instances and Azure DevOps Server instances. And then related to all of this was worrying about disk arrays and RAID configurations and backups and redundancy and failover.

I did *a lot* of sys admin tasks. I spent a lot of time in loud, freezing-cold data centers huddled around server racks. But I didn't think about that stuff as being significant — it was just part of the gig.

But think about now. I can't remember the last time I was in a corporate data center. I can't remember the last time I even *saw* a server. Now I pop into the Azure portal, spin up a VM or an instance of Azure Storage or Cosmos or SQL Server and go. Typically, off and running in a matter of minutes.

And when I'm done with one of those things, I just click delete and they all go away.

That's not easy to do, kids! That ain't nuthin'. Microsoft has developed a system to provision, manage, bill for, monitor, and deprovision all of that stuff. And when you really start thinking about what has to go in to that — I dunno about you — but that just BLOWS MY MIND how complex that is.

But in order to do that, there are tradeoffs. Azure has to be able to generalize and abstract things down to resources that it manages.

Asking the Azure data center automation framework and Azure Portal to *also* provide comprehensive admin UIs for the innards of all these things? Well, I suspect that if they'd tried to pull that off that Azure never would have shipped.

Performance Reasons

There is another Azure architectural reason the two systems are separate. Cosmos DB is designed to handle millions of operations per second, and every single document read has to answer "does this principal have permission?" If that check had to round-trip to Azure's central RBAC service, you'd potentially be adding cross-service latency to every request. So the Cosmos team built their own RBAC system that runs inside Cosmos itself, colocated with the data engine. Role assignments live under the `Microsoft.DocumentDB` provider rather than `Microsoft.Authorization`. The lookup is fast because it never leaves Cosmos.

That explains why the two systems exist. So what about the portal?

Why No Data Plane Admin in the Portal?

So you can't do data plane admin in the Azure Portal. Why? I suspect that it's a little bit philosophical and a little bit practical realities. The Azure Portal is focused on resources because that's what Azure is focused on. The portal (more or less) is focused on driving the stuff that the Azure data center framework does.

If I'm thinking from a product perspective, you have to stay focused and you can't be everything to everyone. You probably *could* implement data plane permissions via the portal but now you're taking on a whole new set of complexities and features. I'd bet that it was considered...and then dropped to the bottom of the backlog. Too hard to pull off and do well.

I do wish that the portal had a prominent message that says something like "hey. Looking to grant data access permissions? Those are all done via CLI-only." That would have saved me a whole lot of confusion.

The good news is that once you know the gap exists, it's not hard to work around. CLI for ad-hoc. Bicep or Terraform for production. Just remember to ignore the IAM blade when it comes to data access. "These aren't the droids you're looking for." Treat the portal as a read-only dashboard for control plane things and you'll be fine.

Reading the Error Messages

Let's go back to that error message from the Quest section, because now you can actually read it. Here it is again:

```
Request is blocked because principal [your-app-identity] does not hav
e
required RBAC permissions to perform action
[Microsoft.DocumentDB/databaseAccounts/readMetadata] on resource [/].
```

Notice that it names `readMetadata` specifically. Not `read`, not `query`, not whatever operation your code was actually trying to do. It's almost always `readMetadata`. This throws people off every time, because the natural assumption is that the named action is the one that failed, and nobody's code is calling something literally named `readMetadata`.

Here's what's actually happening. Before the SDK does anything else, it has to do a handshake with the account to figure out partition key ranges, container routing information, and other metadata about where the data you're asking for physically lives. That handshake calls `readMetadata`. Every real operation — every document read, every query, every change feed subscription — depends on the SDK having done that handshake successfully. If your identity doesn't have at least one of the built-in data roles, `readMetadata` is the first thing that fails, before your code ever gets a chance to attempt whatever it was actually trying to do.

So if you see `readMetadata` in the error, it almost never means something's wrong with your metadata query. It means your identity is missing the basic "I'm allowed to talk to this account at all" permission that every real operation builds on top of. Ninety percent of the time, the fix is "assign the identity Built-in Data Contributor (or Reader) via `az cosmosdb sql role assignment create` and try again."

The other ten percent is usually one of two things. Either the role assignment exists but hasn't propagated yet (Cosmos can take a minute or two to reflect new role assignments — if you just created the assignment and it's still failing, wait two minutes before doing anything else). Or you assigned the role to the wrong principal ID. The most common version of this mistake is grabbing the App Service's *Application ID* instead of its managed identity's *Object ID*. They're different GUIDs. They sit right next to each other in the portal. Only the Object ID works for role assignments. I've made this mistake more than once and I'm the one writing the book about it.

What Each Credential Can Actually Do

Before we get into the library config and the deployment walkthrough, let's put one more table on the page. This one compares what you can do with each kind of credential — because most Cosmos tutorials treat the primary key and a managed identity as two equivalent ways to authenticate, and they're not.

The primary key (the primary *access* key) is a broad credential by design. It can do every data plane operation. It can also do every control plane operation that Cosmos itself manages — create databases, delete containers, rewrite indexing policies, crank throughput to 100,000 RU/s and leave it there. What it *can't* do is anything at the ARM layer: modify the account's networking, change the backup policy, rotate its own key, or delete the account itself. Those still need Azure RBAC on the account resource. Within Cosmos itself, though, the key grants broad access across both planes.

That means when you paste a primary key into appsettings.json, you're not just dropping a secret into a file. You're giving the application that loads that file — and anyone who can read that file — the authority to rewrite every container, drop every database, and reindex every collection in the account. Your simple CRUD app has the permissions of a platform administrator. And there's no way to scope it down. You can't give a service "primary key minus container delete." It's all or nothing.

Managed identity + a data plane role assignment is different. It grants exactly the permissions you named and nothing else. You can *decompose* what used to be a single blunt credential into separately-grantable capabilities. Schema for the deployment pipeline. Data for the app. Reporting access for the dashboard. Nothing for anyone else. That decomposition is the actual win.

Here's the comparison in one place:

Operation	**Primary Key (connection string)**	**Cosmos DB Operator (control plane)**	**Built-in Data Contributor (data plane)**	**Built-in Data Reader (data plane)**
Read documents (point read, query)	☑	✕	☑	☑

Operation	Primary Key (connection string)	Cosmos DB Operator (control plane)	Built-in Data Contributor (data plane)	Built-in Data Reader (data plane)
Read change feed	☑	✕	☑	☑
Create, update, delete documents	☑	✕	☑	✕
Bulk operations, transactional batch	☑	✕	☑	✕
Create or delete a database	☑	☑	✕	✕
Create or delete a container	☑	☑	✕	✕
Modify indexing policy	☑	☑	✕	✕
Modify vector indexing policy	☑	☑	✕	✕
Modify TTL settings	☑	☑	✕	✕
Change throughput (RU/s, autoscale)	☑	☑	✕	✕
Modify unique key constraints (at creation)	☑	☑	✕	✕
Read account keys / connection strings	✕	✕	✕	✕
Rotate account keys	✕	✕	✕	✕

Operation	Primary Key (connection string)	Cosmos DB Operator (control plane)	Built-in Data Contributor (data plane)	Built-in Data Reader (data plane)
Create or remove data plane role assignments	✕	✕	✕	✕
Configure networking, firewall, private endpoint	✕	✕	✕	✕
Configure backup policy, failover regions	✕	✕	✕	✕
Delete the Cosmos account	✕	✕	✕	✕

The bottom six rows are pure ARM operations — they need Azure RBAC roles on the account resource itself (`Contributor` or similar). No Cosmos-specific credential, key or role, can touch them.

And the "who should have what" recommendation becomes:

Identity	Credential approach
You, local dev against a real Cosmos account	`az login` + Cosmos DB Operator + Built-in Data Contributor
Production app (App Service, Functions, Container App)	Managed identity + Built-in Data Contributor — nothing else
Deployment pipeline (Bicep, Terraform, GitHub Actions)	Service principal + Cosmos DB Operator on the account + Contributor on the RG for ARM-level things
Read-only reporting service	Managed identity + Built-in Data Reader

Identity	Credential approach
Nobody, ever, in production	The primary key

That last row is where the contrast hits hardest. The primary key can do everything in the "can do" column, including the schema-level operations that a running app has no business doing. That's not because the key is a bad credential — it's because the key predates the RBAC data plane by years, and it was designed for a time when "can this principal do this operation" was a coarser-grained question than we ask today. RBAC gives you the decomposition the key never could. That's the upgrade path.

The primary key has one honest use: **the emulator.** The emulator ships with a well-known, publicly-documented key. It's not a secret, there's nothing to leak, and RBAC setup against a local emulator would be friction without benefit. Use the key there. Use managed identity everywhere else.

What `DefaultAzureCredential` Actually Does

The mechanism that makes the managed identity path pleasant in .NET is a class called `DefaultAzureCredential`, which lives in the `Azure.Identity` NuGet package. It's what my `Benday.CosmosDb` library uses when you flip the config switch. But before we get to that switch, it's worth understanding what `DefaultAzureCredential` is actually doing, because it's a small piece of magic and the magic is worth knowing.

`DefaultAzureCredential` is a **credential chain**. When your code asks it for a token, it walks through a list of credential sources in order, trying each one, returning the first one that works. The list looks roughly like this:

10. **Environment variables** (things like `AZURE_CLIENT_ID`, `AZURE_CLIENT_SECRET`, `AZURE_TENANT_ID` — the service principal approach, usually set in CI/CD pipelines)
11. **Managed Identity** (is the code running on an Azure resource that has a managed identity? use it)
12. **Azure CLI login** (are you logged in via `az login`? use that identity)
13. **Azure PowerShell login** (same idea, but for `Connect-AzAccount`)
14. **Visual Studio / VS Code signed-in account** (are you signed into an Azure account in your IDE? use that)

15. A few others that are less common.

This chain is why the managed identity story *feels* seamless. The exact same code that runs in production with a managed identity also works on your laptop during development, because locally you're signed into `az login` and the chain falls through to that credential. You don't need one code path for local and another for production. You write:

```
var credential = new DefaultAzureCredential();
```

And that credential works everywhere, because it adapts to its environment. Running in App Service? It uses the managed identity. Running on your laptop? It uses your `az login` session. Running in a GitHub Actions pipeline? It uses the environment variables your workflow set.

This is genuinely lovely when it works. But it can be a little bit maddening when it doesn't. Here's the scenario that gets a little frustrating: since `DefaultAzureCredential` is a chain of credentials, it's entirely possible that it picks one with *some* but not *all* the permissions you need and then it errors out. What is often lost is *which* credentials did it try and which one failed. Since the chain fails through silently, you can get "token acquisition failed" at the end without a clear indication of which link fell over.

There's an environment variable, `AZURE_IDENTITY_LOGGING_ENABLED=true`, that you can set to make the chain verbose about what it tried and what went wrong. File that one away for the day you need it. You'll probably need it some day.

The Local Dev Story

Here's what the local development experience looks like when you go this route.

You open a terminal. You log in:

```
az login
```

Your browser pops up. You authenticate. `az` remembers who you are.

You grant your own user identity the roles you need on the Cosmos account you'll be developing against. For a real account where you're also going to be creating containers and modifying indexing policies — which is most development scenarios — you need both planes:

```
# Control plane: Cosmos DB Operator (so you can create containers, et
c.)
az role assignment create \
  --role "Cosmos DB Operator" \
  --assignee <your-user-object-id> \
  --scope /subscriptions/<sub-id>/resourceGroups/<rg>/providers/
      Microsoft.DocumentDB/databaseAccounts/<account-name>

# Data plane: Built-in Data Contributor (so you can read/write
documents)
az cosmosdb sql role assignment create \
  --account-name <account-name> \
  --resource-group <rg> \
  --scope "/" \
  --principal-id <your-user-object-id> \
  --role-definition-id 00000000-0000-0000-0000-000000000002
```

Notice the two commands are different. The control plane grant uses `az role assignment create` — standard Azure RBAC. The data plane grant uses `az cosmosdb sql role assignment create` — the Cosmos-specific one. Same pattern, different commands, different resource providers under the hood.

Update your `appsettings.json` to remove the `AccountKey` and set `UseDefaultAzureCredential` to `true`:

```
{
  "CosmosConfiguration": {
    "Endpoint": "https://your-account.documents.azure.com:443/"
,
    "DatabaseName": "AppDb",
    "ContainerName": "AppContainer",
    "PartitionKey": "/tenantId,/entityType",
    "UseHierarchicalPartitionKey": true,
    "CreateStructures": true,
    "UseDefaultAzureCredential": true
  }
}
```

No account key. No connection string. No secret anywhere in the file.

One thing to watch out for: `CreateStructures = true` tells the library to create the database and container on startup if they don't already exist. That's a control plane operation, which means it needs the Cosmos DB Operator role to work. That's fine for local dev — you granted yourself Operator above. In production, you'd typically set `CreateStructures` to `false` and let your deployment automation (Bicep, Terraform, a setup script running under a service principal with Operator) handle container creation. The running app only needs data plane Contributor and shouldn't be creating or deleting containers.

Run the app. The credential chain tries managed identity first (you're not on an Azure resource, so that fails immediately), falls through to your `az login` session, grabs a token, hands it to the Cosmos SDK, the SDK makes the request, Cosmos checks the data plane role assignment, sees you have Contributor, lets the request through. Documents flow. You're doing real development against real Cosmos with zero secrets in your config.

When you hand the project off to a teammate, they do the same thing. They `az login` with their account, you grant their account the same two roles, and they're productive. Nobody ever sees a primary key. Nobody ever has to rotate one when somebody leaves the team.

This is the thing tutorials should be teaching, and for the most part they aren't.

The `UseDefaultAzureCredential` Flag in Benday.CosmosDb

Because this pattern is so common in production, my `Benday.CosmosDb` library has a single config flag that turns on the whole story:

```
{
  "CosmosConfiguration": {
    "Endpoint": "https://your-account.documents.azure.com:443/",
    "DatabaseName": "AppDb",
    "ContainerName": "AppContainer",
    "PartitionKey": "/tenantId,/entityType",
    "UseHierarchicalPartitionKey": true,
    "UseDefaultAzureCredential": true
```

```
    }
}
```

When that flag is `false` (the default, for backward compatibility), the library constructs a `CosmosClient` using the account key you provided — the old tutorial path. When it's `true`, the library ignores `AccountKey` entirely and constructs the client using `new DefaultAzureCredential()`. Your code doesn't change. Your repositories work the same way. Your queries run the same way. The library takes care of the switch under the hood.

In the fluent builder style, the same thing looks like this:

```
var config = CosmosConfigBuilder.Create()
    .WithEndpoint("https://your-account.documents.azure.com:443/")
    .UseDefaultAzureCredential()
    .WithDatabase("AppDb")
    .WithContainer("AppContainer")
    .WithPartitionKey("/tenantId,/entityType", useHierarchical: true)
    .Build();
```

One method call. The whole managed-identity-in-production-and-az-login-on-your-laptop story. Nobody has to remember the pattern. Nobody has to paste primary keys into config files.

Turning Keys Off for Good: `disableLocalAuth`

Remember earlier in the chapter when I mentioned that in the SQL Server on-prem days, you'd configure Integrated Security for your app and then — once you were sure everything worked — you'd turn off username/password auth in SQL Server entirely? Locking the other door once you had the Active Directory door open and working.

Cosmos DB has the same move. It's called `disableLocalAuth`.

Here's why it matters. Everything I've shown you up to this point is a recommendation. Your app uses managed identity. Your role assignments are in Bicep. Your developers `az login` locally and never touch a key. Great. But the primary key still exists. It's still in the portal. It still works. Anyone with control plane Contributor rights on the account can copy it and use it right now. A contractor you worked with six months ago, an ex-employee whose service principal never got cleaned up, an automation user that should have been decommissioned three re-orgs ago — if any of those has the key, they have full data plane access and there's nothing stopping them. You've made the RBAC path *possible*. You haven't made the key path *impossible*.

`disableLocalAuth` is how you lock the other door. It's an account-level property. Set it to `true` and key-based authentication stops working entirely. Every request that tries to authenticate with a primary key, a secondary key, or a connection string is rejected. Not rate-limited, not warned about — rejected. The only way to authenticate becomes Entra ID.

```
az resource update \
  --resource-group <your-resource-group> \
  --name <your-cosmos-account-name> \
  --resource-type "Microsoft.DocumentDB/databaseAccounts" \
  --set properties.disableLocalAuth=true
```

Or in Bicep, as part of your account definition:

```
resource account 'Microsoft.DocumentDB/databaseAccounts@2024-05-15' =
{
  name: name
  location: location
  kind: 'GlobalDocumentDB'
  properties: {
    disableLocalAuth: true
    databaseAccountOfferType: 'Standard'
    locations: [ /* ... */ ]
  }
}
```

The flag is reversible — you can flip it back to `false` if something genuinely has to fall back to key auth during an incident — but the right posture for production is "on, and leave it on." Azure Policy even has a built-in policy (*Cosmos DB database accounts should have local authentication methods disabled*) that you can apply at the subscription or management group level. Once that policy is in place, nobody can spin up a new Cosmos account without key auth disabled. The door is locked, and the policy makes sure future doors get locked by default too.

Two things to know before you flip the switch.

It's currently only supported on the NoSQL API. If you're running a Cosmos account for MongoDB, Cassandra, Gremlin, or Table, `disableLocalAuth` either doesn't exist or works differently. Something to factor in if you're picking an API for a new project where this kind of lockdown matters.

Some tooling will break. If your team uses a Cosmos Explorer-style GUI that authenticates with keys, it will stop working against accounts that have local auth disabled. The Azure portal's built-in Data Explorer mostly handles this correctly now — it authenticates using your signed-in Entra ID identity, assuming you've granted yourself the data plane roles. Third-party tools vary. You'll need to migrate those tools to Entra ID or move to ones that already support it. Small transition cost for a meaningfully better posture. Worth paying.

With `disableLocalAuth = true`, your Cosmos account is genuinely a zero-key environment. Every request is authenticated through Entra ID. Every identity has a named, auditable, revocable role assignment. The primary key in the portal still exists but it's functionally decorative — nobody can actually use it to do anything. This is the destination the rest of this chapter has been pointing at.

Same move you made in SQL Server twenty years ago. Same idea. Different era. Same good instinct.

A Quick Summary for Reference

If you're scanning back through this chapter in six months trying to remember how to do the thing, here's the compressed version.

Control plane — account, database, container, indexing policy, throughput. Assigned through standard Azure RBAC via the portal's IAM blade, or via `az role assignment create`. Your running application almost never needs this.

Data plane — document operations. Assigned through Cosmos-specific RBAC via `az cosmosdb sql role assignment create`. Your running application needs this. The portal doesn't surface data plane roles — you'll use the CLI (or Bicep, or Terraform) instead. This is by design, not a bug in your setup.

Default data plane roles: - Reader: `00000000-0000-0000-0000-000000000001` - Contributor: `00000000-0000-0000-0000-000000000002`

The one config flag: `UseDefaultAzureCredential: true` in `Benday.CosmosDb`, or `new DefaultAzureCredential()` in raw SDK code.

Auditing what's assigned: `az cosmosdb sql role assignment list --account-name <acct> --resource-group <rg>`. The portal will never tell you; the CLI is the only source of truth. (More in Chapter 14.)

Reading the error message: If the 403 names `Microsoft.DocumentDB/databaseAccounts/readMetadata`, your identity is missing the basic data plane role entirely — the SDK handshake is what's failing, not whatever your code was actually trying to do.

Locking the door: `disableLocalAuth: true` on the account rejects all key-based authentication outright. Apply it via Bicep, ARM, or `az resource update`. Azure Policy has a built-in policy to enforce it across a subscription. This is the "we're done with keys" setting — the Cosmos version of turning off SQL Server password auth once Integrated Security was working.

The mindset: Managed identity in production, `az login` locally, no primary keys in config files anywhere, ever, once you've moved past the emulator. Deployment automation creates the schema. The running app touches data. Neither can do the other's job.

Next up: Chapter 10, where we pull it all together. The cocktail app on drinkymcdrinkface.com is a complete production Cosmos DB application — three entity types sharing a single container, multi-tenancy done right, traditional search that doesn't need AI, and all of it running on the patterns we've been building since Chapter 1. Hierarchical partition keys, aggregate roots, denormalization, the library, and now managed identity — all in one running system, solving a problem most database books would tell you is too complicated for a single chapter. We'll prove that it isn't.

Chapter 10 Cosmos DB: Designing a Multi-Entity App

Nine chapters. That's a lot of theory.

We've talked about trees and boxes, aggregate roots, hierarchical partition keys, the repository pattern, request units, change feeds, managed identity, and the whole Azure RBAC mess. I've tried to pay all of that off with working code along the way — the `Note` class in Chapter 3, the Person/Note/Comment sample app in Chapters 5 and 6, snippets from Azure Functions in Chapter 8. But those are deliberately small examples. They're the training-wheels versions. Each one is designed to illustrate exactly one thing and nothing else.

That's useful for learning. It's less useful for real, actual dev.

My goal for the next handful of chapters is to talk you through building an actual app called drinkymcdrinkface.com. Seriously. It's a real site. I registered a domain and everything. It's a cocktail recipe search engine. It's simple enough that it doesn't take a ton of explaining but complex enough that we can work through some actual design choices.

Think of it as a case study: ~5,800 real cocktail recipes, a curated ingredient taxonomy, multi-tenancy, a working auth layer, and a domain model. This is a chapter about design decisions.

Quick Overview of the App

Here's what drinkymcdrinkface.com does. You can search cocktails by name ("manhattan"), by a single ingredient ("rye"), by multiple ingredients with AND semantics ("rye AND vermouth"), or by describing what you're in the mood for in natural language ("something dark and smoky with mezcal") and letting AI take over. We'll get to the AI stuff in the Vector Database chapter.

There's a classification taxonomy about ingredients and that means that the app knows that "Old Overholt Rye" and "Rittenhouse 100" are both rye whiskey. Put another way, searching by ingredient type works even if you don't know the specific brand. That ingredient taxonomy is browsable so you can find what you're in the mood for. Also, if you're looking at a recipe and see an ingredient that you don't recognize, you can click it to view what kind of 'thing' it is.

And if you've created an account, logged-in users can favorite recipes and see their favorites on a dedicated page.

Under the hood: it's 5,800 recipe documents, 2,144 ingredient classification documents, whatever user favorites people have created, and ASP.NET Core Identity users and roles — all sharing one Cosmos container, partitioned intelligently so that we use Cosmos DB efficiently.

Here's the whole domain model in one picture before we start picking it apart:

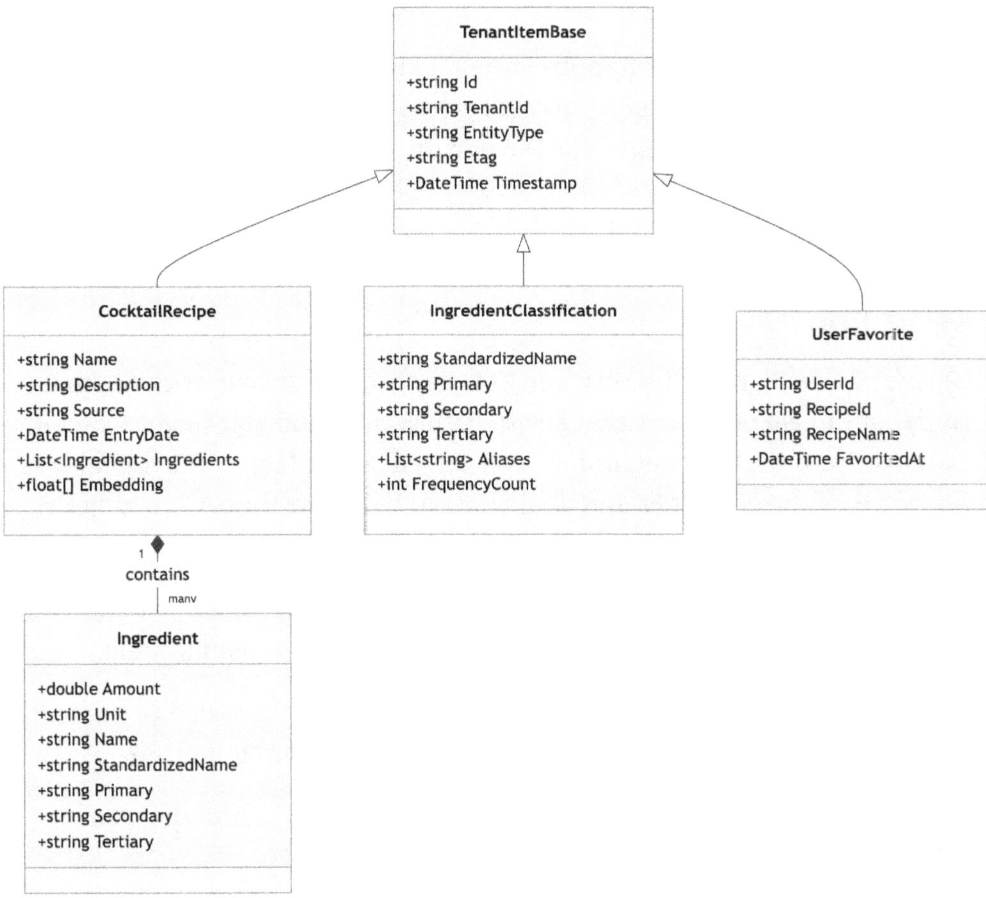

Three classes inherit from `TenantItemBase` — `CocktailRecipe`, `IngredientClassification`, `UserFavorite`. Those are the three aggregate roots, and they're what we'll spend most of this chapter talking about. `Ingredient` is the lone non-aggregate-root in this picture — it lives inside `CocktailRecipe` as a nested value object. We'll get to why in a minute.

One Database, One Container

The first design choice is to have one Cosmos DB database and inside it, only one Cosmos DB container.

This is for cost reasons. Remember that you pay for Cosmos typically on a per-container basis. Each container you provision gets its own throughput allocation (or shares an allocation at the database level), and that allocation is what shows up on your bill. More containers = more throughput pools to pay for.

Also, a Cosmos container can happily store all kinds of documents side-by-side in the same container. Documents in the same container don't have to share a schema. The only thing they share is the partition key path, which we'll get to next.

So: one container, multiple kinds of documents in it. That's the starting point.

The Partition Key

At the risk of — well, more like certainty of — repeating myself, with Cosmos DB you've got to get your partition key structure right and you've got to get it right almost from the very beginning. You can change it later...but you'll also have to recreate the container and all its data at the same time. Changing the partition key is a pain.

That said, we're using the `/tenantId,/entityType` hierarchical partition key for everything. This gives us a clear way to create a multi-tenant system.

You might be thinking — why does a cocktail recipe database need to be multi-tenant? What could possibly be multi-tenant? Who are the "tenants"?

There are two types of tenant in this app: the *system tenant* and the *user tenants*.

The system tenant is where shared data lives — the cocktail recipes, the ingredient taxonomy, anything that the whole app reads from. Every user gets to access data under the system tenant. In our case, the system tenant ID is the literal string `"COCKTAILS"`. In other apps, I often use `"SYSTEM"` but whatever value you choose, I'd suggest making it obvious and create a constant in your application called something like `DefaultTenantId`.

User tenants are per-user. Every authenticated user gets their own tenant, keyed by their Identity user ID. Per-user data — favorites, eventually anything else a user "owns" — gets stored with `TenantId = userId`. Users can't see each other's data because their data lives in different logical partitions. Using `TenantId` as the top of the partition key hierarchy is a key element of NOT accidentally serving up some other user's data. You'd have to mess up and have a cross-partition query in order to even *retrieve* that data. It's not that it makes it impossible for your app to access that data but it does add that little extra layer to help ensure that you don't do something...uhhh..."sub-optimal".

Anyway. Same container. Different tenant IDs at the first level of the partition key. That's how multi-tenancy works in this app and it's a real-world pattern that works great in Cosmos.

That second level of the partition key (`entityType`) is the discriminator for *types* of data. This is what allows us to stuff all kinds of documents into a single Cosmos container without running into partitioning problems. Since we're using hierarchical partition keys, we aim for the `tenantId` first and then the `entityType` second.

So a recipe document goes into the partition `["COCKTAILS", "CocktailRecipe"]`. A classification document goes into `["COCKTAILS", "IngredientClassification"]`. A user favorite goes into `["f8d9a1b2-...", "UserFavorite"]` — under the user's own tenant ID. Identity user records go into their own partition, separately again.

Every query in the app specifies both levels of the partition key. That means every query is scoped to one logical partition. No cross-partition scans. No "let me check every partition for matching documents." One query, one partition.

CocktailRecipe and Ingredient

I've said `CocktailRecipe` is one of the aggregate roots. Why isn't `Ingredient` one too?

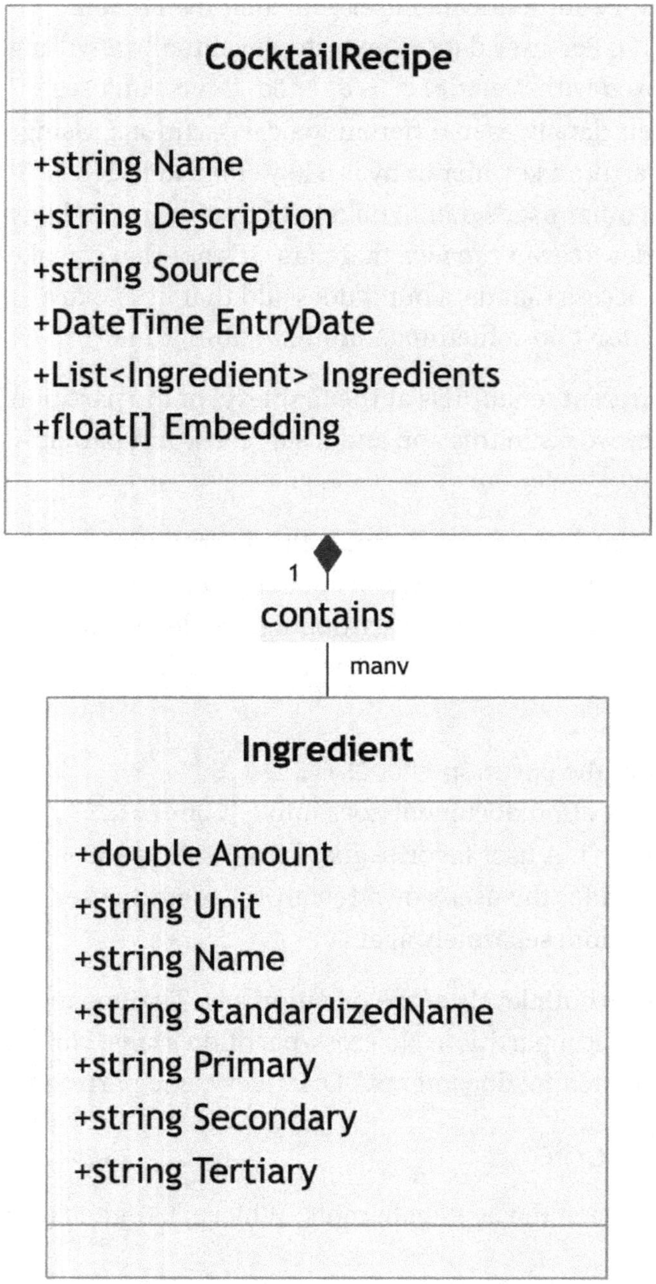

Apply the delete test. If I delete a recipe, should this Ingredient disappear?

The "1.5 oz of Old Overholt Rye" that goes into the "Manhattan" has no meaning outside of that recipe. Therefore, delete it.

Two different recipes that both use 1.5 oz of Old Overholt Rye don't share an `Ingredient` instance — each recipe gets its own copy.

Let's bounce back into relational database thinking for a second. If we were going to model this in a relational database, you *could* probably create a "1.5 oz of Old Overholt Rye" record in an ingredient table and then share that to multiple recipes via foreign key...but why would you? It might save some data storage space but then suddenly, you've got an awkward data integrity nightmare where two separate recipes share the same ingredient record. You *could* normalize that relationship but it would end up adding so much complexity that you'd regret the design decision almost immediately.

Back to Cosmos DB, there's no "look up an Ingredient by ID" use case because there's no Ingredient ID to look up. An Ingredient doesn't have its own identity. It exists *only* in the context of a recipe.

That makes `Ingredient` a *value object*, not an aggregate root. It lives inside the `CocktailRecipe` document as a nested array entry. When you save the recipe, the ingredients go with it. When you delete the recipe, the ingredients go with it.

Here's what `Ingredient` actually looks like in code:

```
public class Ingredient
{
    public double Amount { get; set; }
    public string Unit { get; set; } = string.Empty;
    public string Name { get; set; } = string.Empty;

    // Denormalized snapshot from IngredientClassification
    public string StandardizedName { get; set; } =
        string.Empty;
    public string Primary { get; set; } = string.Empty;
    public string Secondary { get; set; } = string.Empty;
    public string Tertiary { get; set; } = string.Empty;
}
```

The top three properties are the raw ingredient as it appeared in the source recipe — "1.5 oz Old Overholt Rye." The bottom four are denormalized snapshot data: `StandardizedName = "Old Overholt Rye Whiskey"`, `Primary = "Spirit"`, `Secondary = "Whiskey"`, `Tertiary = "Bourbon"`.

Hold that thought about the snapshot fields — we'll come back to them.

`IngredientClassification`

OK, so now that I've said all that about `CocktailRecipe` and `Ingredient`, why is `IngredientClassification` a separate aggregate root?

It's doing two jobs. One is a *definition* job — it's the controlled vocabulary that says "this is what a Bourbon is" and "this is what a Liqueur is." The other is a *cleanup* job — it's where I reconcile the messy ingredient names in the source data against those canonical definitions. Both of those jobs together are what push the classification out into its own document.

The definition job. Classifications are metadata about ingredients, not instances of ingredients in the context of a recipe. The fact that "Old Overholt Rye is a Bourbon" exists independently of any recipe. Delete a Manhattan, and Old Overholt Rye is still a Bourbon. Delete every cocktail that uses it, and it's still a Bourbon. Classifications have their own lifecycle, edited on a different cadence from recipes. And when they change — say, I decide to split `Bourbon` into `Straight Bourbon` and `Bonded Bourbon` — I want that change to propagate to every recipe that uses Rittenhouse without having to track which recipes reference it.

Apply the delete test: if I delete a recipe, should the "Old Overholt Rye is a Bourbon" fact disappear? No. That's a separate aggregate root. The classification is the source of truth. What the recipe holds is just a snapshot.

The cleanup job. The recipes got scraped out of various sources on the internet, and the raw ingredient names are all over the place. "Old Overholt Rye", "Overholt Rye", "Old Overholt", or just "Overholt" — they're all the same thing. That's where the alias list comes in. Each `IngredientClassification` document carries a `List<string>` of aliases, and anything that matches any of those aliases resolves to that classification.

```
public class IngredientClassification : TenantItemBase
{
    public string StandardizedName { get; set; } =
        string.Empty;
```

```
    public string Primary { get; set; } = string.Empty;
    public string Secondary { get; set; } = string.Empty;
    public string Tertiary { get; set; } = string.Empty;
    public List<string> Aliases { get; set; } = new();
    public int FrequencyCount { get; set; }
}
```

Aliases are doing two things at once. They're the data cleanup mechanism — every known variant of an ingredient name resolves to the same canonical entry. And they're also the loose link between `Recipe.Ingredients` (which carries the messy original name from the source recipe) and the canonical `IngredientClassification`. There's no foreign key between the recipe's ingredient and the classification. There's an alias match. At import time, the classifier looks up the raw ingredient name against every alias in every classification, and when it finds a hit, it copies the classification's metadata into the ingredient's denormalized snapshot fields. (We'll come back to those snapshot fields in a minute.)

Why are aliases a `List<string>` on the classification document instead of their own entity? Apply the delete test one more time. If I delete the classification for "Old Overholt Rye Whiskey," should the alias "Old Overholt 100" disappear? Yeah, of course. An alias has no meaning without the classification it points to. It's not data that survives on its own. It's not data you'd query for independently. A separate "Alias" aggregate root would be a classic example of over-decomposition. Aliases are a nested value object inside the classification document. Keep it simple.

The classifier logic at runtime just walks the alias list across every classification, builds a case-insensitive dictionary from `alias → classification`, and uses that dictionary at import and reclassification time. Single-pass, in-memory, rebuilt when the taxonomy changes. Nothing fancy.

Denormalization, and the Guess Behind It

Chapter 6 talked about denormalization as the Cosmos pattern that often makes people coming from relational a little itchy. "Wait, you're storing the ingredient's classification on the ingredient, even though the classification is its own document?" Yes. I know. It violates the RDBMS Prime Directive: "thou shalt not duplicate data, for lo, it invites the discord and debauchery of referential integrity."

But there's a real conversation to have here that I glossed over in Chapter 6, and it's worth having now against a concrete app. There are definitely trade-offs.

The duplication is real. Those four snapshot fields on `Ingredient` — `StandardizedName`, `Primary`, `Secondary`, `Tertiary` — appear on every ingredient on every recipe. Roughly 5,800 recipes, each with 3–8 ingredients, comes out to 20,000+ copies of taxonomy data sitting across the container. Every time I classify "Old Overholt Rye" as `Spirit → Whiskey → Bourbon`, that classification gets copy-pasted into however many recipes use Old Overholt Rye. Multiply across the whole ingredient list and it's a lot of duplicated data.

But then again, at worst, we're probably looking at a handful of megabytes of duplicated data. The current charge per gigabyte in Cosmos is $0.25 USD per month. The cost of that duplicated data is probably well under a penny per month.

There's an obvious alternative. Skip the duplication snapshot data entirely. Load every classification into an in-memory hashtable at app startup, keyed by alias. At recipe render time, look up each ingredient's name against the hashtable and get the classification back. No duplication. No stale snapshots. No reclassify command.

But then that alternative has its own costs and complexity. Now I have a cache. The cache has to be warmed at startup. The cache has to be invalidated when classifications change. If the app runs across multiple processes, every process has its own copy of the cache, and keeping them in sync is its own problem. Cache management probably (once again) doesn't move the needle on our bill but the complexity added to the app isn't free.

So I made a guess. It's one of those things that software architects never like to admit. In the absence of a clear decision, I made a guess. And my guess is that classifications change rarely — probably once every few months as I tune the taxonomy — but recipe rendering happens constantly, and every recipe render needs to display canonical ingredient names. Rare expensive write operations versus frequent cheap reads. That shape says "denormalize." The cost of updating a lot of documents when the taxonomy changes is paid rarely.

The cost of reading the canonical name at render time is practically zero, because the document already contains it.

If classifications changed every hour — if users were editing the taxonomy through a UI all the time — the math would flip. I'd probably be on the cache side. But they don't.

I could be wrong. And with all of these types of decisions, I could be totally wrong. But if I'm wrong, the likely fix (ironically) is probably even more duplication — just add the IngredientClassification's Id value to the recipe Ingredient. That'll formalize the connection and give a nice tight way to bulk reclassify all those recipes. Or I move to the cache idea. Or I quit software entirely and go raise goats or something. I dunno. Everything is a trade-off.

Here's the part I'm even less sure about. The denormalized snapshot makes *recipe display* easy — every recipe document has everything it needs. It does not make *taxonomy browsing* easy. "Show me all recipes that use Bourbon" is a query that scans the ingredients across many recipe documents. It works. It's not a point read against some indexed structure. If the app eventually gets enough traffic that taxonomy browsing becomes slow, my next move is probably (like I said a moment ago) to add a denormalized copy of `IngredientClassification.Id` onto each ingredient. That would let the taxonomy pages query by ID instead of by string match, which is more surgical.

But I haven't done that yet because I don't know if it'll actually matter. It's hard to predict performance problems before they happen. For now, the denormalized `StandardizedName/Primary/Secondary/Tertiary` fields get me the payoff I care about (easy recipe rendering) without the complexity of yet another denormalized field or caching structure. If taxonomy browsing becomes a problem later, I've got options.

That's honestly how most of these decisions go. You guess about the rate-of-change. You pick the design that matches your guess. You build the escape hatch (the `reclassify` command, or "I could add this field later") so that if you guessed wrong, you can recover...or just quit and go raise goats.

`UserFavorite` and the User-Tenant Payoff

I wanted to have a feature that allowed users to create a list of favorite cocktail recipes. Maybe they're actual favorites. Maybe they're more of a 'to do' list. But

I needed a way to start storing user specific data. Which brings us to the `UserFavorite` class.

`UserFavorite` is another of the aggregate roots in the domain model. It's an aggregate root because a favorite has its own lifecycle, isn't owned by a recipe or a taxonomy document, and gets created and deleted independently.

This `UserFavorite` data is the first obvious element of multi-tenancy in our app. So where in the hierarchical partition key does a favorite go?

Remember the "two-tenant" setup from earlier. Recipes and classifications live under the system tenant — `tenantId = "COCKTAILS"`. Favorites are different. Favorites are *user* data. Each user's favorites belong to that user. So `UserFavorite` documents set `TenantId = userId`. Not `"COCKTAILS"`. The Identity user's ID goes directly into the hierarchical partition key.

The hierarchical partition key for a favorite is `["f8d9a1b2-...", "UserFavorite"]`, not `["COCKTAILS", "UserFavorite"]`.

Why does that matter? Because the question "what does this user need to see?" is a per-user question, not a global question. The "My Favorites" page loads *my* favorites only — not everyone's favorites simply *filtered* to mine. That filter-to-mine pattern is an expensive one. It cross-partitions, scans all favorites, and discards 99.99% of them just to show a user his or her data. The per-user partition pattern is a much more efficient approach. It reads the partition for exactly one user, reads the data, and returns it. One partition, one query.

Same container as the recipes and classifications. Different tenant. Different scope of query. This is the user-tenant half of the multi-tenancy pattern showing up in code.

> ***A Little Added Safety***
>
> *This multi-tenant partition key approach also helps out in another way that has nothing to do with application performance. It gives you a layer of defense against accidentally serving up the wrong data to a user. If User A saw User B's cocktail recipe favorites, it's probably not the end of world. Not great. Definitely a bug. But not a crisis. On the other hand, if this were something more sensitive like a medical record management system or a banking app, there'd be Big Problems™ to deal with.*

There's a denormalization beat here too:

```
public class UserFavorite : TenantItemBase
{
    public string UserId { get; set; } = string.Empty;
    public string RecipeId { get; set; } = string.Empty;
    public string RecipeName { get; set; } =
        string.Empty;  // denormalized
    public DateTime FavoritedAt { get; set; }
}
```

`RecipeName` is a snapshot of the recipe's name at the time the favorite was created. The My Favorites page renders entirely from `UserFavorite` documents. It never goes back to the `CocktailRecipe` entity type for lookups. Single-partition query, zero cross-entity reads, full page rendered.

If a recipe gets renamed later, the favorite keeps showing the old name until the user re-favorites it. That's fine. The trade is "slightly stale favorite names" in exchange for "My Favorites loads in one partition read."

Another opportunity for denormalization for UserFavorites would be to take a snapshot of the ingredients. This would allow us to fetch all the user's favorites and display them along with the ingredients. That might be a good feature for v2.

Auth: Identity in the Same Container

If we're going to store favorites on a per-user basis, we're going to need to know who the user is. That means adding authentication and authorization to the app. Since I'm deploying drinkymcdrinkface.com to an Azure App Service, I've got about a half-zillion options for how to get authentication up and running. Once again, there are trade-offs but the easiest option in this case is using ASP.NET Core Identity.

By the way, if you'd like an overview of ASP.NET Core Identity, I've got an overview video up on YouTube.

The cocktail app has user authentication — registration, login, passkey support, an admin dashboard. That's all handled by ASP.NET Core Identity, backed by `Benday.Identity.CosmosDb.UI`, a NuGet package I wrote that plugs Identity's stores into Cosmos DB and ships a prebuilt set of Razor Pages for the UI.

Registration looks like this in `Program.cs`:

```
builder.Services.AddCosmosIdentityWithUI(cosmosConfig);
```

One line. That's the whole auth wiring. Under the hood, `AddCosmosIdentityWithUI` does all the Identity plumbing — stores, schemes, password hashers, the login and registration pages, the passkey pages, the admin dashboard. All of it configured against the same `CosmosConfig` the rest of the app uses.

"The same `CosmosConfig`." Read that again. ASP.NET Core Identity has a bunch of data that it needs to store in whatever persistence option you use — SQL Server, Cosmos DB, etc. That means that the Identity user documents, role documents, and claim documents are all (by default) going into the same Cosmos container as the recipes, classifications, and favorites. One container. Different entity types. Same hierarchical partition key scheme.

My identity library is built on top of the Benday.CosmosDb library that we've been talking about in this book. It happily uses the same `/tenantId,/entityType` partition key config that we've been using so far. The `EntityType` discriminator is what makes this work. Cosmos doesn't care that an `IdentityUser` and a `CocktailRecipe` are different shapes. The partition routing is what matters, and the partition routing is happy to have different shapes in different partitions.

First reaction from most people: that's insane. Authentication data and application data in one container? Aren't those supposed to live in different databases?

In a relational world, yah...maybe. It could be a separate database in SQL Server or maybe a separate schema namespace to keep it separated. But in Cosmos, that argument mostly evaporates. There's no schema at the container level. Documents are JSON. Partition routing is per-document. A well-designed hierarchical partition key keeps an Identity query from ever touching cocktail data and vice versa.

The practical upside is significant. One container to provision. One RBAC surface to configure. One throughput pool to manage. No "users database" and "app database" separation that would require two sets of Azure resources, two connection strings, two sets of permissions, and two places where things could go wrong.

This is exactly the kind of architectural simplification the aggregate-root-and-hierarchical-partition-key pattern is supposed to enable. It's counterintuitive the first time you see it. Then you stop worrying about it and it's just how you build apps.

Five Entity Types, One Container, One Running System

Let's recap what's now sitting in the container:

Entity Type	Tenant ID	Count	Partition shape
`CocktailRecipe`	`"COCKTAILS"`	~5,800	Single logical partition
`Ingredient Classification`	`"COCKTAILS"`	~2,144	Single logical partition
`UserFavorite`	user's Identity ID	N per user	One partition per user
`IdentityUser`	(library-managed)	N users	(library-managed)
`IdentityRole`	(library-managed)	Handful	(library-managed)

Five entity types. One container. Zero cross-partition queries at runtime when the app is used normally. The recipe-search page reads from one partition. The My Favorites page reads from one partition. The taxonomy browser reads from one partition. Login checks read from one partition. Every page, one partition.

This isn't theoretical. I'll show you the RU charges from a real session against the deployed database in Chapter 11, where we get into the query layer. The short version: the most expensive query in the app is about 250 RUs, and that's the natural-language vector search that has to scan a lot of document content. The cheapest queries — point reads like "is this recipe favorited?" — are 1 RU. An entire typical user session, clicking around the app for a few minutes, runs on less RU than a single inefficient query would burn in a relational app doing the same work.

The container is partitioned well because the domain was modeled well. The aggregate roots are in the right places. The denormalization is in the right places. The multi-tenancy lives at the right level of the partition key. The queries that fall out of that design stay inside a single partition because the design was built so they could.

None of this is magic. It's the direct, mechanical consequence of applying aggregate-root thinking to document design, and then laying the documents into a hierarchical partition key that matches the access patterns of the app.

If you finish this chapter thinking "okay, I could do this for my domain" — that's the win. Pick up a pen. Write down your domain model. Ask "if I delete this, should that disappear?" Draw the aggregate-root boundaries. Decide what goes in a tenant and what goes in a per-user partition. Denormalize the snapshots that your queries need. Put it all in one container unless you have a specific reason not to.

That's the pattern. There might be trade-offs. Try to think them through and plan your architectural escape route. But also, don't over build and over plan. Try some stuff, run some profiling on your app, and see what actually works.

Next up: Chapter 11, where we finally dig into the query layer. LINQ vs. raw Cosmos SQL, when to reach for which, how `Benday.CosmosDb` instruments the ones that go through it, and the category of bug that happens when LINQ *doesn't* go through it. I'll also explain why I built `ICosmosQueryLogSink` into the library — because once you have a real production app with a hundred different queries, pulling query diagnostics out of the general log stream stops being a viable strategy. Chapter 11 is where we solve that.

The cocktail app is the running example from here to Chapter 13. Same container. Same partition layout. Same denormalized snapshots. Different capabilities layered on top.

Chapter 11 Cosmos DB: Querying Cosmos — LINQ, SQL, and Knowing What Runs

Chapter 7 showed you what queries *cost*. This chapter shows you what queries *are*.

In Chapter 7 we ran a test harness, measured RU charges for every operation, and came back with hard numbers. Point reads cost 1 RU. A cross-partition scan of 1,000 documents costs... well, it depends. We also introduced the idea of LINQ's `IQueryable` and deferred execution. Let's apply some of that thinking to a real app.

Now that you've seen the cocktail app's design in Chapter 10 — three aggregate roots, one container, hierarchical partition keys — we can talk about the query layer that runs on top of it. Specifically: LINQ vs. raw Cosmos SQL, when to reach for which, how the Cosmos LINQ provider actually translates your code into SQL, what "deferred execution" means when there's a real database on the other end of the wire, the category of bug that happens when your LINQ bypasses the library, and how `ICosmosQueryLogSink` gives you structured observability over the whole thing.

What's ICosmosQueryLogSink?

Before we get into the actual content of this chapter, I should probably talk about how I'm getting my timing numbers, RU counts, and SQL on each of my calls to Cosmos DB. In my `Benday.CosmosDb` library, I have an optional diagnostic setting that allows you to log details of the queries that run through the library. If you run your data operations through a `CosmosRepository<T>` repository, under the surface, that repository takes a parameter of type `Benday.CosmosDb.Diagnostics.ICosmosQueryLogSink`.

When the repository makes calls against Cosmos DB, it captures information about the operation and then outputs it to `Microsoft.Extensions.Logging.ILogger` and also to `ICosmosQueryLogSink`. Keen-eyed observers will notice that I'm logging two different ways and wonder why.

Logging to `ILogger` means that the information ends up getting buried in the log stream for your app. Pretty much everything in .NET is writing Debug, Info, Warning, and Error messages to ILogger. It's great for getting a unified log stream for the app, but it's kind of a pain when you want to do specific performance analysis things. For example, having a nice, structured way to know what your query's timing numbers, RU counts, and SQL are.

By default, the `Benday.CosmosDb` library turns off the `ICosmosQueryLogSink`. More precisely, it registers a "no op" implementation of the sink that does nothing. This is what you'll want to use in production.

```
namespace Benday.CosmosDb.Diagnostics;

public sealed class NoOpCosmosQueryLogSink : ICosmosQueryLogSink
{
    public static readonly NoOpCosmosQueryLogSink Instance = new();

    private NoOpCosmosQueryLogSink() { }

    public void Record(CosmosQueryDiagnostics diagnostics)
    {
    }
}
```

But when you're in development and you want to know EXACTLY what your application is doing, you can configure your application to log all this data to a file by using the `WithQueryLogSink<FileCosmosQueryLogSink>()` option on `CosmosRegistrationHelper`.

```
var helper = new CosmosRegistrationHelper(
    builder.Services, cosmosConfig);

builder.Services.Configure<CosmosFileLogSinkOptions>(
options =>
{
    options.FilePath = "logs/cosmos-queries.ndjson";
    options.QueueCapacity = 100;
});

helper.WithQueryLogSink<FileCosmosQueryLogSink>();
```

That writes the operations to an **NDJSON** (Newline Delimited JSON) log file so you can easily access all that query diagnostic info. We'll dig into what the data actually looks like and how to use it later in the chapter, but throughout the examples that follow, when I say "I looked at the sink output," this is what I mean.

LINQ vs. Raw SQL

When I wrote the cocktail app (https://www.drinkymcdrinkface.com), I used a combination of queries that use LINQ and some that use raw Cosmos SQL. Why I did it that way is a mix of preference, expediency, and also sometimes technical limitations. Plus, a bunch of logging features that exist in the `Benday.CosmosDb` library that I wanted to standardize on.

Preference-wise, when I'm coding C# against Cosmos DB (or also SQL Server) I tend to use LINQ queries — under the surface, that's typically some kind of `IQueryable`.

For example, here's `SearchByTitleAsync` — a title search. LINQ.

```
public async Task<List<CocktailRecipe>> SearchByTitleAsync
(
    string searchText, string tenantId)
{
    var context = await GetQueryContextAsync(tenantId);

    var query = context.Queryable
        .Where(x => x.Name.Contains(
            searchText, StringComparison.OrdinalIgnoreCase
));

    return await GetResultsAsync(
        query, nameof(SearchByTitleAsync),
        context.PartitionKey);
}
```

Clean. Readable. One LINQ `Where` clause, one call to `GetResultsAsync`. The library handles the partition key, logs the RU charge, captures the generated

SQL. Everything gets taken care of in a standardized way without a whole lot of extra, duplicated code.

But then there's the `SearchBySingleIngredientAsync` method that finds recipes that contain a specific ingredient. When I originally wrote this, I reached for raw SQL because I needed to get into the nested `Ingredients` array on each recipe. My thinking was: LINQ can't express `JOIN i IN c.ingredients` directly, so I need to write the SQL myself. Here's what I wrote:

```
public async Task<List<CocktailRecipe>>
    SearchBySingleIngredientAsyncUsingSql(
    string ingredientName, string tenantId)
{
    var partitionKey = GetPartitionKey(tenantId);

    var queryText = @"
        SELECT DISTINCT VALUE c FROM c
        JOIN i IN c.ingredients
        WHERE c.entityType = 'CocktailRecipe'
        AND c.tenantId = @tenantId
        AND CONTAINS(i.name, @ingredientName, true)";

    var queryDef = new QueryDefinition(queryText)
        .WithParameter("@tenantId", tenantId)
        .WithParameter("@ingredientName",
            ingredientName.Trim());

    var iterator = GetContainer().
        GetItemQueryIterator<CocktailRecipe>(
            queryDef,
            requestOptions: new QueryRequestOptions {
                PartitionKey = partitionKey });

    return await GetResultsAsync(iterator,
```

```
        nameof(SearchBySingleIngredientAsync));
}
```

`JOIN i IN c.ingredients` iterates the nested ingredients array — that's a Cosmos SQL cross-apply, not a relational JOIN — and `DISTINCT VALUE c` deduplicates because a recipe might match the ingredient twice. Both queries end up calling `GetResultsAsync`, which means both get instrumented — RU charge, duration, partition key, cross-partition detection.

I was happy with this. It worked. It was readable. I moved on.

But Wait — LINQ Can Do This Too

But a little later, I started wondering if I could just do a LINQ query against the Ingredients collection. So I went back and tried a LINQ version just to see what would happen. It turns out that LINQ *could* get to the same result through a different "door": LINQ's `Any()` method.

```
public async Task<List<CocktailRecipe>>
     SearchBySingleIngredientAsyncUsingLinq(
         string ingredientName, string tenantId)
{
    var trimmed = ingredientName.Trim();

    var queryContext = await GetQueryContextAsync(tenantId
);

    var query = queryContext.Queryable
        .Where(x => x.Ingredients.Any(
            i => i.Name.Contains(trimmed,
                StringComparison.OrdinalIgnoreCase)))
        .OrderBy(x => x.Name);

    return await GetResultsAsync(
        query,
        GetQueryDescription(
             nameof(SearchBySingleIngredientAsyncUsingLinq
)),
```

```
        queryContext.PartitionKey);
}
```

That compiles. That runs. And when I looked at the `ICosmosQueryLogSink` output, here's the SQL it generated:

```
SELECT VALUE root FROM root
JOIN (
    SELECT VALUE EXISTS(
        SELECT VALUE i0 FROM root
        JOIN i0 IN root["ingredients"]
        WHERE CONTAINS(i0["name"], "bourbon", true)
    )
) AS v0
WHERE v0
ORDER BY root["name"] ASC
```

That is definitely not what I would have written by hand. It's wrapping an `EXISTS` inside a `JOIN` subquery, aliasing the boolean result as `v0`, and then filtering `WHERE v0`. To me it looks a little circuitous and it's not really how I probably ever would have thought about doing it but it works.

Both versions return the same 463 results for a "bourbon" search. So I rigged up a head-to-head test — run both versions back-to-back against the same data and compare the diagnostics from the sink:

Version	Generated SQL Strategy	RUs	Duration	Results
LINQ (`Any()`)	EXISTS subquery	41.48	562ms	463
Raw SQL	JOIN + DISTINCT	79.19	414ms	463

The LINQ version costs almost **half the RUs**. The slightly ugly generated SQL wins.

Why? `EXISTS` short-circuits. It walks the ingredients array and the moment it finds a match, it stops. The `JOIN` approach cross-applies *every* ingredient in *every* recipe, produces a row for every match, and then `DISTINCT` has to collapse all those duplicates back down. A recipe with three bourbon ingredients generates three intermediate rows in the JOIN version and one boolean in the EXISTS version.

I only discovered this because I had the query log sink running and could compare the RU charges side by side. The developer instinct — "I'll write the SQL myself, I know what I'm doing" — actually produced a worse query.

But that raises one those really important questions that has been hiding in plain sight the whole time: how did LINQ turn `x.Ingredients.Any(...)` into that SQL? What's actually going on between the C# LINQ code and the SQL that Cosmos ran?

How LINQ-to-Cosmos Actually Works

Here's where I'm going to nerd out for a minute, because understanding this mechanism is what makes the rest of the chapter click.

In Chapter 7, I did a sidebar on how LINQ works — how it rides on top of `IEnumerable<T>` and the Iterator Pattern, and how `IQueryable<T>` lets you define a *potential* query that doesn't run until you need results. What I didn't get into was *why* those two interfaces behave so differently, even when the code you write looks identical.

We Need the Func. Gotta Have That Func.

As noted software architect and funk legend George Clinton once wrote, we need the Func and gotta have that Func. He was talking about something else entirely but the principle applies.

These two lines of C# look darned similar:

```
// Against a List<T> (IEnumerable)
var results = myList.Where(x => x.Name.Contains("bourbon"));

// Against a Cosmos queryable (IQueryable)
var results = context.Queryable.Where(x => x.Name.Contains("bourbon"));
```

Same `Where`. Same lambda. Same syntax. But the compiler does something fundamentally different with each one.

For the `IEnumerable` version, the lambda compiles into a `Func<T, bool>` — executable code. A function. .NET iterates through your list, calls that function on each item, and keeps the ones where it returns true. The lambda *runs* on every element in memory. It's just code calling code. (Gotta have that `Func<T, bool>`.)

For the `IQueryable` version, the compiler doesn't produce a `Func` at all. Instead, it produces an `Expression<Func<T, bool>>` — a *data structure* that describes the lambda. That `x => x.Name.Contains("bourbon")` gets turned into a tree of objects: a `MethodCallExpression` wrapping a `LambdaExpression` wrapping a `MemberExpression` (the property access on `.Name`) wrapping a `ConstantExpression` (the `"bourbon"` value). It's objects all the way down.

That's the trick. Same syntax, completely different compilation. `IEnumerable` gets a function to execute. `IQueryable` gets a *description* of a function — an **expression tree** — that it hands off to a provider for translation. The lambda becomes data instead of code.

The Provider Walks the Tree

The Cosmos LINQ provider — a key part of the `Microsoft.Azure.Cosmos` SDK — walks that expression tree, node by node, and emits a string of Cosmos SQL. `Where(x => x.Name == "Manhattan")` becomes `SELECT VALUE root FROM root WHERE root["name"] = "Manhattan"`. The LINQ syntax on the C# side is just the authoring surface. What actually hits the database is always SQL.

That's what happened with the ingredient search. I wrote `.Where(x => x.Ingredients.Any(i => i.Name.Contains(...)))`. The Cosmos LINQ provider's expression tree walker hit the `Any()` node, recognized it had a handler for `Enumerable.Any`, and translated it into the `EXISTS` subquery wrapped in that `JOIN ... AS v0` structure. Circuitous-looking SQL, yes — but the provider chose `EXISTS` because it's the semantically correct translation of "does any element in this collection match?", and that `EXISTS` is why it outperformed my hand-written `JOIN + DISTINCT`.

Why does this matter beyond the cocktail app? Because the translation has limits.

That expression tree walker was written by developers at Microsoft. They had to write a handler for every .NET method they wanted to support. `String.Contains`? Yes, they wrote a translation for that — it maps to Cosmos's `CONTAINS` function. `String.StartsWith`? Yes. `Enumerable.Any`? Yes. `Enumerable.All`? *No*. `String.IsNullOrEmpty`? *No*. Those throw at runtime. Not at compile time. At *runtime*. You write what looks like perfectly valid C#, the compiler is happy, and then you run it and the Cosmos SDK says "I don't know how to translate this to SQL" and hands you an exception.

Here's what the `All()` error actually looks like:

```
Microsoft.Azure.Cosmos.Linq.DocumentQueryException:
'Method 'All' is not supported.'
   at Microsoft.Azure.Cosmos.Linq.ArrayBuiltinFunctions.Visit(
       MethodCallExpression methodCallExpression,
       TranslationContext context)
```

You can see exactly where the translation failed: `ArrayBuiltinFunctions.Visit`. The SDK's expression tree walker hit a `MethodCallExpression` for `All()` and simply didn't have a handler for it.

This is why abstractions leak. It's not a bug. It's a fundamental consequence of the design: someone has to write a translation for every operation, and the surface area of .NET is enormous. The Cosmos SDK team can't cover all of it, so they cover the common stuff and leave the rest unimplemented — ya know — just to keep us on our toes. Joking aside, supporting every single possible thing is a lot of work and there are probably zillions of edge cases and piles of things that just simply don't have a good option for translation. Even for Microsoft: there are only so many minutes in the day.

The practical takeaway: if you're writing a LINQ query and it compiles, that does *not* guarantee that it will run. LINQ-to-Cosmos is a *runtime* translation, not a compile-time one. The first time you find this out is usually when production throws an exception you've never seen in local testing because you never hit that code path with the right data.

Multi-Ingredient Search: And Then It Gets Weirder

When I saw the single-ingredient results, I decided to try an experiment for another query in the app. The cocktail app also has a multi-ingredient search

— "find recipes that contain rum AND bourbon." The raw SQL version builds dynamic `EXISTS` subqueries, one per ingredient:

```
SELECT * FROM c
WHERE c.entityType = 'CocktailRecipe' AND
      c.tenantId = @tenantId
AND EXISTS(SELECT VALUE i FROM i IN c.ingredients
           WHERE CONTAINS(i.name, @ingredient0, true))
AND EXISTS(SELECT VALUE i FROM i IN c.ingredients
           WHERE CONTAINS(i.name, @ingredient1, true))
ORDER BY c.name
```

Can LINQ do this too? My first instinct was to try LINQ's `All()` method:

```
var query = context.Queryable
    .Where(x => x.Ingredients.All(i =>
        cleaned.Any(ing =>
            i.Name.Contains(ing,
            StringComparison.OrdinalIgnoreCase))));
```

And there's the speed bump: `Method 'All' is not supported.` — the exact exception I just described. `Any()` has a handler in the expression tree walker. `All()` doesn't.

But you don't need `All()`. You already know `Any()` works. And chaining multiple `.Where()` calls AND-s them together — that's just how LINQ composition works. So the trick is to loop over the search terms and add one `.Where()` per ingredient:

```
public async Task<List<CocktailRecipe>>
    SearchByIngredientsAsyncUsingLinq(
        params string[] ingredientNames)
{
    var cleaned = (ingredientNames ?? Array.Empty<string>(
))
        .Where(x => string.IsNullOrWhiteSpace(x) == false)
        .Select(x => x.Trim().ToLowerInvariant())
        .Distinct().ToArray();
```

```
    if (cleaned.Length == 0)
        return new List<CocktailRecipe>();

    var queryContext = await GetQueryContextAsync(
        ApiConstants.DefaultTenantId);

    IQueryable<CocktailRecipe> query =
         queryContext.Queryable;

    foreach (var term in cleaned)
    {
        var captured = term; // capture for closure
        query = query.Where(x =>
            x.Ingredients.Any(i =>
                i.Name.Contains(captured,
                    StringComparison.OrdinalIgnoreCase)));
    }

    query = query.OrderBy(x => x.Name);

    return await GetResultsAsync(
        query,
        GetQueryDescription(),
        queryContext.PartitionKey);
}
```

Each `.Where()` adds another EXISTS subquery. Nothing hits the database until `GetResultsAsync` — you're just stacking filters on the `IQueryable`. (We'll talk about that "nothing hits the database until" part in the deferred execution section coming up.)

The `var captured = term` line matters, by the way. Without it, the closure captures the loop variable itself, and by the time the query executes, every EXISTS clause would use whatever `term` was on the last iteration. Classic C# closure-over-loop-variable gotcha.

So how did the head-to-head come out? "rum AND bourbon":

Version	RUs	Duration	Results
LINQ (chained `Where` → EXISTS)	18.29	93ms	49
Raw SQL (dynamic EXISTS)	18.48	79ms	49

Basically a dead heat. Both approaches ended up generating EXISTS subqueries — they converged on the same strategy. The LINQ version produces `WHERE (v0 AND v1)` with JOINed boolean subqueries; the raw SQL does `AND EXISTS(...) AND EXISTS(...)` directly. Different SQL syntax, same execution cost.

So Which One Do You Pick?

There *can* be performance differences between the SQL approach and the LINQ approach. Sometimes one can be surprisingly faster or use different amounts of RUs. It really depends on how well the "expressionizer" logic is in the SDK provider — the thing that walks your expression tree and emits SQL — does with your particular query scenario. Sometimes Microsoft's translation produces better SQL than what you'd write by hand (the single-ingredient EXISTS story). Sometimes it produces equivalent SQL (the multi-ingredient story). Sometimes it can't translate at all (the `All()` story).

But then again, there's the "heat death of the universe" problem.

Remember Chapter 7? We spent a whole section talking about how some optimizations matter at a universal scale and are completely irrelevant at the scale most of us mere humans actually operate at. The difference between 41 RUs and 79 RUs matters if you're running that query ten million times a day. But for most apps, both numbers are completely fine and nobody will ever notice.

So sometimes you'll pick one approach over the other not because it's faster, but because writing it the other way ends up yielding incomprehensible code. The chained-WHERE LINQ version for multi-ingredient search is readable. The dynamically-built EXISTS SQL is *also* readable. But some queries — conditional aggregation, vector distance, projections to different shapes — only exist in raw SQL, and trying to force them through LINQ would produce something nobody could maintain.

My advice: use LINQ when it's clear. Drop to raw SQL when LINQ can't do it or when the LINQ version turns into spaghetti. And either way, look at the sink output so you know what actually ran and how it performs.

A Note on Query Plan Caching

One more thing worth noting about the LINQ vs. raw SQL choice, and this one's a little subtle. The raw SQL versions use parameterized queries (`@ingredientName`, `@ingredient0`, `@ingredient1`). The LINQ-generated SQL inlines the values directly (`"bourbon"`, `"rum"`).

That matters because of how Cosmos handles query plans. Before Cosmos can execute a query, it has to build a query plan — and building that plan requires a network round-trip to the Cosmos DB gateway. Cosmos caches these plans, keyed by the query text string. A parameterized query like `CONTAINS(i.name, @ingredientName, true)` is the same query text regardless of whether you're searching for "bourbon" or "rye" or "mezcal" — one plan, cached, reused for every search. A LINQ-generated query with inlined values produces a different query text for every search term — `CONTAINS(i0["name"], "bourbon", true)` is a different cache key than `CONTAINS(i0["name"], "rye", true)`. Each unique search term misses the cache and triggers another gateway round-trip.

At the scale where the RU difference between EXISTS and JOIN+DISTINCT matters — millions of queries a day — the plan-caching difference matters too. At normal scale, probably not. But it's one more thing the sink output can help you watch for.

The LINQ provider could parameterize the generated SQL — emit `@p0` instead of `"bourbon"` and attach the value as a query parameter. The `parameters` field in the sink output is already there, it's just empty for LINQ queries. EF Core already does exactly this for SQL Server. The Cosmos LINQ provider just... doesn't, at least not yet.

Deferred Execution

Chapter 7 introduced this, but it was a sidebar. Now we're going to live in it for a minute because it drives the whole query-composition pattern in the library.

Deferred execution means: constructing a LINQ query in code doesn't actually cause it to run. Nothing hits the database until something *forces* execution —

`ToListAsync()`, `CountAsync()`, `FirstOrDefaultAsync()`, `foreach`, anything that actually needs the results.

```
var context = await GetQueryContextAsync(tenantId);

// This doesn't run a query. This builds a description of
one.
var query = context.Queryable
    .Where(x => x.Name.Contains(searchText,
        StringComparison.OrdinalIgnoreCase))
        .OrderByDescending(x => x.Timestamp);

// THIS runs the query. Right here. Not before.
return await GetResultsAsync(query,
    nameof(SearchByTitleAsync), context.PartitionKey);
```

The first three lines create an `IQueryable<T>`. No RUs consumed. No network call. The query is just a data structure sitting in memory — an expression tree, waiting. `GetResultsAsync` is the trigger. That's where the expression tree gets walked, the SQL gets generated, the HTTP request goes to Cosmos, and you start paying.

For in-memory `IEnumerable` — like a `List<T>` — deferred execution is invisible because the "database" is just RAM and there's a less obvious cost. The `Func` runs against each element as the iterator pulls them. For `IQueryable` against a real database, the `Expression` sits there doing nothing until something forces the provider to translate and execute it. That's what makes composition cheap — you can build a query across multiple methods, add filters conditionally, stack `Where` clauses, and pay nothing until you pull the trigger.

The multi-ingredient search from earlier is deferred execution in action. That `foreach` loop that stacks `.Where()` calls? Each iteration adds a filter to the expression tree. No database call. No RUs. Just building up the description, one `Any()` clause at a time. The query doesn't fire until `GetResultsAsync` at the end — and when it does, Cosmos gets one SQL statement with all the EXISTS subqueries already composed.

But here's the flip side: deferred execution also means you need to know *exactly where* the trigger is. And sometimes it's not where you think.

Two Ways LINQ Goes Sideways

The cocktail app taught me two things about how LINQ can not-entirely-succeed in the context of a library like `Benday.CosmosDb`. Both are real bugs I hit. Both are the kind of thing where you stare at the code for ten minutes saying "that looks right" before you realize what's happening.

The Library Can't See It

`CountAsync()` is a LINQ extension method. You call it on an `IQueryable<T>` and it returns an `int`. Sounds great. Here's the problem: `CountAsync()` executes the query *itself*. It already has everything it needs under the surface so it calls into the Cosmos SDK directly, gets the results, counts them, and returns the number.

The library — `Benday.CosmosDb` — never sees the execution. It never gets to log the RU charge. It never captures the query text. It never detects whether the query went cross-partition. As far as the library is concerned, nothing happened.

```
// The library sees this — it goes through GetResultsAsync
var results = await GetResultsAsync(
    query, "SearchByTitle", partitionKey);

// The library does NOT see this —
// CountAsync runs the query itself
var count = await query.CountAsync();
```

Same `IQueryable`. Same database. One goes through the library's instrumentation pipeline; the other doesn't. This is what I mean by "knowing when your query runs." The query *runs*. You just don't know about it.

The fix in `Benday.CosmosDb` is `ExecuteScalarAsync` — a method on the repository that wraps scalar operations (count, first-or-default, any) and runs them through the same diagnostics pipeline as everything else. But you have to know to use it instead of reaching for the LINQ extension directly.

The SQL Isn't What You'd Necessarily Write

The second issue is subtler. When LINQ *does* translate your code to SQL, the resulting SQL might not be what you'd write by hand. It's *equivalent* — it returns the same results — but it's not *identical*. And sometimes the difference matters.

I hit this with `GetByPrimaryAsync` when I needed to find ingredient classifications where the `Secondary` field was either null, empty, or missing entirely. My first attempt used LINQ:

```
var query = context.Queryable
    .Where(x => string.IsNullOrEmpty(x.Secondary));
```

This threw at runtime. `String.IsNullOrEmpty` doesn't have a Cosmos LINQ translation. Fair enough. So I rewrote it:

```
var query = context.Queryable
    .Where(x => x.Secondary == null || x.Secondary == "");
```

This *worked*, but the generated SQL was:

```
WHERE (root["secondary"] = null OR root["secondary"] = "")
```

The SQL I would've written by hand was:

```
WHERE (NOT IS_DEFINED(root["secondary"]) OR root["secondary"] = ''
)
```

Those aren't the same thing. `root["secondary"] = null` matches documents where the field exists and has an explicit JSON `null` value. `NOT IS_DEFINED(root["secondary"])` matches documents where the field doesn't exist at all. In a Cosmos container with documents that evolved over time — some imported early before a field was added, some imported later — you might have both flavors. The LINQ version misses the "field doesn't exist" case.

This didn't cause a production bug for me because all my documents happened to have the field. But it *could* have. And the only reason I caught it was that I was staring at the generated SQL in the log sink output and comparing it to what I expected.

Inside the Sink: What the Data Looks Like

I introduced `ICosmosQueryLogSink` at the top of this chapter and I've been referencing the sink output all along. Now let's look at what's actually in the data.

Here's the interface:

```
public interface ICosmosQueryLogSink
{
    void Record(CosmosQueryDiagnostics diagnostics);
}
```

One method. Synchronous. Fire-and-forget. The library calls `Record` on the thread that executed the query and moves on. If the sink throws, the library catches it and logs a warning. A broken sink never prevents a query from completing.

And here's what `CosmosQueryDiagnostics` carries:

```
public sealed class CosmosQueryDiagnostics
{
    public CosmosQueryEventKind EventKind { get; init; }
    public DateTimeOffset Timestamp { get; init; }
    public string RepositoryName { get; init; }
    public string QueryDescription { get; init; }
    public string? QueryText { get; init; }
    public IReadOnlyDictionary<string, object?>? Parameters
        { get; init; }
    public PartitionKey PartitionKey { get; init; }
    public double RequestCharge { get; init; }
    public TimeSpan Duration { get; init; }
    public int ResultCount { get; init; }
    public bool IsCrossPartition { get; init; }
    public string? IndexMetrics { get; init; }
}
```

Repository name, query description (typically `"RepositoryName - MethodName"`), the generated SQL text, query parameters, partition key, RU charge, wall-clock duration, result count, whether it was a cross-partition execution, and — when enabled — the raw index utilization metrics from Cosmos. Everything you need to understand what happened, packaged as *data*, not as a log line.

Event Kinds

The `EventKind` field distinguishes three types of events:

`PointOperation` — a single-document operation: save, delete, or point-read. No query text (there's no SQL involved — it's just an ID and a partition key).

`FeedResponsePage` — one page of results from a multi-page query. Cosmos paginates large result sets, and the library iterates through the pages. Each page gets its own event with that page's RU charge and result count.

`QueryTotal` — the summary for the completed query. Emitted exactly once per query execution, with the total RU charge, total result count, and total duration across all pages. For scalar operations (`CountAsync`, `FirstOrDefaultAsync` via `ExecuteScalarAsync`), this is the *only* event emitted — there are no pages.

For most analysis, you filter to `QueryTotal` events. That gives you one row per query execution with the full cost. The `FeedResponsePage` events are there if you need to understand pagination behavior or identify queries with unexpectedly many pages.

What the File Output Looks Like

`FileCosmosQueryLogSink` writes each event as a single line of JSON (NDJSON format). Events go into an in-memory queue from `Record()` and get written to disk by a background thread, so the library's query-execution path is never blocked on file I/O. If the queue fills up (default capacity is 10,000), new events are dropped rather than blocking — a stuck disk shouldn't grow memory without bound.

> ***WARNING: Don't Use This in Production!***
>
> *This file-based logging is only for development use. It's not optimized for running under load or on a server. For example, I run almost everything that I do on Azure App Services using the "run from zip" option. I suspect that FileCosmosQueryLogSink would throw endless exceptions in that configuration.*

> *If you think you'd like something that runs in production, drop a [feature request](#) in the* **`Benday.CosmosDb`** *repo on GitHub.*

Here's a real `QueryTotal` entry from an actual session:

```
{
  "eventKind": "QueryTotal",
  "timestamp": "2026-04-20T19:27:57.220Z",
  "repositoryName": "CosmosDbPersonRepository",
  "queryDescription": "CosmosDbPersonRepository - GetAllAsync",
  "queryText":
"SELECT VALUE root FROM root ORDER BY root[\"timestamp\"] DESC",
  "parameters": {},
  "partitionKey": "[\"SYSTEM\",\"Person\"]",
  "requestCharge": 1,
  "durationMs": 5.131,
  "resultCount": 1,
  "isCrossPartition": false,
  "indexMetrics": null
}
```

Look at what you can see: this was a `GetAllAsync` call on the `Person` repository. It generated a `SELECT VALUE root` query ordered by timestamp descending. It ran against the `["SYSTEM","Person"]` partition — both levels of the hierarchical partition key specified, so no cross-partition scan. It cost 1 RU, took 5 milliseconds, and returned 1 document.

Compare that to what `ILogger` gave you: a line that said `"Request Charge (GetAllAsync): 1 RUs"`. Same information, technically. But the structured version is data you can query, sort, filter, and aggregate. Export the file into a spreadsheet, sort by `requestCharge` descending, and your most expensive queries are right there at the top. Filter by `isCrossPartition == true` and you've found the queries that need partition key work. Filter by `repositoryName` and you've isolated a single entity type's behavior.

Point-read entries look slightly different:

```
{
  "eventKind": "PointOperation",
```

```
  "timestamp": "2026-04-20T19:27:57.179Z",
  "repositoryName": "CosmosTenantItemRepository`1",
  "queryDescription":
"CosmosTenantItemRepository`1 - SaveAsync",
  "queryText": null,
  "parameters": null,
  "partitionKey": "[null]",
  "requestCharge": 1,
  "durationMs": 9.988,
  "resultCount": 0,
  "isCrossPartition": false,
  "indexMetrics": null
}
```

No queryText — point operations don't have a SQL query, just an ID lookup. The SaveAsync operation cost 1 RU and took about 10 milliseconds.

Writing Your Own Sink

The interface is intentionally simple — one method, synchronous, fire-and-forget — so you can build whatever you need. Want to push diagnostics into Application Insights as custom events? Write a sink that calls TelemetryClient.TrackEvent(). Want to aggregate in memory and dump a summary at shutdown? Write a sink that accumulates into a ConcurrentDictionary keyed by query description. Want to fail tests if any query exceeds 50 RUs? Write a sink that throws in your test project.

The contract is:

- Record is called synchronously from the query thread. Don't do slow I/O inline — buffer and flush from a background worker (like FileCosmosQueryLogSink does).
- Exceptions from Record are caught, logged as warnings, and suppressed. A broken sink must not prevent queries from completing.
- The library registers NoOpCosmosQueryLogSink by default. You override it with helper.WithQueryLogSink<YourSink>().

Index Metrics: Which Indexes Did My Query Actually Use?

Everything we've looked at so far tells you *what* ran and *what it cost*. But there's a question the sink couldn't answer until recently: did the query actually use the indexes I set up?

Back in Chapter 7, we talked about custom indexing policies — how excluding unqueried properties from your index can cut write costs by 80%. The advice was "index what you query on, exclude everything else." Good advice. But how do you *verify* that your queries are hitting the indexes you think they're hitting? And how do you find out if Cosmos wishes you had an index that you don't?

That's what `IndexMetrics` is for. The Cosmos SDK has a feature called `PopulateIndexMetrics` that you can set on `QueryRequestOptions`. When it's on, Cosmos returns a blob of data with every query response that tells you exactly which indexes were utilized and which indexes it *recommends* you add. The `Benday.CosmosDb` library now captures that data and flows it through the sink.

It's off by default — and it should be. Turning on `PopulateIndexMetrics` has measurable RU and latency overhead. This is a development and investigation tool, not a production setting. You turn it on, run your app through its paces, look at the output, and turn it off.

To enable it, use `ConfigureDiagnosticsDefault` on `CosmosRegistrationHelper`:

```
helper.ConfigureDiagnosticsDefault(options =>
{
    options.CaptureIndexMetrics = true;
});
```

That turns it on for every entity type. If you only want it for a specific entity — maybe you're investigating one slow query and don't want the overhead everywhere — use `ConfigureDiagnostics<TEntity>` instead.

Once it's on, the `indexMetrics` field in the sink output goes from `null` to a JSON string with two sections: `UtilizedIndexes` and `PotentialIndexes`.

The examples in this section come from the `Benday.CosmosDb` sample app (Person, Note, Comment) rather than the cocktail app. I added this feature to the library after the cocktail app work was done, and the sample app was the faster way to exercise it. The data is different but the diagnostics work exactly the same way — same sink, same NDJSON format, same fields.

Here's a `GetAllAsync` on the Note repository, ordered by timestamp descending:


```
{
  "eventKind": "QueryTotal",
  "repositoryName": "CosmosTenantItemRepository`1",
  "queryDescription": "CosmosTenantItemRepository`1 - GetAllAsync",
  "queryText": "SELECT VALUE root FROM root ORDER BY root[\"timestamp\"] DESC",
  "partitionKey": "[\"SYSTEM\",\"Note\"]",
  "requestCharge": 2.92,
  "isCrossPartition": false,
  "indexMetrics": {
    "UtilizedIndexes": {
      "SingleIndexes": [
        { "IndexSpec": "/timestamp/?" },
        { "IndexSpec": "/tenantId/?" },
        { "IndexSpec": "/entityType/?" }
      ],
      "CompositeIndexes": []
    },
    "PotentialIndexes": {
      "SingleIndexes": [],
      "CompositeIndexes": [
        {
          "IndexSpecs": ["/tenantId ASC", "/entityType ASC",
            "/timestamp ASC"],
          "IndexImpactScore": "High"
        }
      ]
```

```
    }
  }
}
```

(I've pretty-printed the `indexMetrics` value here for readability. In the actual NDJSON file, it's a JSON string on one line.)

Read this from top to bottom. `UtilizedIndexes` tells you the query used three single-property indexes: `/timestamp`, `/tenantId`, and `/entityType`. That's Cosmos saying "I had indexes on these properties and I used them." Good.

`PotentialIndexes` is where it gets interesting. Cosmos is saying: "You don't have a composite index on `/tenantId ASC, /entityType ASC, /timestamp ASC`, and if you added one, it would have a **High** impact on this query's performance." A composite index lets Cosmos satisfy the filter *and* the sort in a single index scan instead of using three separate indexes and combining the results. For a query that runs frequently, that's worth paying attention to.

Now compare that to a `GetAllByParentIdAsync` on the Comment repository from the same session:


```
{
  "UtilizedIndexes": {
    "SingleIndexes": [
      { "IndexSpec": "/tenantId/?" },
      { "IndexSpec": "/parentId/?" },
      { "IndexSpec": "/entityType/?" },
      { "IndexSpec": "/parentEntityType/?" }
    ],
    "CompositeIndexes": []
  },
  "PotentialIndexes": {
    "SingleIndexes": [],
    "CompositeIndexes": []
  }
}
```

`PotentialIndexes` is empty. Cosmos used the indexes it had and didn't wish for anything else. That's the "you got it right" signal.

So the workflow is: turn on `CaptureIndexMetrics`, exercise your application through its normal query patterns, look at the sink output, and pay attention to any `PotentialIndexes` entries with "High" impact scores. Those are Cosmos telling you where you're leaving performance on the table. Fix the ones that matter, turn off `CaptureIndexMetrics`, and move on.

When to Drop to Raw SQL

Earlier in this chapter I thought I had a clean list of "use raw SQL when..." rules. Then I ran the head-to-head comparisons and the list got shorter. Turns out LINQ can do more than I would have initially guessed — `Any()` handles nested array queries, and chaining `.Where()` handles dynamic composition. But there are still things that only raw SQL can do.

You need `VectorDistance`. The vector similarity search uses Cosmos's `VectorDistance()` SQL function. No LINQ mapping exists. This is always raw SQL. (We'll see this in Chapter 12.)

You need conditional aggregation. `GetEmbeddingStatsAsync` uses `SUM(c.embedding != null ? 1 : 0)` — the standard Cosmos idiom for conditional counting. LINQ can't express a ternary inside a SUM.

You need `NOT IS_DEFINED`. As we saw earlier, LINQ's `== null` check and Cosmos SQL's `NOT IS_DEFINED` are different things. If you need to distinguish between "field is null" and "field doesn't exist," you need raw SQL.

You need projections to a different shape. If the query returns something other than the repository's entity type — a scalar, a custom projection, a count — raw SQL with `QueryDefinition` is usually cleaner than fighting with LINQ's `Select`.

The LINQ version becomes incomprehensible. Sometimes you *can* express something in LINQ, but the result is so convoluted that nobody — including you in six months — will be able to read it. Readability counts. Additionally, if that LINQ starts looking convoluted, think about what is going to happen when that expression tree gets converted into SQL. It might *work* but end up creating something that is completely bonkers once it turns into SQL.

When none of those apply — simple filters, ordering, nested array searches with `Any()`, even dynamic multi-condition composition — LINQ is the better default. It's more readable, it stays inside the library's `GetQueryContextAsync` / `GetResultsAsync` pipeline automatically, and as we saw, sometimes the SDK's translation actually outperforms hand-written SQL.

The Practical War Stories

Let me close with two specific bugs from the cocktail app that I think are worth knowing about, because they're the kind of thing that'll bite you if you're not looking for them.

The `GetCountAsync` Story

I needed a simple count of how many recipes existed. Should be easy, right? I wrote something like this:

```
var context = await GetQueryContextAsync(tenantId);
var count = await context.Queryable.CountAsync();
```

This worked. But as we discussed, it bypasses the library's instrumentation — `CountAsync()` is a LINQ extension that runs the query directly. So I switched to `ExecuteScalarAsync`, which routes the execution through the library's pipeline:

```
var context = await GetQueryContextAsync(tenantId);
var count = await ExecuteScalarAsync(
    context.Queryable, q => q.CountAsync(),
    nameof(GetCountAsync), context.PartitionKey);
```

And it blew up. Null reference exception inside `ToQueryDefinition()`. Not from my code — from deep inside the Cosmos SDK.

The issue: `ExecuteScalarAsync` internally calls `ToQueryDefinition()` to capture the SQL text for diagnostics. But `CountAsync()` on a bare queryable — one with no `Where` clause, no `OrderBy`, nothing composed on top — produces a queryable that `ToQueryDefinition()` doesn't know how to handle. It's a degenerate case: a queryable that's *too* simple.

The fix was to add a trivially-true `Where` clause to make the queryable non-trivial:

```
var context = await GetQueryContextAsync(tenantId);
var count = await ExecuteScalarAsync(
    context.Queryable.Where(x =>
        x.EntityType ==
            context.Queryable.First().EntityType),
    q => q.CountAsync(),
    nameof(GetCountAsync), context.PartitionKey);
```

Ugly? A little. But it works, it goes through the library's diagnostic pipeline, and the `Where` clause doesn't change the result because the partition key already scopes to the right entity type. The lesson: when the SDK's internal plumbing expects a "real" query and you hand it a bare queryable, things break in surprising ways.

The `GetEmbeddingStatsAsync` Story

I wanted to know: how many recipes have embeddings, and how many don't? This is useful during the batch embedding process — run the stats, see how many are left, decide whether to kick off another batch.

The query I needed in SQL was:

```
SELECT
    COUNT(1) AS totalCount,
    SUM(c.embedding != null ? 1 : 0) AS withEmbedding,
    SUM(c.embedding = null ? 1 : 0) AS withoutEmbedding
FROM c
WHERE c.entityType = 'CocktailRecipe'
AND c.tenantId = 'COCKTAILS'
```

That `SUM(c.embedding != null ? 1 : 0)` is the standard Cosmos idiom for conditional aggregation. It's the equivalent of SQL Server's `SUM(CASE WHEN ... THEN 1 ELSE 0 END)`. LINQ can't express this — there's no `Sum` overload that takes a ternary conditional. This is the kind of query that LINQ will never be able to do because the expressiveness gap between "what .NET methods exist" and "what Cosmos SQL can do" is just too wide.

Raw SQL. Parameterized. Through the library's diagnostics. Done.

What You Now Know

Three chapters ago, you knew how Cosmos DB is structured. Two chapters ago, you knew what queries cost. One chapter ago, you knew how the cocktail app was designed. Now you know what's actually running underneath.

LINQ is great until it isn't. Raw SQL is ugly until you need it. And sometimes the LINQ version that generates weird-looking SQL actually outperforms the hand-crafted version you were so proud of. The Cosmos LINQ provider is doing heroic work translating expression trees to SQL, but it can't translate everything, and the things it *can* translate don't always map one-to-one. Deferred execution is what makes query composition cheap, but it also means you have to track *when* the query fires — because if it fires outside the library's pipeline, nobody's watching.

`ICosmosQueryLogSink` is the answer to "what happened?" It captures every query as structured data — method name, SQL text, parameters, partition key, RU charge, duration, cross-partition flag, and index utilization — and gives you a single place to look when something is slow, expensive, or wrong. Without it, I'd never have discovered that my "better" hand-written SQL was costing twice the RUs.

Next up: Chapter 12, where we add vector search to the same container. The cocktail app gets natural-language search — "something dark and smoky with mezcal" — and the whole AI integration costs about a penny. Same partition layout. Same query patterns. One new concept: embeddings. That's the chapter you demo at conferences.

Chapter 12 Cosmos DB: Vector Search — Adding AI to the Same Container

It's the age of artificial intelligence, right? So how could anyone possibly do anything without talking about AI even if it's not especially relevant? AI all the time. With an extra helping of AI with some whipped cream and AI cherries on top. As you can tell, I'm a little burned out on hearing "AI" every 9 seconds. And I'm well and truly done with all the products that make an API call to an LLM, rebrand themselves as an AI company, and proceed to get endless venture capital cash.

But for Cosmos DB, there really is a legitimate AI angle. Cosmos DB supports three key things that help enable AI features and AI integrations in your apps: **vector search, vector indexing, and vector similarity queries**.

At the end of Chapter 11, I teased the idea that we'll add AI-powered vector search to the cocktail database app for about $0.01. And here it begins.

Vector Distance Searches

Everything in the cocktail app up to this point has been keyword search. Search by title matches text. Search by ingredient matches text. Even the multi-ingredient AND search — fancy as the queries can get — just matches text. If you search for "bourbon," you get recipes with the word "bourbon" in the ingredients.

If you search for something that's a little more natural language-y like "something dark and smoky", you'd get nothing. The word "dark" doesn't appear in any ingredient name. Neither does "smoky." The search engine so far is literally literal.

Vector search changes that. Instead of matching *text*, it matches *meaning*. "Something dark and smoky with mezcal" has zero keyword overlap with "Oaxacan Old Fashioned" — but they're conceptually close. Vector search finds that connection. And the wild part is: it happens inside the same Cosmos container, using the same partition layout, queried with the same Cosmos SQL. No separate vector database. No Pinecone. No Qdrant. Just a `float[]` property on the recipe document and a SQL function called `VectorDistance`.

What's an Embedding?

So what we're trying to do is enable search based on fuzzy *meaning* rather than boolean "does this string exist" text searches. Now I don't know about you but as a long time software developer when I hear someone say "yah...we're going to search on 'meaning'", I kind of shudder. It's one of those things that a non-programmer says that sounds so completely obvious to other humans but to a programmer it begs the question: "what is meaning and how do we store it?"

We need some kind of storable abstraction that represents this vague notion of 'meaning'. And then we need a way to essentially compare one meaning (our search query) to all the meanings (the cocktail recipes) that are stored in our Cosmos DB container.

Sounds impossible. And on that note, I'm done writing and this book is over. Thanks so much for coming. Good luck.

OMG I *wish* I could do that. Wouldn't that be kind of hilarious? The author of a book hits something that's too difficult and they just 'nope out' of the book and fill the rest of the pages with "lorem ipsum" text. Ehhh I'm just gunna go for it.

Lorem ipsum dolor sit amet, consectetur adipiscing elit, sed do eiusmod tempor incididunt ut labore et dolore...I'm just kidding. Continuing on.

The meaning is generated by an AI model and it's known as an **embedding** or a **vector**.

An embedding is a list of numbers — a *vector* — that represents the meaning of a piece of text. You feed a string into an embedding model, and it hands you back an array of floating-point numbers. For the model we're using (`text-embedding-3-small` from Azure OpenAI), that array is 1,536 numbers long.

Those numbers aren't human-readable. You can't look at position 847 of the array and say "ah, that's the bourbon-ness dimension." But the model has learned, from training on enormous amounts of text, to place semantically similar things near each other in that 1,536-dimensional space. "Rye whiskey" and "bourbon" end up close together. "Smoky mezcal cocktail" and "Oaxacan Old Fashioned" end up close together. "Gin and tonic" and "margarita" end up farther apart. The embedding is essentially the AI model's interpretation of the recipe.

In order to determine similarity, you do some math and compare the vectors. Out of that comparison comes a similarity score. In Cosmos DB, there's a function that's available via SQL query called `VectorDistance` that compares two vectors and returns the semantic similarity score.

Sort the results by that generated similarity score and that's your semantic search engine. I've got to say that I was seriously surprised by how simple this was to implement.

What Gets Embedded (And Why It Matters)

The most important design decision in the whole vector search feature isn't the model or the database configuration or the query syntax. It's *what text you feed into the embedding model.* Get this wrong and your search results will be garbage regardless of how good the model is.

Here's the method that builds the embedding text for each recipe:

```
public static class RecipeEmbeddingHelper
{
    public static string GetEmbeddingText(CocktailRecipe recipe)
    {
        var ingredientDescriptions = recipe.Ingredients
            .Where(i => string.IsNullOrWhiteSpace(i.Name) == false)
            .Select(i => string.IsNullOrWhiteSpace(i.Secondary)
                ? i.Name
                : $"{i.Secondary} ({i.Name})");

        var ingredients = string.Join(", ", ingredientDescriptions);

        var name = recipe.Name?.Trim() ?? string.Empty;
        var description = recipe.Description?.Trim() ?? string.Empty;

        if (ingredients.Length == 0)
        {
            return $"{name}: {description}".Trim(':', ' ');
        }

        return
$"{name}: {description} Ingredients: {ingredients}".Trim(
            ':', ' ');
```

```
    }
}
```

Here's an example using the recipe for a "Tailspin".

```
Tailspin

Ingredients:
1 oz Gin · Gin
0.75 oz Sweet vermouth · Vermouth
0.75 oz Green chartreuse · Herbal Liqueur
1 dash Orange bitters · Bitters

Instructions:
Stir in mixing glass and garnish with lemon twist, cherry,
or olive.
```

Using that recipe as a source, output that gets fed in for the embedding becomes the following:

```
Tailspin: Stir and strain Ingredients: Gin (Gin), Vermouth
(Sweet vermouth), Herbal Liqueur (Green chartreuse)
```

Notice the ingredient format: `Herbal Liqueur (Green chartreuse)`. That's the taxonomy `Secondary` category followed by the raw ingredient name. This is the key design decision and it's the whole reason the ingredient classification system from Chapter 10 exists.

Without the taxonomy context, the embedding text would be:

```
Tailspin: Stir and strain Ingredients: Gin, Sweet vermouth
, Green chartreuse
```

That would work for recipes where the ingredient names are obvious — everybody knows gin is a spirit. But what about "Carpano Antica"? Or "Punt e Mes"? Or "Dolin Blanc"? Those are all vermouths, but the embedding model probably won't know that. By prepending the category — `Vermouth (Carpano Antica)`, `Vermouth (Punt e Mes)`, `Vermouth (Dolin Blanc)` — we're teaching the model that these are all the same *kind* of thing. The embedding will capture "vermouth-ness" even for obscure brand names.

This is what I mean when I say the embedding text is the most important design decision. The model can only work with what you give it. If you give it brand names it doesn't recognize, the embeddings will be noisy. If you give it category + brand name, the embeddings capture the *flavor profile* of the recipe, not just its ingredient list.

I have unit tests for this:

```
[Fact]
public void
GetEmbeddingText_IncludesSecondaryContextForClassifiedIngredients()
{
    var recipe = new CocktailRecipe
    {
        Name = "Tailspin",
        Description = "Stir and strain",
        Ingredients =
        {
            new Ingredient { Name = "Gin", Secondary = "Gin" },
            new Ingredient { Name = "Sweet vermouth",
                 Secondary = "Vermouth" },
            new Ingredient { Name = "Green chartreuse",
                 Secondary = "Herbal Liqueur" }
        }
    };

    var text = RecipeEmbeddingHelper.GetEmbeddingText(recipe);

    Assert.Equal(
        "Tailspin: Stir and strain Ingredients: Gin (Gin), Vermouth (
Sweet vermouth), Herbal Liqueur (Green chartreuse)",
        text);
}

[Fact]
public void
GetEmbeddingText_FallsBackToNameOnlyForUnclassifiedIngredients()
{
```

```
    var recipe = new CocktailRecipe
    {
        Name = "Mystery",
        Description = "Stir",
        Ingredients =
        {
            new Ingredient { Name = "Obscure bitters", Secondary = ""
}
        }
    };

    var text = RecipeEmbeddingHelper.GetEmbeddingText(recipe);

    Assert.Equal("Mystery: Stir Ingredients: Obscure bitters", text);
}
```

When an ingredient doesn't have a classification (the `Secondary` field is empty), the helper falls back to just the raw name. Better to give the model something than nothing.

Container Setup: The Vector Policies

Before you can query vector embeddings with `VectorDistance`, you need to configure two things on your container: a **vector embedding policy** and a **vector indexing policy**.

A note on timing: Microsoft's docs have been inconsistent about whether you can add these to an existing container. Several pages say the policies must be set at container creation time. I can tell you from experience that this isn't true — I added the vector policies to the cocktail app's container well after it was created and already had thousands of documents in it. Here's exactly how I did it.

Step 1: Open the Azure Portal

The first step is to open the Azure Portal (https://portal.azure.com), navigate to your Cosmos DB account, and then navigate to the Data Explorer.

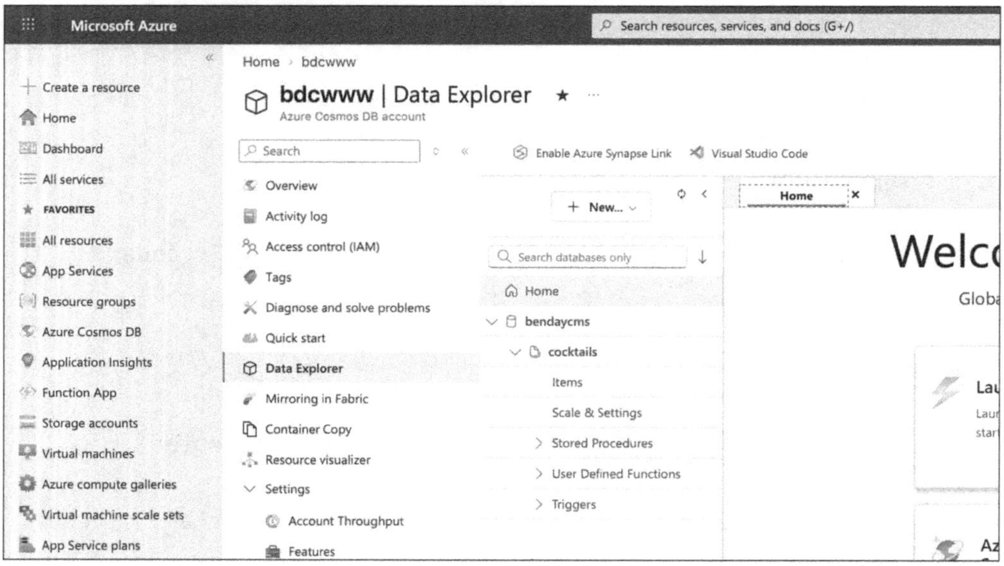

Step 1: Navigate to the Azure Portal

Step 2: Open the Container Policies Tab

Once you're navigated to your Cosmos DB account's Data Explorer, expand your database and container in the left nav. You should now see **Scale & Settings**.

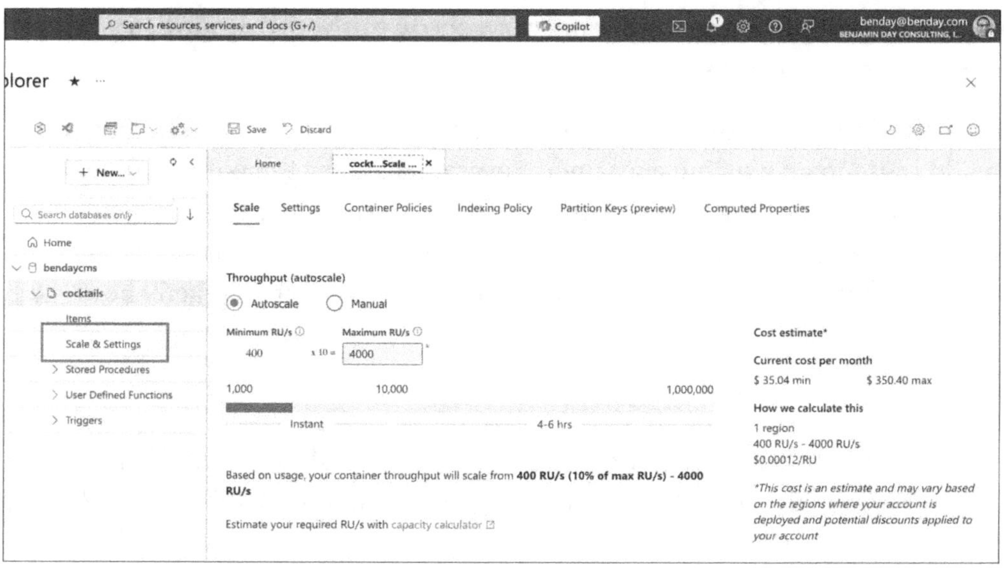

Step 2.1: Scale & Settings

Select the **Container Policies** tab, then the **Vector Policy** sub-tab. If you haven't configured vector search yet, you'll see an empty page with an "Add vector embedding" button.

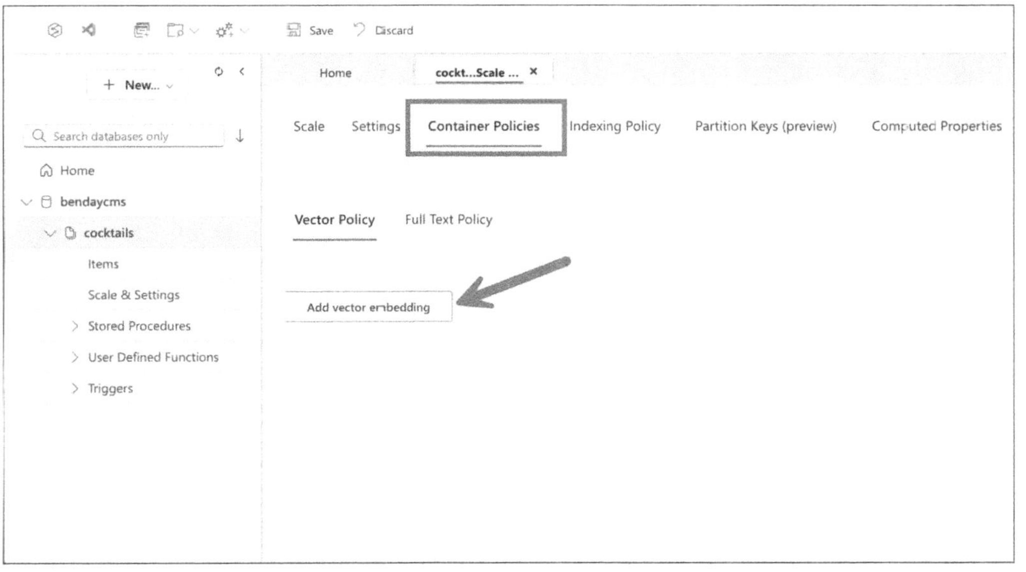

Step 2.2: Container Policies

Step 3: Add a Vector Embedding

Click **Add vector embedding**. The portal opens a form with four fields, pre-populated with defaults that you'll need to change. The defaults — path `/vector1`, distance function `euclidean`, dimensions `0` — aren't what you want.

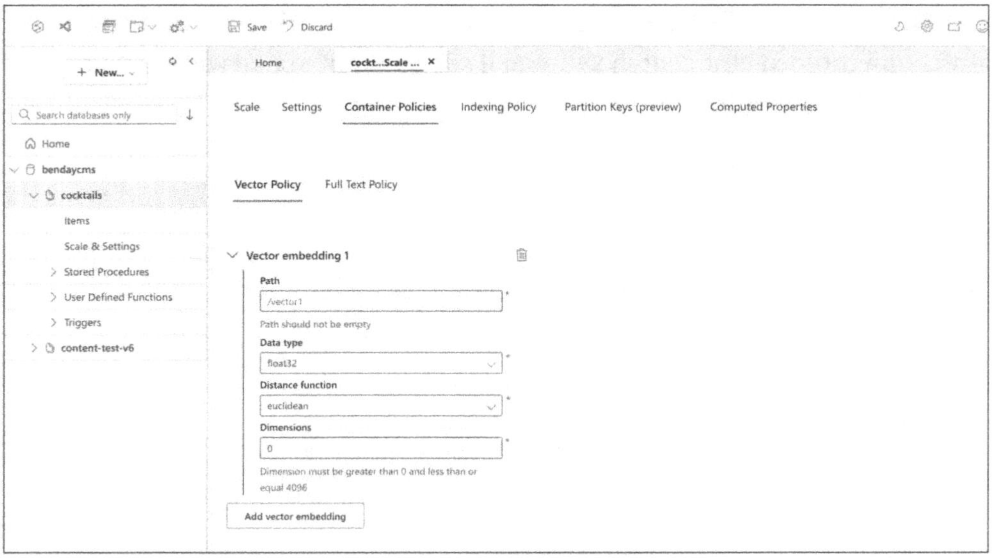

Step 3: The Empty Vector Embedding Form

Step 4: Configure the Embedding

Fill in the actual values for your embedding:

- **Path:** `/embedding` — the JSON path where the vector array lives on your documents
- **Data type:** `float32` — matches what `text-embedding-3-small` produces
- **Distance function:** `cosine` — the standard choice for text embeddings. Cosine distance measures the angle between vectors rather than the absolute distance, which means it's insensitive to vector magnitude and only cares about direction
- **Dimensions:** `1536` — the output size of `text-embedding-3-small`

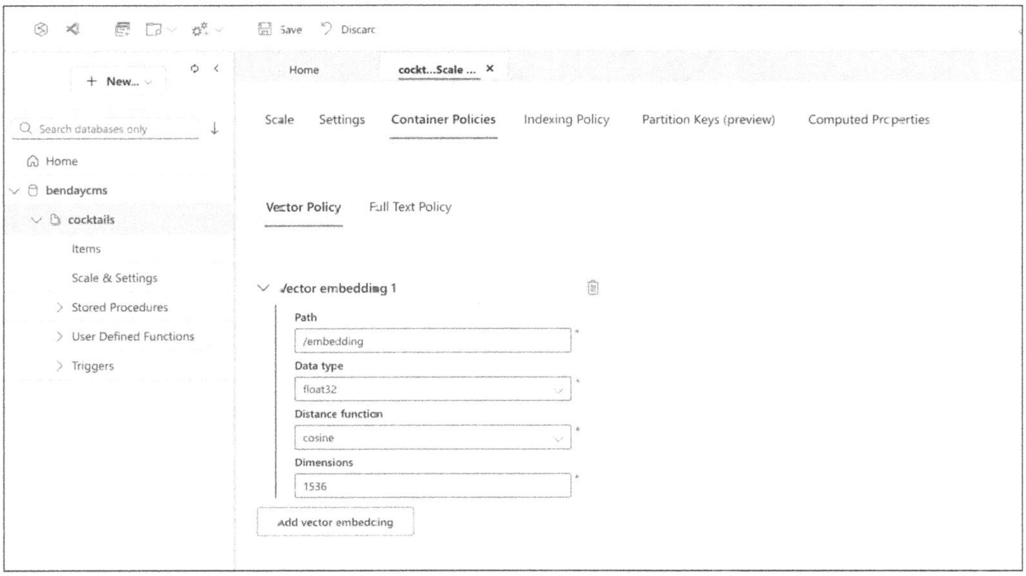

Step 4: Configure the Vector Policy

Step 5: Save the Vector Policy

Click **Save** in the toolbar. After saving, the fields become read-only — the policy is now part of your container configuration.

Step 6: Update the Indexing Policy

Now switch to the **Indexing Policy** tab. This is a JSON editor. Before adding vector search, your indexing policy looks something like this — the default `/*` included path, `_etag` excluded, nothing else:

Step 6.1: Configure the Indexing Policy

You need to make two changes to this JSON. First, add `/embedding/*` to the `excludedPaths` array — this prevents Cosmos from trying to create standard range indexes over each of the 1,536 float values in the embedding array, which would be pointless and expensive. Second, add a `vectorIndexes` section with the path and index type:

```
"excludedPaths": [
    { "path": "/\"_etag\"/?" },
    { "path": "/embedding/*" }
],
"vectorIndexes": [
    {
        "path": "/embedding",
        "type": "diskANN"
    }
]
```

`DiskANN` is Microsoft Research's approximate nearest-neighbor indexing algorithm — it's designed for disk-resident vectors and gives you fast approximate results without loading every vector into memory. The alternative is `flat`, which does exact nearest-neighbor search by comparing your query vector against every single document. For 5,800 recipes, `flat` would probably be fine. For a million documents, you want DiskANN.

Click **Save** again. The updated indexing policy now includes the vector index and the embedding exclusion:

Step 6.2: Save the Indexing Policy

That's it. Your existing container — with all its existing data — is now configured for vector search. No migration, no new container, no data movement. The documents that don't have an `embedding` property yet are fine; they'll just be skipped by the `IS_DEFINED(c.embedding)` filter in the vector search query.

The Embedding Pipeline

With the container configured, we need to actually generate the embeddings. This is a batch process — run it once to populate all the vectors, then again whenever new recipes are added.

The Azure OpenAI Service

The embedding service wraps the Azure OpenAI client:

```
public class AzureOpenAIEmbeddingService : IEmbeddingService
{
    private readonly EmbeddingClient _client;
    private readonly int _dimensions;

    public AzureOpenAIEmbeddingService(
        IOptions<AzureOpenAIOptions> options,
        ILogger<AzureOpenAIEmbeddingService> logger)
    {
        var config = options.Value;
        _dimensions = config.EmbeddingDimensions;

        var azure = new AzureOpenAIClient(
            new Uri(config.Endpoint),
            new ApiKeyCredential(config.ApiKey));

        _client = azure.GetEmbeddingClient(
             config.EmbeddingDeployment);
    }

    public async Task<float[]> GetEmbeddingAsync(
        string text,
        CancellationToken cancellationToken = default)
    {
        var options = new EmbeddingGenerationOptions
        {
            Dimensions = _dimensions
        };

        var response = await CallWithRetryAsync(
            async () => await _client.GenerateEmbeddingAsync(
                text, options, cancellationToken),
            cancellationToken);

        return response.Value.ToFloats().ToArray();
```

```
    }
}
```

The configuration is minimal:

```
{
  "AzureOpenAI": {
    "Endpoint": "https://your-instance.openai.azure.com/",
    "ApiKey": "",
    "EmbeddingDeployment": "text-embedding-3-small",
    "EmbeddingDimensions": 1536
  }
}
```

`text-embedding-3-small` is the model. It's fast, it's cheap, and the quality is more than sufficient for ingredient-level semantic search. The 1,536-dimension output is the standard dimension for this model.

The `CallWithRetryAsync` method handles transient errors — 429 rate limits and 5xx server errors — with exponential backoff. When you're embedding 5,800 recipes in parallel, you're going to hit rate limits. The retry logic waits and tries again.

The Batch Command

The batch embedding is a CLI command:

```
await Parallel.ForEachAsync(toEmbed, parallelOptions,
      async (recipe, ct) =>
{
    var text = RecipeEmbeddingHelper.GetEmbeddingText(
        recipe);
    var vector = await embeddingService.GetEmbeddingAsync(
        text, ct);
    recipe.Embedding = vector;

    var pk = new PartitionKeyBuilder()
        .Add(recipe.TenantId)
        .Add(nameof(CocktailRecipe))
```

```
        .Build();

    await UpsertWithRetryAsync(container, recipe, pk, ct);

    var soFar = Interlocked.Increment(ref done);
    // progress reporting every 50 recipes...
});
```

The pattern is: find recipes without embeddings, generate their embedding text, call Azure OpenAI, write the vector back to the recipe document, upsert it. `Parallel.ForEachAsync` with a configurable degree of parallelism (default 5) keeps the throughput reasonable without overwhelming either the OpenAI rate limit or the Cosmos RU budget.

The command also has a status mode:

```
cocktails embed /status

  With embedding    : 5823
  Without embedding : 0
  Total             : 5823
```

That's the `GetEmbeddingStatsAsync` query from Chapter 11 — the conditional aggregation with `SUM(IS_DEFINED(c.embedding) AND ARRAY_LENGTH(c.embedding) > 0 ? 1 : 0)`. Now you know what it's for.

The Cost

Embedding 5,823 recipes with `text-embedding-3-small` costs fractions of a penny. The Azure OpenAI pricing for `text-embedding-3-small` is based on token count, and our embedding texts are short — a recipe name, a description, and a handful of ingredient strings. The total token count for the entire corpus is tiny by LLM standards.

The Cosmos side has a cost too — each upsert to write the embedding vector back to the recipe document costs a few RUs — but the total for 5,823 upserts is well under a dollar at standard provisioned throughput.

The point is: the expensive part of AI isn't what you'd expect. The one-time cost to embed your entire corpus is negligible. The ongoing cost is the vector *queries* — and we'll see those numbers in a minute.

The Recipe Document

The embedding lives directly on the recipe document. No separate vector store, no sidecar collection, no external index. Just a property:

```
public class CocktailRecipe : TenantItemBase
{
    public string Name { get; set; } = string.Empty;
    public string Description { get; set; } = string.Empty;
    public string Source { get; set; } = string.Empty;
    public DateTime EntryDate { get; set; }
    public List<Ingredient> Ingredients { get; set; } = new();

    /// <summary>
    /// Vector embedding of the recipe
    /// (name + description + ingredients
    /// with category context) used for
    /// similarity / natural-language search.
    /// Populated via text-embedding-3-small (1536 dims).
    /// Empty array until embeddings are generated.
    /// </summary>
    public float[] Embedding { get; set; } = Array.Empty<float>();
}
```

`float[]` — 1,536 floats, approximately 6 KB when serialized to JSON. That's the overhead per document. For 5,823 recipes, that's about 35 MB of embedding data total in the container. Not nothing, but well within Cosmos's comfort zone.

The `Embedding` property defaults to `Array.Empty<float>()`. Recipes that haven't been embedded yet just have an empty array. The vector search query filters these out with `IS_DEFINED(c.embedding) AND ARRAY_LENGTH(c.embedding) > 0`.

The VectorDistance Query

Here's the single query that powers all the search modes. This is what Chapter 11 called out as a "must use raw SQL" case — `VectorDistance` has no LINQ mapping.

```
var queryText =
    $@"SELECT TOP @limit c.id, c.tenantId, c.entityType, c.name,
              c.description, c.source, c.entryDate, c.ingredients,
              VectorDistance(c.embedding, @queryVector) AS score
       FROM c
       WHERE {BaseWhere}
       AND IS_DEFINED(c.embedding) AND ARRAY_LENGTH(c.embedding) > 0
       {excludeClause}
       ORDER BY VectorDistance(c.embedding, @queryVector)";

var definition = new QueryDefinition(queryText)
    .WithParameter("@tenantId", tenantId)
    .WithParameter("@limit", limit)
    .WithParameter("@queryVector", queryVector);
```

A few things worth pointing out:

The projection deliberately excludes the embedding array. The SELECT lists every field *except* `c.embedding`. Each embedding is 1,536 floats — about 6 KB of JSON. If you're returning 8 results, that's 48 KB of data you'd pull across the wire just to throw away. The caller doesn't need the embedding vectors; it needs the recipe names and ingredients to display.

`VectorDistance` appears twice — once in the SELECT (to get the score) and once in the ORDER BY (to sort by similarity). Cosmos is smart enough to compute it once. The score comes back as a cosine similarity value roughly between 0 and 1, where higher means more similar.

The `@queryVector` parameter is a `float[]`. The Cosmos SDK handles serializing it into the query. You don't need to convert it to JSON yourself.

The exclude clause is optional — when searching for "recipes similar to a Manhattan," you want to exclude the Manhattan itself from the results. When doing a natural language search ("something dark and smoky"), there's nothing to exclude.

Cosine Similarity: Wait, This Is Just Geometry?

If you're like me, the "vector" thing didn't really click until I saw the word "cosine." It's probably been easily 36 years since I sat in my high school geometry class — so suffice it to say, it's been a while. But when I realized what `VectorDistance` is actually computing, I had one of those moments where I just kind of sat back in my chair and said "wait...seriously? That's how this works?"

That revelation was quickly followed up by "whew...uhhh...I don't remember *anything* about what cosine means." Appropriately enough, my solution to not remembering this was to ask Claude to teach it to me. Those mysterious "sin", "cos", and "tan" buttons on your calculator? They compute different types of ratios on a triangle. A lot of people remember what these calculations are using the "SOH-CAH-TOA" mnemonic.

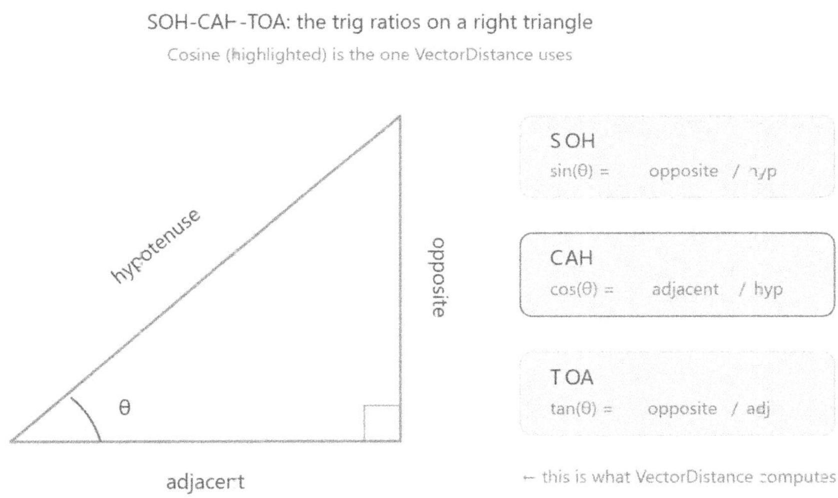

Sine, Cosine, and Tangent

What we're doing with vector similarity is measuring the angle between two arrows.

Picture two arrows — vectors — both starting from the same point, pointing out into space. Each arrow represents a recipe's embedding. The *direction* the arrow points encodes the meaning — the flavor profile, the ingredient types, the character of the cocktail. The angle between the two arrows tells you how similar the meanings are.

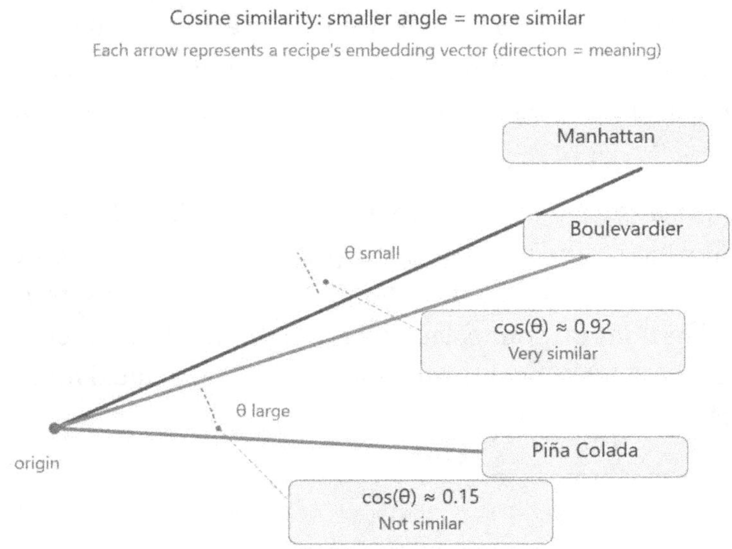

Cosine Similarity between Cocktail Recipes

If two arrows point in exactly the same direction, the angle between them is 0°. The cosine of 0° is 1.0 — perfect similarity. If two arrows point in completely unrelated directions — 90° apart — the cosine of 90° is 0. No relationship.

That's it. That's the whole thing. All of this AI-powered semantic search magic is — at its core — the cosine function from high school trigonometry. Cosine is adjacent over hypotenuse. The cosine of the angle between two arrows in 1,536-dimensional space.

BTW, that "θ" in the "cos(θ)" — that's the Greek letter "theta". Theta refers to the value of the angle that we're referring to.

The reason cosine works so well for text embeddings is that it only cares about *direction*, not *length*. Two recipe vectors might have different magnitudes for reasons that don't mean anything semantically — maybe one recipe had a longer description, maybe one had more ingredients. Cosine ignores all of that and just asks: are these arrows pointing the same way?

In practice, when you see a similarity score of 0.92, that means the two arrows are nearly parallel — the recipes have very similar flavor DNA. A score of 0.45

means they're kind of related but pointing in noticeably different directions. A score near 0 means they have essentially nothing in common.

And you never have to compute any of this yourself. `VectorDistance` does it. But knowing what it's actually doing — comparing the angle between two directions in high-dimensional space using a function you learned in 10th grade — makes the whole system a lot more understandable while still preserving the pure, amazing magic of the calculation.

Triangle math stuff from geometry helps me to compare cocktail recipe similarity. I never saw that coming.

The Projection Problem (And the Fix)

In the earlier version of this code, this query bypassed the `Benday.CosmosDb` library's diagnostics entirely. The reason was purely mechanical: the library's `GetResultsAsync` methods were generic on the repository's entity type — `CocktailRecipe` — but this query projects to a different shape. It returns a `SimilarityRow` that has a `Score` field instead of an `Embedding` field.

The types didn't match, so the query had to use `container.GetItemQueryIterator<SimilarityRow>()` directly, which meant the `ICosmosQueryLogSink` never saw it. Chapter 11 made a whole point about knowing what runs — and here was a query running in the dark.

The fix was adding a `GetResultsAsync<TResult>(QueryDefinition, ...)` overload to the library that's generic on the *row type* rather than locked to the repository's entity type. Same diagnostics pipeline, different deserialization target:

```
var rows = await GetResultsAsync<SimilarityRow>(
    definition, GetQueryDescription(), pk);

return rows.Select(row => new RecipeSimilarityResult
{
    Recipe = new CocktailRecipe
    {
        Id = row.Id.SafeToString(),
        Name = row.Name.SafeToString(),
        Description = row.Description.SafeToString(),
```

```
        Ingredients = row.Ingredients ?? new()
        // ... other fields
    },
    Score = row.Score
}).ToList();
```

Now the sink sees the SQL text, the RU charge, and the duration. And those numbers are worth seeing.

What Vector Search Costs

From the query log sink — a real session browsing around the cocktail app:

Query	RUs	Duration	Results
Title search ("manhattan")	11.34	379ms	17
Single ingredient ("rye") LINQ	201.09	2,686ms	687
Multi-ingredient ("rum" + "bourbon")	28.29	246ms	49
Vector similarity (TOP 8)	**430.95**	**641ms**	**8**

Vector search is expensive per query — about 431 RUs to find the 8 nearest neighbors out of 5,823 recipes. That's the cost of computing `VectorDistance` across every embedded document in the partition. It's consistent too — across seven `GetSimilarAsync` calls in the same session, the charge was between 419 and 431 RUs every time.

But here's the context. A vector search runs maybe once per user action — "show me similar recipes" or "search by description." It's not running in a loop. A title search or ingredient search might run on every keystroke if you have autocomplete wired up, but a vector search runs when the user clicks a button. At that frequency, 431 RUs is completely manageable.

The "heat death of the universe" framing from Chapter 11 applies here too. If you're running vector queries millions of times a day, the RU cost matters and you'd want to look at DiskANN tuning, result caching, or reducing the dimension count. For the cocktail app's scale — a few thousand users a day, maybe a few hundred vector queries — 431 RUs is pocket change.

Three Ways to Search

The same `GetSimilarAsync` method powers all three search modes. The only difference is where the query vector comes from.

Similarity Search: "Find Recipes Like This One"

The user is looking at a recipe — say, a Manhattan — and wants to find similar cocktails. The query vector is the Manhattan's own embedding, already stored on the document:

```
// Look up the source recipe
var source = await repo.GetByNameAsync("Manhattan");

// Use its embedding as the query vector
var results = await repo.GetSimilarAsync(
    source.Embedding,
    limit: 8,
    excludeRecipeId: source.Id);
```

The results share *flavor DNA* without any keyword overlap. A Manhattan (rye, sweet vermouth, bitters) returns things like the Boulevardier (bourbon, sweet vermouth, Campari) and the Rob Roy (Scotch, sweet vermouth, bitters). The embedding model understands that these are structurally similar cocktails even though the specific spirits are different — because the embedding text included the taxonomy categories, and "Whiskey (Old Overholt Rye)" and "Whiskey (Famous Grouse Scotch)" are nearby in embedding space.

Natural Language Search: "Something Dark and Smoky"

This is the one that I'm really looking forward to adding to a talk and demoing at a conference. I think this'll be a wow moment. (Or maybe it won't and I'm just a complete and total nerd.) The user types a free-text description of what they're in the mood for. We embed that text and use the resulting vector as the query:

```
// Embed the user's description
var queryVector = await embeddingService.GetEmbeddingAsync
(
    "something dark and smoky with mezcal");
```

```
// Search by semantic similarity
var results = await repo.GetSimilarAsync(
     queryVector, limit: 8);
```

“Something dark and smoky with mezcal” has zero keyword overlap with any recipe in the database. But the embedding model places it near recipes that contain mezcal, mole bitters, coffee liqueur, dark spirits — the conceptual neighborhood of “dark and smoky.” The search works not because of text matching but because of *meaning* matching.

The cost is one additional embedding call — the user’s query text gets sent to Azure OpenAI, which returns a vector, and then that vector goes into the same `VectorDistance` query. The embedding call takes about 100–200ms and costs a fraction of a cent.

Opposites Shouldn’t Attract But Do Anyway

There is one downside to the way it’s currently written. If I say “I’d like something dark and smoky without Cynar or Fernet,” it returns me a whole bunch of recipes that contain Cynar and Fernet Branca. (I like flavors that are “herbal” but I don’t particularly care for “bitter.”)

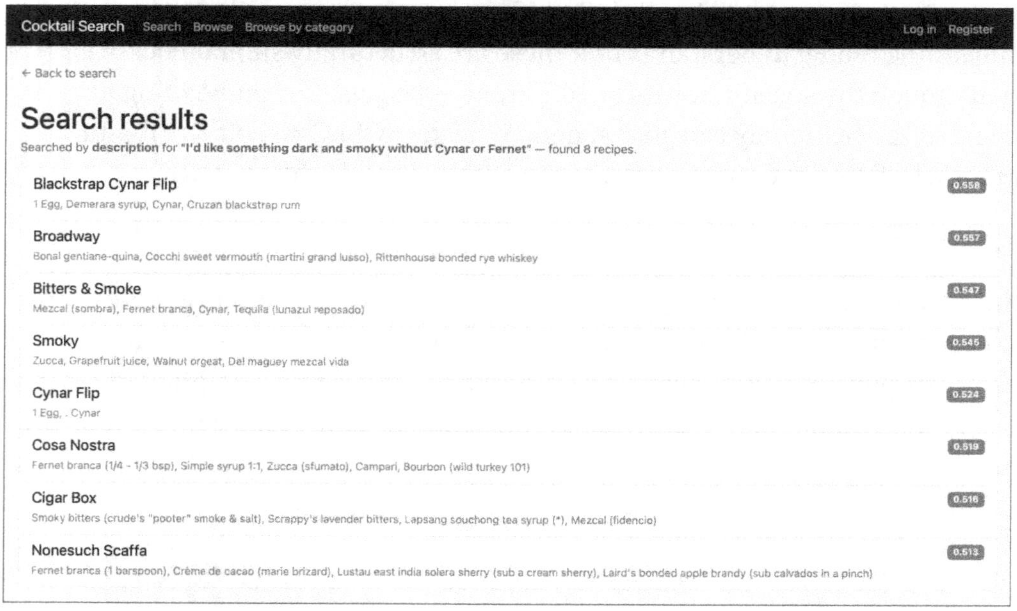

The AI Queries Don’t Handle ‘Without’ Well

The issue is that embedding models capture *what the text is about*, not the logical intent behind it. "Something dark and smoky with Cynar" and "something dark and smoky without Cynar" produce nearly identical embeddings — because both texts are *about* Cynar. The model sees "dark," "smoky," "Cynar," and "Fernet" as the meaningful content words and places the query vector right next to recipes containing those ingredients. The word "without" barely moves the needle.

We started out this chapter by trying to pin down an abstraction for *meaning*. Perhaps we should have been saying *about* instead — "what is this text *about*?" versus "what does this text *mean*?" The model that we're using (an embedding model) tends to see that "without Cynar or Fernet" part of the query as something that should attract results that *contain* rather than don't contain those ingredients. It's because those words generate more relative similarity rather than less.

This is a known limitation of pure vector search, and it's why applications often using a hybrid search model. In that hybrid search model, you actually do something more like two queries rather than just one. The positive part of the query — "dark and smoky, herbal" — is a great fit for vector similarity. The negative part — "not Cynar, not Fernet" — is a great fit for a traditional keyword exclusion filter. Combining the two, you'd embed the positive description for the `VectorDistance` ranking and add `NOT EXISTS` or `NOT CONTAINS` clauses to the WHERE to filter out the ingredients you don't want. The vector finds the neighborhood; the filter trims the results.

I haven't built that combined mode yet, but the plumbing is all there — it'd just be another WHERE clause on the same query or a filter in-memory on the results.

Hybrid Search: Filter Then Rank

The third mode combines a traditional filter with vector similarity. "Show me gin cocktails similar to a Manhattan." The gin part is a keyword filter; the similar-to-Manhattan part is a vector search.

This can be done by adding filter clauses to the `VectorDistance` query's WHERE — `AND EXISTS(SELECT VALUE i FROM i IN c.ingredients WHERE CONTAINS(i.name, 'gin', true))` before the ORDER BY. You get the precision of keyword filtering with the intelligence of semantic ranking.

What You Now Know

The cocktail app now has four search modes: title, single ingredient, multi-ingredient, and natural language. The first three are keyword searches — they match text. The fourth matches *meaning*. All four use the same Cosmos container, the same partition layout, and the same `ICosmosQueryLogSink` diagnostics pipeline.

Vector search in Cosmos isn't a separate product or a separate database. It's a property on your document, a policy on your container, and a SQL function in your query. The embedding model — `text-embedding-3-small` — does the hard work of turning text into vectors. What you feed it matters more than any other decision in the pipeline. The taxonomy `Secondary` categories in the cocktail app are what make the embeddings smart enough to know that Punt e Mes and Sweet Vermouth are the same kind of thing.

The cost model is two-layered: a one-time batch cost to embed your corpus (negligible), and an ongoing per-query cost to search it (~431 RUs for TOP 8 across 5,823 recipes). Both are manageable at the scale most apps operate at.

One thing that came up during development: the vector search query originally bypassed the library's diagnostics because it projected to a different row type than the repository's entity type. That bugged me. I added a `GetResultsAsync<TResult>` overload so projected queries go through the same sink as everything else. The Chapter 11 principle — *know what runs* — applies to vector queries just as much as to LINQ.

Next up: Chapter 13, where we address the biggest criticism people throw at Cosmos DB — "you can't do reporting." Spoiler: the criticism is aimed at the wrong target. The cocktail app's data mirrors into Fabric with zero lines of ETL code, and suddenly you've got Power BI dashboards over the same recipe data you've been searching all along.

Chapter 13 Making the Case for Cosmos: Loss Aversion, Tradeoffs, and the Right Tool for the Job

This chapter is going to be about engineering tradeoffs and I'm going to use the topic of reporting with Cosmos DB as the scenario. But first, I want to talk about psychology. Specifically, the psychology of loss aversion.

The 95/5 Problem

Loss aversion is a well-documented finding in behavioral psychology. The short version: humans feel losses roughly twice as intensely as equivalent gains. If I hand you $100, you feel good. If I take $100 away from you, you feel *terrible* — and the terrible feeling is about twice as strong as the good feeling. The gain and the loss are the same dollar amount, but they don't register the same way in your brain.

This isn't a character flaw. It's not a sign of weakness or irrationality. It's how human brains are wired. Daniel Kahneman and Amos Tversky documented this in their prospect theory work in the late 1970s, and it's been replicated across decades of research. We are, at a neurological level, more sensitive to losing things than to gaining them.

Let's say you're evaluating *something* in order to make a decision — it's an important decision but it's not life or death so there's some ambiguity. And to make it a little more interesting, let's say that we know that there isn't a totally clear answer. There's no outcome that's going to be obviously right or obviously wrong. But whatever outcome you pick, it gives you 95% of what you need but is missing 5%.

Now you'd think a rational person would weigh the 95% gain against the 5% loss and conclude "that's a great deal." But that's not what happens. What happens is that the 5% loss *dominates* your thinking. The missing piece feels enormous. The 95% you're gaining fades into the background because gains just don't register as intensely as losses.

And there's a second layer that makes this worse: humans are generally bad at perceiving long-term, gradual costs. We're great at spotting acute, immediate problems. "I can't do X right now" is clear, sharp, and urgent. But "this decision will slowly accumulate long-term consequences over next 3 years" is fuzzy and abstract. The acute problem is up-in-our-face and hard to ignore. The chronic problem is quietly over the horizon.

We humans consistently make decisions based on what's on fire and up close.

Now why is a chapter that's nominally about reporting starting with a discussion of psychology?

Because I wanted you to notice something important BEFORE I say the next bit.

The Reveal

Ready? Here goes.

Cosmos DB isn't particularly good at reporting.

I'm going to guess that you had a little "gah!" moment. A little moment of "oh crap...we can't use this thing" or "maybe I should pick a relational database for our app instead" or "oh man! I don't want to bother having to sell this to my boss or my team...I'll just pick relational and no one will blink an eye."

It's perfectly natural. Remember the 95/5 problem. Yeah. There it is. That's it in a nutshell.

Assuming you're reading this book from start to finish, you've just spent twelve chapters reading about Cosmos DB. And now I want to let you in on a little bit of my mindset. As I've written these chapters, I've made a specific effort to write about Cosmos DB in a certain way and at the same time use that same treatment for relational databases. I tried to be be neutral on what The Right Choice™ is while emphasizing the capabilities and benefits of Cosmos DB. I really wanted to avoid dunking on relational databases and relational design because that's just not valuable. I want you to be able to craft strong architectural arguments and communicate them using *positive* linguistic frames.

I focused on the gains but also tried hard to NOT frame the relational database side as "losses". No judgements. Just the facts. And the facts just are what they are.

This is the first chapter where I'm saying there's anything like a *loss*. And this loss is coming in on the Cosmos DB side. The thing I've written twelve chapters about.

So here's what I want you to notice. Twelve chapters of gains — no impedance mismatch, no DTOs, no adapter layers, domain objects that serialize directly to storage, horizontal scalability, vector search for a penny. I laid all of that out, carefully, over tens of thousands of words. And then one sentence — "Cosmos DB isn't particularly good at reporting" — and there's a decent chance that one sentence carries more emotional weight than the other twelve chapters combined.

That's the 95/5 problem in action. Twelve chapters of gain. One sentence of loss. And the loss is probably winning.

I'm not saying the reporting limitation doesn't matter. It does. I'm saying that your emotional response to hearing about it is probably disproportionate to its actual impact — and if you don't notice that disproportion, it'll drive your architecture decisions in ways that likely aren't in your best interest.

So let's slow down. Let's look at the full picture instead of focusing on our ancient lizard-brain reacting to what's on fire.

Making the Business Case

One of the things I've been trying to do throughout this book — and I'm going to be more explicit about it now — is help you build the vocabulary to make the business case for your architectural decisions. Not just to other developers, but to the people in your organization who don't think in terms of partition keys and RUs. The managers, the VPs, the product owners. The people who hear "we can't do reporting" and think "then why are we using this?"

If you're an architect or a tech lead, the technical analysis is only half the job. The other half is communication — explaining *why* a short-term limitation doesn't justify abandoning a long-term architectural advantage, in language that doesn't require the listener to understand document databases. That's a skill most of us never got trained on, and it's the skill that determines whether your good technical decisions actually survive contact with the rest of the organization.

The framework I'm about to walk you through isn't just a tool for your own thinking. It's a communication framework. It gives you a structure for having that conversation in a meeting, with a slide deck, or in a Slack thread with your VP — not just in your own head.

The Acute/Chronic Tradeoff Test

Here's a thinking framework I use when I'm evaluating technology decisions where one option has an obvious, visible limitation. I call it the Acute/Chronic Tradeoff Test, and it's designed to counteract exactly the bias we just talked about.

Step 1: Name the acute pain.

What's the thing you can't do right now? Be specific. Not "reporting is hard" — that's too vague to evaluate. Something oriented on business problems like: "I can't run a GROUP BY across my recipe data and therefore I can't get a dashboard for the product team." Or: "My VP wants a chart showing sales by region and I can't produce one without writing some awkward C# code." Specificity matters because vague fears feel bigger than they are. The "business value" focus helps you stay focused on strategic things ("what does the business need?") versus tactical things ("what's the syntax for my query?").

Step 2: Find & name the chronic costs of the alternative.

What ongoing complexity are you signing up for if you switch technologies to solve the acute pain? Not the migration cost — that's a one-time expense. I'm talking about the *permanent* operational cost. The things you'll be paying for every sprint, every release, every maintenance window, for the life of the project.

It's entirely possible that you come up with nothing. Maybe there simply AREN'T long term chronic costs and issues. If that's the case, that makes your decisions a whole lot easier. But let's assume that that isn't the case and that there actually are some lingering, nagging concerns. In my experience, just about every choice in tech has trade-offs.

Step 3: Ask whether the acute pain has a targeted solution.

Can you solve the specific gap without adopting the full chronic cost? For example, can you get the reporting without encountering the impedance mismatch problem and having to add entities and adapters to your application? If a targeted solution exists, you don't *have to* make the binary choice. This is the step most people skip, because loss aversion makes the decision feel urgent — and urgency kills exploration.

Once again, it's one of those ways that the ancient structures in our brains that have kept life living for a couple billion+ years sometimes nuke our ability to make good decisions. Stress — and make no mistake, that's stress — tends to push our decisions toward "expedient" rather than "well-reasoned".

Step 4: Check your weighting.

Are you overweighting the acute loss relative to the chronic gain you'd be giving up? Here's a test: would you describe the tradeoff the same way if someone laid out both sides on paper with dollar amounts and time estimates? Or does the acute pain just *feel* bigger?

This framework isn't a rule that says "always ignore the acute pain." Sometimes the acute pain really is a dealbreaker. If your application's primary purpose is analytical reporting, then Cosmos DB could unambiguously be the wrong tool and no framework will change that. The test says: before you react to the pain, check whether you're seeing the full picture.

And this generalizes well beyond databases. Microservices vs. monolith: the acute appeal of independent deployability can hide the chronic cost of distributed coordination and operational complexity. Rewrite vs. refactor: the acute satisfaction of starting clean can hide the chronic cost of re-discovering everything the old system encoded in its quirks and edge cases. Build vs. buy: the acute sense of control from building your own can hide the chronic cost of maintaining it forever versus forever having to pay licenses for that off-the-shelf system.

In each case, the acute feeling is real — but so is the chronic cost that the acute feeling obscures.

Applying the Test: Cosmos Reporting vs. the Relational Retreat

Let's apply the framework to the decision in front of us.

Step 1 — the acute pain: Cosmos DB doesn't do analytical queries well. It just *doesn't*. The end. You can't easily answer "what are the most popular base spirits across all recipes" or "which ingredients appear together most frequently" or let a product manager explore the data ad hoc with filters they didn't plan for in advance. That's a real limitation, and I can't pretend otherwise.

Step 2 — the chronic cost of retreating to relational: What you're signing up for when you say "let's just use SQL Server instead":

DTOs and adapter layers for every entity. Remember Chapter 1? Domain models are trees. Relational databases store boxes. You chop the tree into boxes to save, reassemble boxes into a tree to read. That impedance mismatch requires adapter code for every entity, and that adapter code needs to be written, tested, maintained, and debugged. Permanently. For every entity. Forever. If that sounds dramatic, think about how many hours you've spent in your career debugging Entity Framework mappings, writing migration scripts, and fixing bugs where a property got mapped to the wrong column. Now multiply that by the life of the project. Just because we've been working this way and writing code this way for years doesn't mean that we should *continue* writing code this way indefinitely.

But it's not just the impedance mismatch. When your application grows and you need to scale, relational databases present compounding complexity. Scaling data writes means replication or sharding. Replication or sharding means coordinating distributed transactions. Distributed transactions mean your referential integrity enforcement — the thing that made relational attractive in the first place — starts working against you. The very features that make set operations powerful are the features that make horizontal scaling expensive and fragile.

It's not just one liability. It's scalable data writes PLUS transactional integrity PLUS referential integrity enforcement. Those three things interact and compound. Each one is manageable in isolation. Together, at scale, they're the reason "scaling a relational database" is a recognized engineering specialty with its own job titles...with some real, practical, technical limits.

Compare that to what you've been building for twelve chapters. Domain objects that serialize directly to JSON and get stored as-is. No DTOs. No adapter layers. No entity configuration files. No migration scripts. Horizontal scalability without distributed transaction complexity. The tree goes in, the tree comes out. That's not a marginal improvement — that's potentially thousands of hours of developer time and operational headache over the life of a project. Having written both kinds of systems, it feels *amazing* to not have to write all that boilerplate stuff just so that the app is long-term maintainable.

But all of that chronic gain gets eclipsed the moment someone says "I need a report."

The right-tool reframe: Here's the thing. If you're trying to hire a new developer for your team, do you pass on that candidate because they're not a world-class violinist? Do you pass on them because they've never visited Zimbabwe? Because they don't like blue cheese? No. And why not? Because those things aren't relevant to the job.

In the case of reporting in Cosmos DB, or JSON document storage and retrieval in SQL Server, you need to ask yourself if this tool is the RIGHT tool for the job at hand. Cosmos DB's job is transactional document storage and retrieval. SQL Server's job is... well, lots of things, but one of them is set-based analytical operations. Using Cosmos for reporting is like hiring that developer and then being disappointed they can't improvise a frickin' sick cadenza off of Vivaldi.

Using SQL Server for horizontally-scaled document persistence is like hiring a violinist and being disappointed they can't write a React component.

Step 3 — the targeted solution: Does one exist? Can you solve the reporting gap without adopting the full chronic cost of relational? (Or to put it in the reverse, can you solve the ORM mismatch problem without choosing Cosmos DB?)

Yes. We'll get to that in the next chapter. But first, let's understand *why* Cosmos DB is bad at reporting — because the architectural explanation will make the solution make a lot more sense.

Why Cosmos DB Is Bad at Reporting (And Why That's Probably By Design)

Before we get to the solution, let's understand the problem honestly. Not as some kind of garment-rending, overwrought apologia, but as a structural analysis. Understanding *why* Cosmos DB is bad at reporting will make the solution make more sense.

Relational: Set Operations Live Next to the Data

Relational databases are good at analytical queries because of a fundamental architectural property: all the data lives in one logical pile. Tables sit together in a shared storage space. When you run a GROUP BY query, the database engine walks through the relevant table or tables, computes the aggregation, and returns the answer. The set operations and the data are *direct neighbors*. The computation happens right next to the storage.

That proximity is genuinely powerful for analytics. You can do enormous amounts of data munging without ever leaving the context of the database. You can join tables, aggregate across millions of rows, compute running totals, rank results, and return computed answers — all without the data leaving the database engine. You return *answers*, and not the raw data that then has to be analyzed out-of-band by your application. If you need that kind of thing, it's a real structural advantage. It's arguably the relational database's super power.

But the Achilles heel of relational databases is that they don't scale all that efficiently. To generalize it: they scale *up* rather than *out*. (BTW, that's the expensive kind of scaling.)

Cosmos: Sharding Inverts the Tradeoff

Cosmos DB's architecture inverts this. Data is sharded across partitions by design. Rather than the data being in one bit pile, the data gets spread out on to multiple sub-instances of Cosmos running on relatively inexpensive hardware. That's scale *out* rather that *up* and that's the inexpensive kind of scaling.

That data partitioning (sharding) is what makes it horizontally scalable — writes distribute across partitions and instances, no single partition becomes a bottleneck, and you can scale to enormous throughput without the compounding complexity of distributed transactions and referential integrity enforcement that relational databases face...at the expense of pretty much *not* being able to do distributed transactions and engine-enforced referential integrity.

But that sharding creates a structural problem for analytical queries. When you want to do set-based operations, the data might live across multiple partitions, and the database engine has to gather it into working memory before it can compute your answer. That's essentially the same work your application would do if it just read all the data out and analyzed it in C#. The Cosmos database engine is doing the same gather-then-compute that you could do at the app layer — which raises the question of what value the database engine is adding for that workload.

This is — I think — why the suite of set-based operations in Cosmos DB is somewhat underwhelming. Why invest serious engineering effort into building sophisticated aggregation, join, and windowing capabilities into a product whose architecture makes those operations structurally awkward? Why build something into the product to support a workload that the product is, pretty much by design, not optimized for?

This isn't a knock on Cosmos DB. It's actually a sign of good product judgment. The Cosmos team seems to have decided — correctly, I'd argue — that if the database engine is going to do the same gather-then-compute work that your application could do, why would we think that we could solve that better than your app? There's not much point pretending the database is adding unique value there or solving it more efficiently. Better to be excellent at what the architecture supports (transactional document operations) than to be mediocre at a whole bunch of stuff.

The Cost Problem (Even Within a Single Partition)

Even within a single logical partition, analytical queries have a cost problem. All 5,800 recipes in the cocktail app sit at `["COCKTAILS", "CocktailRecipe"]` — one logical partition. A GROUP BY query to count recipes by base spirit isn't a cross-partition scan. But it still reads every document in that partition and charges RUs proportional to the data touched. You're running an analytical workload on a transactional engine at transactional prices. Do it once, fine. Put it behind a dashboard that auto-refreshes every five minutes, and those RUs add up. (Remember the "heat death of the universe" problem though…this might still be a valid approach.)

Things Cosmos Simply Can't Do

And some things Cosmos genuinely cannot do at all. Joins. "Which ingredients appear together most frequently" requires a self-join across the ingredients arrays within each recipe — you'd need to compare every ingredient to every other ingredient in the same recipe, across all recipes. Cosmos doesn't support that kind of join. "How many recipes does each ingredient classification map to" requires joining recipe data with taxonomy data. Same container, different entity types, no real join capability. To answer these questions today, you'd have to read all the relevant documents into your application's memory and do the work in C#.

The Practical Honesty Moment

Now, here's a practical honesty moment. A lot of datasets are smaller than people think. The cocktail database is 5,800 recipes at roughly 1 to 2 kilobytes each — that's about 11.6 MB on the high side. That fits comfortably in memory on even a small Azure App Service SKU. I'm always a little surprised by how small my datasets *actually* are. You could, in theory, just read the whole thing into memory and analyze it with LINQ in C#. It'd be super-fast and your RU count would be zero for just about everything.

But. Your dataset might be a LOT bigger. Your analysis might be more complex. And more importantly, you probably don't want to write and maintain custom C# code for every analytical question a product manager might ask next Tuesday and for the rest of time.

For the rest of this chapter and the next, we're going to assume that you don't have the luxury of reading your entire dataset into memory — that you actually need a proper analytics solution.

The Scalability Irony

Here's the thing I find structurally fascinating about this whole situation.

The same architectural property that makes relational databases a scalability liability for transactions is what makes them an asset for analytics. All the data in one logical blob means writes contend with each other, integrity enforcement compounds the scalability cost, and horizontal scaling requires increasingly expensive engineering and hardware. That's bad for transactions at scale. But all the data in one logical blob also means set operations can reach everything without gathering data from across a distributed system. That's great for analytics.

Cosmos DB flips that tradeoff. Sharding means writes scale horizontally and cheaply. Sharding also means set operations have to gather before they can compute. The tradeoff is symmetric: you can't have both "writes distribute without coordination" and "set operations reach everything without gathering" in the same architecture. Physics, not product management or tech skills, is the constraint.

Which means the question isn't "which database architecture is better?" It's "which database architecture is better *for the specific workload*?" And the answer is: it depends on the workload. Use the right tool for the job.

Which brings us to the next question: do you need to *own and operate* a relational database to get the analytical benefit? Or is there a way to get the set-operations-living-next-to-the-data experience on top of your Cosmos data, without maintaining a separate database and without building an ETL pipeline?

That's what the next chapter is about.

Chapter 14 Cosmos DB: Reporting with Fabric

In the last chapter, we built a framework for thinking about architectural tradeoffs — the Acute/Chronic Tradeoff Test. We named the acute pain (Cosmos DB isn't good at reporting), named the chronic cost of retreating to relational (impedance mismatch, scalability complexity, operational burden that compounds forever), and asked whether a targeted solution exists that solves the acute pain without adopting the chronic cost.

This chapter is Step 3: the targeted solution.

Microsoft Fabric with Cosmos DB mirroring gives you the set-operations-living-next-to-the-data experience on top of your Cosmos data, without maintaining a separate relational database and without building an ETL pipeline. Let me show you what that looks like.

Enter Microsoft Fabric

Here's what Fabric mirroring does, in plain language rather than marketing language: it creates a copy of your data in a format optimized for reporting. Cosmos does what Cosmos is good at and then – over here and separated – you get a copy of your data that you can use for reporting using T-SQL.

Sounds great, right? Use the right tool(s) for the job(s). So how's it work?

Fabric mirroring continuously replicates your Cosmos DB data into something called OneLake — Microsoft's unified data lake. Your JSON documents get converted to Delta Lake tables in Parquet format, which is a columnar, analytics-optimized format. The replication happens in near real-time. And here's the critical part: **it doesn't consume Request Units on your Cosmos DB account.**

Why doesn't this use your Cosmos DB RUs? How does that magic trick pulled off? We haven't discussed backup and restore options for Cosmos DB yet but there's an option called **continuous backup**. The Fabric replication process rides on top of Cosmos DB's continuous backup feature as its source. So continuous backup writes the changes to something external to the live Cosmos container(s) and then Fabric replication uses that separated, inert copy of the data for replication. That way, there's zero impact on the transactional workloads.

Once your data is mirrored into OneLake, Fabric gives you a SQL analytics endpoint. From this point, it starts looking quite a bit like SQL Server queries. Each Cosmos container shows up as a table — and you can query it with T-SQL. (Actual, real T-SQL.) GROUP BY, JOIN, aggregate functions, window functions — all the set-based operations that Cosmos can't do or does awkwardly. The operations run in Fabric's compute, not Cosmos's, so you don't burn RUs.

What this means architecturally: your operational data stays in Cosmos, stored as trees, optimized for transactional document operations. Fabric automatically maintains an analytical copy, stored as tables, optimized for set-based operations. Two copies of the data, each in the format that suits its purpose. No code to write. No ETL pipeline to maintain. No sync jobs to monitor at 2 AM.

This is the "right tool for the job" principle in action. Your Cosmos app keeps all its architectural advantages — no impedance mismatch, no DTOs, no adapters, domain objects stored as-is. And your reporting needs get met by a purpose-built analytical engine. Both tools doing what they're good at. Neither being asked to do what they're not particularly great at.

Let me show you what this looks like with the cocktail app.

Setting Up the Demo: Mirroring the Cocktail App

Here's what you need to get started.

Prerequisites

Cosmos DB continuous backup. Continuous backup is a prerequisite for mirroring because it's how Fabric taps into the change stream. If you don't already have it enabled, you'll need to migrate your account to continuous backup mode. Fair warning: enabling continuous backup is irreversible — once it's on, you can't turn it off. The good news is that the 7-day retention tier is free, so there's no cost impact.

A Microsoft Fabric trial. This is free for 60 days. No credit card required beyond whatever Azure account you already have. Go to app.fabric.microsoft.com, sign in with your Microsoft account, and activate the trial. It takes about two minutes. With the current version of the UI, the free trial signup is a little bit hidden. Click on your profile picture in the upper right of the screen and then you'll see your Profile card. The "free trial" button should be visible in the bottom right.

Public network access on your Cosmos DB account. At least for the initial setup. If you're using private endpoints in production, Fabric does support that (it went GA in March 2026), but the setup is more involved and this isn't a networking chapter. Keep it simple for now.

Create a Fabric Workspace

From the Fabric portal page, you'll need to create a workspace. Click on the **New workspace** button.

That should pop open the **Create a workspace** dialog. The one I created for the cocktail database app is called "DrinkDb".

If you're planning to use the Fabric trial, be sure to scroll down on this dialog and choose **Fabric Trial**. Then you'll click the **Apply** button.

Create a Mirrored Azure Cosmos DB

After the workspace is created, you should see a screen that looks something like the following.

Next you'll need to create a new item in this workspace. Click the **New Item** button.

That'll pop up the **New item** dialog and one of the items you can pick is **Mirrored Azure Cosmos DB**.

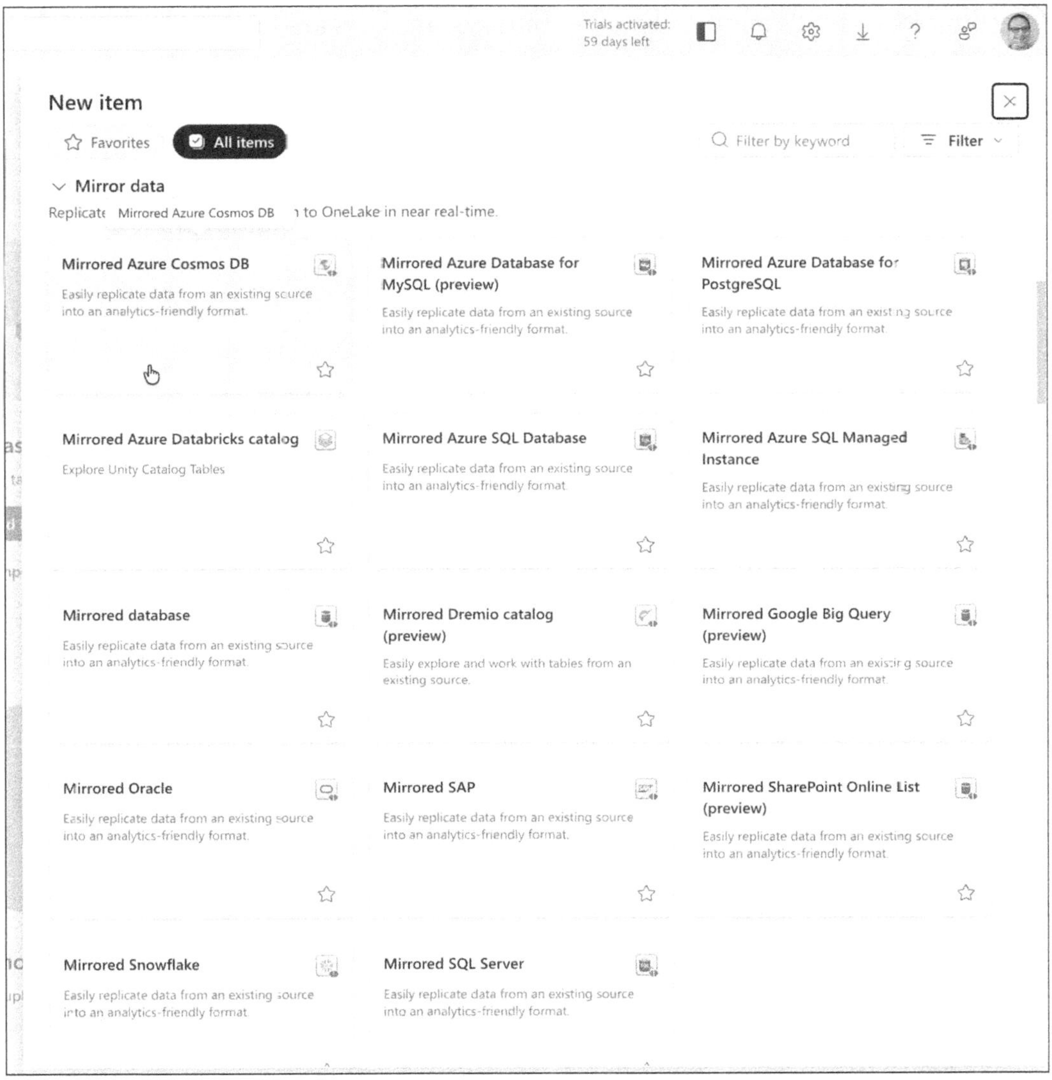

Choose Mirrored Azure Cosmos DB

That'll show you the first page of the **New mirrored Azure Cosmos DB for NoSQL** flow. Under **New sources** click the **Azure Cosmos DB v2** button.

Now you'll configure the Cosmos DB source. Provide your Cosmos DB endpoint URL and an account key. For the privacy level, select **Organizational** — this allows the data to be combined with other sources in your Fabric workspace, which you'll want if you ever extend your analytics beyond this single mirror. (If you prefer Entra ID authentication instead of account keys, that's supported too — but account keys are the simplest path for getting started.)

Click **Connect**, then select the database that contains your cocktail data. Then you'll see the **Choose data** page along with the list of containers in your database. Select the container(s) you want to mirror. In our case, that's the single container called **cocktails** with all our entity types — recipes, classifications, user favorites.

Click **Connect** on the **Choose data** page. You should now see the **Destination** page. I named the destination **DrinkDb Mirror**. Click the **Create mirrored database** button.

And that's just about it for the mirror creation. It should be started.

Monitoring the Replication

Then you wait. Two to five minutes for the initial sync.

The Fabric portal shows a replication monitor with a status indicator and row counts. The status of "Running" was a tiny bit confusing to me initially. It means that the replication monitor is monitoring. The **Rows replicated** count and the **Last completed** date help you to understand what the current state of the replication is. When the status shows "Running" and the row counts show your data (in my case, 8,012 rows — that's the ~5,800 recipes plus ~2,144 ingredient classifications plus user favorites), you're done.

That's it. Zero lines of code. No pipeline. No configuration files. No Azure Functions. No scheduled jobs. Your cocktail data is now continuously replicated into an analytics-ready format, and it'll stay in sync as you add, modify, or delete documents in Cosmos.

How Fabric Flattens Your Documents

Before we start querying, it's worth understanding what Fabric did to your JSON documents during the mirroring. This will make the T-SQL syntax make a lot more sense.

Fabric promoted every top-level property from your JSON documents into its own column on a single table. So `entityType`, `tenantId`, `name`, `description`, `ingredients`, `primary`, `secondary`, `tertiary` — they're all direct columns on the `cocktails` table. There's no wrapper object. There's no `doc` column that contains the whole JSON. It's flat.

The nested stuff — specifically the `ingredients` array inside each recipe — Fabric stores as a JSON string in a varchar column. It's the raw JSON array, but it's a string, not a structured type. To work with it, you'll use `OPENJSON` and `CROSS APPLY` to unpack it, and `JSON_VALUE` to extract specific properties from each element. If you've worked with JSON in SQL Server, you'll recognize the pattern. If you haven't, you'll pick it up from the examples below.

One other thing to notice: because all entity types live in the same Cosmos container, they all land in the same table. `CocktailRecipe` rows, `IngredientClassification` rows, `UserFavorite` rows — they're all in `[bendaycms].[cocktails]`, distinguished by the `entityType` column. This means you'll filter by `entityType` in every query. It also means you can *join across entity types* — which, as we're about to see, is something Cosmos can't do.

Querying with T-SQL: The "Wait, I Can Do That?" Moment

This is where it gets fun...and familiar. (Funmiliar?)

In the Fabric portal, click **Query in T-SQL** from the mirrored database view. This opens the SQL analytics endpoint. Each Cosmos container appears as a table, and you can write T-SQL against it.

Let me show you some queries that would be painful or impossible directly against Cosmos.

Query 1: Most Popular Ingredient Categories

"What are the most common ingredient categories across all recipes?"

In Cosmos, this query scans every document in the `["COCKTAILS", "CocktailRecipe"]` partition and charges RUs proportional to all the data touched. Do it once, and it's fine. Put it behind a dashboard that refreshes automatically, and you're paying transactional prices for analytical work, repeatedly.

In the SQL analytics endpoint:

```
SELECT TOP 20
    JSON_VALUE(i.value, '$.primary') AS primary_spirit,
    COUNT(DISTINCT c.id) AS recipe_count,
    AVG(ingredient_counts.cnt) AS avg_ingredients
FROM [bendaycms].[cocktails] c
CROSS APPLY OPENJSON(c.ingredients) AS i
JOIN (
    SELECT id, COUNT(*) AS cnt
    FROM [bendaycms].[cocktails]
    CROSS APPLY OPENJSON(ingredients)
    WHERE entityType = 'CocktailRecipe'
    GROUP BY id
) ingredient_counts ON c.id = ingredient_counts.id
WHERE c.entityType = 'CocktailRecipe'
  AND JSON_VALUE(i.value, '$.primary') IS NOT NULL
GROUP BY JSON_VALUE(i.value, '$.primary')
ORDER BY recipe_count DESC
```

No RU cost on Cosmos. The query runs entirely in Fabric's compute. And you can run it as many times as you want — there's no meter ticking on your transactional database.

A few things jump out from the results. "Spirit" leads at 3,868 recipes, which makes sense — it's the broadest primary classification. "Liqueur" at 3,158 is a close second. And there's a row with a blank `primary` value and 2,997 recipes — ingredients where the primary classification was never set. Within five minutes of querying our data analytically, we've already found a data quality issue we didn't know about. That, by itself, is a pretty good argument for having an analytical layer on top of your operational data.

The average ingredients column shows 4-6 across the board, which feels right for cocktail recipes. Simpler drinks (Spirits) average around 4 ingredients; recipes using Bitters or Syrups tend to have 5 — probably because they're being added as modifiers to more complex drinks.

Query 2: Ingredient Co-occurrence — What Goes With What?

"Which ingredients appear together most often?"

This is the killer query. It requires comparing every ingredient in a recipe against every other ingredient in the same recipe, across all 5,800+ recipes. That's a self-join on a nested array. Cosmos DB cannot do joins. This query is *structurally impossible* in Cosmos.

```
SELECT TOP 20
    JSON_VALUE(i1.value, '$.standardizedName') AS ingredient_1,
    JSON_VALUE(i2.value, '$.standardizedName') AS ingredient_2,
    COUNT(*) AS co_occurrence_count
FROM [bendaycms].[cocktails] c
CROSS APPLY OPENJSON(c.ingredients) AS i1
CROSS APPLY OPENJSON(c.ingredients) AS i2
WHERE c.entityType = 'CocktailRecipe'
  AND JSON_VALUE(i1.value, '$.standardizedName') < JSON_VALUE(i
2.value, '$.standardizedName')
  AND JSON_VALUE(i1.value, '$.standardizedName') IS NOT NULL
  AND JSON_VALUE(i2.value, '$.standardizedName') IS NOT NULL
  AND JSON_VALUE(i1.value, '$.standardizedName') <> ''
  AND JSON_VALUE(i2.value, '$.standardizedName') <> ''
GROUP BY JSON_VALUE(i1.value, '$.standardizedName'), JSON_VALUE
(i2.value, '$.standardizedName')
ORDER BY co_occurrence_count DESC
```

The < comparison prevents duplicates — "Lemon Juice + Simple Syrup" and "Simple Syrup + Lemon Juice" are the same pairing, so we only count it once. The `IS NOT NULL` and `<> ''` filters exclude ingredients with missing standardized names.

The results are interesting. The most common pairings are modifiers, not base spirits — Angostura Bitters with Lime Juice (231 recipes), Lemon Juice with Simple Syrup (210), Lime Juice with Pineapple Juice (170). That tells you something about how cocktails are actually constructed: the base spirit varies, but the supporting cast is remarkably consistent. That's a genuine analytical insight you'd never get from Cosmos directly.

Query 2b: Spirit Pairings Specifically

We can refine the co-occurrence query to look specifically at which base spirits get combined:

```
SELECT TOP 20
    JSON_VALUE(i1.value, '$.standardizedName') AS spirit_1,
    JSON_VALUE(i2.value, '$.standardizedName') AS spirit_2,
    COUNT(*) AS co_occurrence_count
FROM [bendaycms].[cocktails] c
CROSS APPLY OPENJSON(c.ingredients) AS i1
CROSS APPLY OPENJSON(c.ingredients) AS i2
WHERE c.entityType = 'CocktailRecipe'
  AND JSON_VALUE(i1.value, '$.primary') = 'Spirit'
  AND JSON_VALUE(i2.value, '$.primary') = 'Spirit'
  AND JSON_VALUE(i1.value, '$.standardizedName') < JSON_VALUE(i
2.value, '$.standardizedName')
  AND JSON_VALUE(i1.value, '$.standardizedName') <> ''
  AND JSON_VALUE(i2.value, '$.standardizedName') <> ''
GROUP BY JSON_VALUE(i1.value, '$.standardizedName'), JSON_VALUE
(i2.value, '$.standardizedName')
ORDER BY co_occurrence_count DESC
```

The counts here are lower — which itself is an insight. Most cocktails have a single base spirit. Multi-spirit recipes (like a Vieux Carré or a Long Island Iced Tea) are relatively uncommon. I expected stronger pairing signals and instead learned something about the structure of the dataset. Five minutes of ad hoc querying and I'm already learning things about my own data that I didn't know.

Notice what we just did: we went from "structurally impossible in Cosmos" to "let me refine my analysis with a WHERE clause" with about 10 minutes of setup. That's the power of having set operations next to the data.

Query 3: Cross-Entity Join — Recipes Per Classification

"How many recipes use each ingredient classification?"

This query joins recipe data with classification data. In Cosmos, these are different entity types in the same container — `CocktailRecipe` and `IngredientClassification`. Cosmos stores them side by side but can't join across them. In the SQL analytics endpoint, they're all rows in the same table, and T-SQL joins work naturally.

```
SELECT TOP 30
    ic.[primary] AS category,
    ic.secondary AS subcategory,
    COUNT(DISTINCT c.id) AS recipe_count
FROM [bendaycms].[cocktails] c
CROSS APPLY OPENJSON(c.ingredients) AS i
JOIN [bendaycms].[cocktails] ic
    ON ic.entityType = 'IngredientClassification'
    AND ic.secondary = JSON_VALUE(i.value, '$.secondary')
WHERE c.entityType = 'CocktailRecipe'
  AND JSON_VALUE(i.value, '$.secondary') IS NOT NULL
  AND JSON_VALUE(i.value, '$.secondary') <> ''
GROUP BY ic.[primary], ic.secondary
ORDER BY recipe_count DESC
```

Amaro leads at 1,524 recipes — which surprised me. Rum, Vermouth, Whiskey, and Gin round out the top five. The category/subcategory breakdown gives you a genuine picture of the collection's composition, and it came from a cross-entity join that is completely impossible in Cosmos. Two different entity types, same container, joined on a shared property, results in 1.5 seconds.

Query 4: Ad Hoc Exploration

Here's the scenario that matters most in real life. A product manager walks over (or Slacks you or hits you up on Teams, because who walks anywhere anymore) and says: "Hey, can you show me all the gin recipes that have exactly three ingredients? I'm curious what the simplest gin cocktails look like."

Nobody designed for this query. Nobody anticipated it. In Cosmos, you'd need to write a new C# query method, test it, deploy it, and expose it through some UI or API. In the SQL analytics endpoint:

```
SELECT c.name, c.description
FROM [bendaycms].[cocktails] c
CROSS APPLY OPENJSON(c.ingredients) AS i
WHERE c.entityType = 'CocktailRecipe'
  AND JSON_VALUE(i.value, '$.standardizedName') = 'Gin'
GROUP BY c.id, c.name, c.description
HAVING (
    SELECT COUNT(*)
    FROM OPENJSON(c.ingredients)
) = 3
ORDER BY c.name
```

It's the kind of question people ask when they can see their data and start getting curious. That ad hoc explorability is the superpower of set-based analytics — and it's the thing Cosmos architecturally can't provide.

These queries aren't exotic. They're the kind of things any product team asks eventually. The point isn't that Fabric is magic — it's that set-based analytical queries belong in a set-based analytical engine. The right tool for the job.

What About Power BI?

From the SQL analytics endpoint, you can build Power BI reports using DirectLake mode — the reports read directly from the mirrored data in OneLake with no import step, no scheduled refresh, and no intermediate copy. When the underlying Cosmos data changes, the mirror syncs, and the report reflects the change.

I'm not going to walk through the Power BI stuff because this is a Cosmos DB book. But the path from "working T-SQL queries" to "interactive dashboard" is straightforward and covered in Microsoft's Fabric mirroring tutorial. Get that SQL analytics endpoint working and those T-SQL queries and you're most of the way there.

What It Costs

I want to be honest about cost because cost is a real concern and hand-waving doesn't help anybody.

Mirroring compute — the replication from Cosmos to OneLake — is free. Microsoft doesn't charge for the Fabric compute that keeps your mirror in sync.

Mirroring storage — the data stored in OneLake — is free up to a limit based on your Fabric capacity SKU. For the trial capacity (F64), that limit is 64 TB. The cocktail app's data is roughly 12 MB. We're not going to hit that limit.

Cosmos continuous backup — which is a prerequisite for mirroring — is free at the 7-day retention tier. If you want 30-day retention, that has a cost, but it's a Cosmos cost, not a Fabric cost.

T-SQL query compute — running queries in the SQL analytics endpoint — is charged at regular Fabric capacity rates. During the 60-day trial, this is included.

The comparison: Running analytical queries directly against Cosmos costs RUs every time. Building an ETL pipeline to SQL Server costs developer time to build, developer time to maintain, Azure SQL pricing for the database, and the permanent operational burden of keeping the pipeline working. Fabric mirroring costs essentially nothing for the replication, and Fabric compute for the queries you run. For a dataset at our scale, the cost is negligible. For larger datasets, the math gets *more* favorable — because the alternative (reading everything into app memory, or maintaining an ETL pipeline) gets proportionally more expensive while mirroring stays cheap.

The Closing Argument

Chapter 1 started with the observation that relational databases exist because storage cost $700,000 per gigabyte in 1970. Normalization was an economic necessity. The impedance mismatch — chopping trees into boxes — was the price of affordable storage.

Thirteen chapters later, we've built applications where domain objects serialize to JSON and get stored directly. No adapter layers. No entity configuration files. No migration scripts. The tree goes in, the tree comes out. You've added AI-powered vector search to a working cocktail app for about a penny. You've instrumented your queries so you know exactly what runs and what it costs. You've designed a multi-entity, multi-tenant application with three entity types in one container and zero cross-partition queries.

All of that — all thirteen chapters of it — would have been thrown away the moment someone said "I need a report" and you decided to retreat to SQL Server. The reporting gap was the last legitimate objection to Cosmos DB for the kinds of applications this book is about. And the answer turned out not to be "go back to relational" but "add a purpose-built analytical layer that maintains itself."

Remember the Acute/Chronic Tradeoff Test from the last chapter. It works here — Fabric is the targeted solution that solves the acute pain without adopting the chronic cost. But it works beyond here too. Whenever you feel the pull of a sharp, visible limitation driving a big architectural decision, slow down. Name the chronic cost of the alternative. Check whether a targeted solution exists. Check whether you're overweighting the loss.

Relational databases are great technology — for the things they're great at. Cosmos DB is great technology — for the things it's great at. The mature architectural position isn't "pick one." It's: use the right tool for the job, and understand that the right tool for transactions and the right tool for analytics don't have to be the same system.

They just have to be connected. And it turns out, connecting them takes about five clicks and zero lines of code.

This is the final numbered chapter of Azure Cosmos DB for .NET Developers*.* *The book continues with* Appendix A: Cosmos DB Query Cookbook *and* Appendix B: Cosmos DB Operations Reference.

Appendix A — Query Cookbook

This is Appendix A of [Azure Cosmos DB for .NET Developers](). Previous: [Chapter 14: Reporting with Fabric]().

This isn't a chapter. It's a reference shelf.

Every entry follows the same pattern: here's the problem, here's the query, here's why it works. The examples draw from the cocktail app (Chapters 10–12) and the Person/Note/Comment sample app (Chapters 5–6). Bookmark this page. You'll be back.

SELECT vs. SELECT VALUE

The problem: You ran a query expecting a number or a list of documents, and instead you got a JSON object wrapper you didn't ask for.

What's happening:

```
SELECT COUNT(1) FROM c
WHERE c.entityType = 'CocktailRecipe'
```

Returns this:

```
[{ "$1": 5800 }]
```

That's an object with an auto-generated property name. Not the number `5800`. If you're deserializing this into a C# `int`, it won't work.

```
SELECT VALUE COUNT(1) FROM c
WHERE c.entityType = 'CocktailRecipe'
```

Returns this:

```
[5800]
```

That's the raw scalar. `SELECT VALUE` unwraps the result — it gives you the *value* instead of an object containing the value. Same thing applies when you're selecting documents:

```
-- Returns documents wrapped in an object: [{ "c": { ... } }]
SELECT c FROM c WHERE c.entityType = 'CocktailRecipe'
```

```
-- Returns the documents directly: [{ ... }]
SELECT VALUE c FROM c WHERE c.entityType = 'CocktailRecipe'
```

The rule of thumb: If you want to deserialize the results directly into your C# model (or into a scalar), use `SELECT VALUE`. If you need to project into a custom shape with named properties, use `SELECT` with aliases.

Cross-reference: Chapter 7 (query cost comparisons), Chapter 11 (LINQ vs. raw SQL).

SELECT DISTINCT VALUE

The problem: You're searching nested arrays with `JOIN` and getting duplicate results.

In the cocktail app, searching for recipes that contain "lime" looks like this:

```
SELECT VALUE c FROM c
JOIN i IN c.ingredients
WHERE c.entityType = 'CocktailRecipe'
AND CONTAINS(i.name, 'lime', true)
```

If a recipe has both "Lime Juice" and "Lime Wheel" in its ingredients, the JOIN matches twice, and you get the same recipe document twice in your results.

The fix:

```
SELECT DISTINCT VALUE c FROM c
JOIN i IN c.ingredients
WHERE c.entityType = 'CocktailRecipe'
AND CONTAINS(i.name, 'lime', true)
```

`DISTINCT VALUE` deduplicates at the document level. Two matches in the same recipe, one result. This is the standard pattern for any query that JOINs into nested arrays.

RU note: `DISTINCT` adds a small amount of processing overhead. It's worth it. The alternative is deduplicating in your application code, which means you've already paid the RU cost to read the duplicates and transfer them across the wire.

Cross-reference: Chapter 11 (ingredient search queries).

CONTAINS with Case-Insensitive Search

The problem: Your text search is case-sensitive and users are annoyed.

```
-- Case-sensitive: searching for "bourbon" won't match
-- "Bourbon"
SELECT VALUE c FROM c
WHERE CONTAINS(c.name, 'bourbon')
```

The fix: The third parameter. It's a boolean.

```
SELECT VALUE c FROM c
WHERE CONTAINS(c.name, 'bourbon', true)
```

That `true` enables case-insensitive matching. It's easy to miss in the docs because the parameter is optional and not exactly advertised.

In C# with the SDK:

```
var query = context.Queryable
    .Where(x => x.Name.Contains(
        searchText, StringComparison.OrdinalIgnoreCase));
```

The Cosmos LINQ provider translates `StringComparison.OrdinalIgnoreCase` into that `true` third parameter. This is one of those cases where LINQ actually gives you a cleaner syntax than the raw SQL.

Cross-reference: Chapter 11 (SearchByTitleAsync).

Parameterized Queries

The problem: You're building query strings with string concatenation, and you're inviting both SQL injection and poor query plan caching.

Don't do this:

```
// NO. BAD. STOP.
var queryText =
    $"SELECT VALUE c FROM c WHERE c.name = '{userInput}'";
```

Do this:

```
var queryText = "SELECT VALUE c FROM c WHERE c.name = @name";

var queryDef = new QueryDefinition(queryText)
    .WithParameter("@name", userInput);

var iterator = container.GetItemQueryIterator<MyDocument>(
    queryDef,
    requestOptions: new QueryRequestOptions {
        PartitionKey = partitionKey });
```

Parameters are prefixed with @. You chain `.WithParameter()` calls for each one. The SDK handles escaping and type conversion.

Why it matters beyond security: Cosmos DB caches query plans based on the query text. If you concatenate values into the string, every distinct value produces a distinct query plan. With parameters, the query text stays the same and the plan gets reused. On a high-throughput system, this is measurable.

Cross-reference: Chapter 11 (SearchBySingleIngredientAsync raw SQL example).

Cosmos JOIN Is Not Relational JOIN

The problem: You wrote `JOIN` expecting it to work like SQL Server, and the results make no sense.

The critical distinction: In a relational database, `JOIN` connects rows from two different tables. In Cosmos DB, `JOIN` iterates a nested array *within* a single document. It's a cross-apply, not a relational join. There is no "join between documents" in Cosmos DB.

```
-- This iterates the ingredients array inside each recipe
SELECT c.name AS recipe, i.name AS ingredient
FROM c
JOIN i IN c.ingredients
WHERE c.entityType = 'CocktailRecipe'
```

For a recipe named "Margarita" with three ingredients, this produces three rows — one per ingredient. The `JOIN` expands the nested array into a flat result set. It's the same concept as `CROSS APPLY` in SQL Server or `SelectMany` in LINQ.

The implications: You can't join CocktailRecipe documents with IngredientClassification documents, even though they're in the same container. If you need to correlate data across entity types, you either do it in your application code or you use Fabric (Chapter 14). This is a structural limitation of the database architecture, not a missing feature.

Cross-reference: Chapter 10 (multi-entity design), Chapter 13 (why Cosmos is bad at reporting), Chapter 14 (Fabric for cross-entity analytics).

EXISTS Subqueries for Multi-Value AND Search

The problem: You want to find recipes that contain *both* bourbon AND bitters. A single `JOIN` with an `OR` gives you recipes that have *either*. You need AND logic across multiple values in a nested array.

The pattern:

```
SELECT DISTINCT VALUE c FROM c
WHERE c.entityType = 'CocktailRecipe'
AND EXISTS (
    SELECT VALUE 1 FROM i IN c.ingredients
    WHERE CONTAINS(i.name, 'bourbon', true)
)
AND EXISTS (
    SELECT VALUE 1 FROM i IN c.ingredients
    WHERE CONTAINS(i.name, 'bitters', true)
)
```

Each `EXISTS` subquery independently checks whether the ingredients array contains a match. Stacking them with `AND` means the recipe must match *all* of them. Add more `EXISTS` clauses for more ingredients.

In C# with dynamic query building:

```
var sb = new StringBuilder();
sb.Append("SELECT DISTINCT VALUE c FROM c ");
sb.Append("WHERE c.entityType = 'CocktailRecipe' ");
sb.Append("AND c.tenantId = @tenantId ");

var queryDef = new QueryDefinition(""); // placeholder
```

```
int paramIndex = 0;

foreach (var ingredient in ingredients)
{
    var paramName = $"@ingredient{paramIndex}";
    sb.Append(
        $"AND EXISTS (SELECT VALUE 1 FROM i IN c.ingredien
ts ");
    sb.Append($"WHERE CONTAINS(i.name, {paramName}, true))
");
    paramIndex++;
}

queryDef = new QueryDefinition(sb.ToString())
    .WithParameter("@tenantId", tenantId);

paramIndex = 0;
foreach (var ingredient in ingredients)
{
    queryDef = queryDef.WithParameter(
        $"@ingredient{paramIndex}", ingredient.Trim());
    paramIndex++;
}
```

Yes, it's dynamic SQL. But it's parameterized dynamic SQL. The query structure varies by ingredient count, but the values are always parameters.

LINQ alternative: You can also do this with chained `.Where(x => x.Ingredients.Any(...))` calls. As discussed in Chapter 11, the LINQ version actually works well here and sometimes outperforms hand-written SQL because the SDK generates some clever projections.

Cross-reference: Chapter 11 (LINQ vs. raw SQL head-to-head on ingredient search).

String Functions and LIKE

The problem: You're coming from SQL Server and you want to use `LIKE '%something%'` or call string functions you're used to.

What Cosmos DB has:

`CONTAINS(str, substr)` does substring matching, optionally case-insensitive with the `true` third parameter. `STARTSWITH(str, prefix)` does prefix matching and also has the case-insensitive option. `ENDSWITH(str, suffix)` does suffix matching. `STRINGEQUALS(str1, str2, ignoreCase)` does case-insensitive equality without paying for a full `CONTAINS` scan. Beyond those, you've got the usual suspects: `UPPER`, `LOWER`, `LENGTH`, `SUBSTRING`, `REPLACE`, `CONCAT`, `TRIM`, `LTRIM`, `RTRIM`, `LEFT`, `RIGHT`.

What about LIKE? Cosmos DB does have a `LIKE` operator, and it supports % (any characters) and _ (single character) wildcards. But here's the thing: `CONTAINS` is usually the better choice for substring matching. `LIKE '%bourbon%'` and `CONTAINS(c.name, 'bourbon')` do the same work, but `CONTAINS` reads better and has the handy case-insensitive third parameter. `LIKE` is most useful when you need pattern matching that isn't a simple substring — things like `LIKE 'Mar%'` for prefix matches (although `STARTSWITH` is cleaner for that too).

What's expensive: Any function that has to evaluate against every character of every string in every document. `CONTAINS` on a large field is inherently more expensive than `STARTSWITH` because `STARTSWITH` can short-circuit once the prefix doesn't match, while `CONTAINS` has to scan the entire string. If performance matters and a prefix match is sufficient, prefer `STARTSWITH`.

Aggregate Functions and Cross-Partition Behavior

The problem: You need COUNT, SUM, or AVG, and you're not sure what happens when the data spans partitions.

The basics:

```
-- Count all recipes
SELECT VALUE COUNT(1) FROM c
WHERE c.entityType = 'CocktailRecipe'
```

```
-- Average ingredient count (using a subquery)
SELECT VALUE AVG(ARRAY_LENGTH(c.ingredients)) FROM c
WHERE c.entityType = 'CocktailRecipe'
```

Available aggregates: COUNT, SUM, AVG, MIN, MAX.

Cross-partition behavior: If your query doesn't specify a partition key, aggregates run as a cross-partition query. The engine fans out to each partition, computes a partial aggregate on each, and then combines the results. For COUNT, SUM, MIN, and MAX, the combination is straightforward. For AVG, the engine needs to compute the sum and count on each partition and then combine them — which it handles correctly, but the RU cost is proportional to the number of partitions touched.

The RU trap: That cross-partition aggregation can be expensive on high-throughput accounts with many physical partitions. If you find yourself running frequent aggregate queries across all partitions, that's a signal that you want an analytical layer (Chapter 14) rather than running analytics on the transactional engine.

Conditional aggregation: Cosmos supports ternary expressions inside aggregates:

```
SELECT
    COUNT(1) AS totalCount,
    SUM(c.embedding != null ? 1 : 0) AS withEmbedding,
    SUM(c.embedding = null ? 1 : 0) AS withoutEmbedding
FROM c
WHERE c.entityType = 'CocktailRecipe'
AND c.tenantId = 'COCKTAILS'
```

This is the Cosmos equivalent of `SUM(CASE WHEN ... THEN 1 ELSE 0 END)` in SQL Server. LINQ can't express this — there's no `Sum` overload that takes a ternary. Raw SQL only.

Cross-reference: Chapter 7 (RU cost of aggregates), Chapter 11 (GetEmbeddingStatsAsync), Chapter 13 (why analytics belong in Fabric).

DateTime Math

The problem: You need to query by date range, and Cosmos DB's date handling is… not intuitive.

Background: Cosmos DB stores a system property called `_ts` on every document. It's a Unix timestamp — seconds since epoch. It's not a string, not a DateTime, not an ISO 8601 value. It's an integer. Every query involving "when was this last modified" eventually touches this property.

Querying items modified in the last N days:

```
SELECT VALUE c FROM c
WHERE c._ts > DateTimeToTimestamp(
    DateTimeAdd("dd", -2, GetCurrentDateTime())
) / 1000
```

Querying items modified in the last N minutes:

```
SELECT VALUE c FROM c
WHERE c._ts > DateTimeToTimestamp(
    DateTimeAdd("mi", -5, GetCurrentDateTime())
) / 1000
```

That `/1000` is critical. `GetCurrentDateTime()` returns an ISO 8601 string. `DateTimeAdd` adds an interval to it using string codes. `DateTimeToTimestamp` converts the result to *milliseconds* since epoch. But `_ts` is in *seconds*. So you divide by 1000. Miss that division and your comparison is off by a factor of a thousand. You'll either get zero results or all results. Ask me how I know.

The interval codes: `"yyyy"` (year), `"mm"` (month), `"dd"` (day), `"hh"` (hour), `"mi"` (minute), `"ss"` (second), `"ms"` (millisecond). Yes, month is `"mm"` and minute is `"mi"`. Don't confuse them. You will confuse them. You will debug it for 30 minutes before you notice.

If you store your own date fields as ISO 8601 strings on your documents, you can compare them directly using string comparison because ISO 8601 sorts lexicographically:

```
SELECT VALUE c FROM c
WHERE c.createdDate > '2026-01-01T00:00:00Z'
```

This works as long as your dates are consistently formatted with the `Z` suffix and zero-padded. If they're not — fix that first.

OFFSET/LIMIT

The problem: You want pagination and you're reaching for `OFFSET 20 LIMIT 10` like you would in SQL Server.

The syntax:

```
SELECT VALUE c FROM c
WHERE c.entityType = 'CocktailRecipe'
ORDER BY c.name
OFFSET 20 LIMIT 10
```

This *works*, but there's a gotcha that'll get you on cost. Cosmos DB doesn't have an index cursor that efficiently skips to row 20. It processes all 20 skipped documents and charges you RUs for them. `OFFSET 1000 LIMIT 10` reads 1,010 documents and charges accordingly. On page 100 of a 10-items-per-page result set, you're reading 1,000 documents to show 10.

The better approach for deep pagination: Continuation tokens. The SDK returns a continuation token with each page of results. You pass it back to get the next page. The engine picks up where it left off without re-reading skipped documents.

```
var options = new QueryRequestOptions
{
    MaxItemCount = 10,
    PartitionKey = partitionKey
};

string? continuationToken = null;

// First page
var iterator = container.GetItemQueryIterator<CocktailRecipe>(
    queryDef, continuationToken, options);

var response = await iterator.ReadNextAsync();
continuationToken = response.ContinuationToken;
```

```
// Store continuationToken somewhere (session, URL parameter, etc.)

// Next page
iterator = container.GetItemQueryIterator<CocktailRecipe>(
    queryDef, continuationToken, options);
```

When OFFSET/LIMIT is fine: Small datasets, shallow pagination (first few pages), admin UIs where cost isn't critical. For user-facing pagination over large datasets, use continuation tokens.

The `Benday.CosmosDb` library wraps this in a `GetPagedResultsAsync` method that handles the continuation token management, and the `ICosmosQueryLogSink` logs the RU cost per page so you can see exactly what each page request costs.

Cross-reference: Chapter 7 (RU costs scale with documents read).

ORDER BY and Composite Indexes

The problem: Your query with `ORDER BY` is slow, expensive, or throwing an error about missing indexes.

The basics: Cosmos DB can sort by any property that's included in the index. By default, all properties are indexed with range indexes, so single-property `ORDER BY` works out of the box:

```
SELECT VALUE c FROM c
WHERE c.entityType = 'CocktailRecipe'
ORDER BY c.name ASC
```

When you need a composite index: The moment you sort by *two or more properties*, or when you filter on one property and sort by another that's not the filter property, Cosmos DB may need a composite index. Without one, you'll get an error like: "The order by query does not have a corresponding composite index that it can be served from."

Creating a composite index requires updating your container's indexing policy. In the Azure portal, go to your container → Settings → Indexing Policy, and add a composite index:

```
{
    "indexingMode": "consistent",
```

```
    "includedPaths": [{ "path": "/*" }],
    "excludedPaths": [{ "path": "/\"_etag\"/?" }],
    "compositeIndexes": [
        [
            { "path": "/entityType", "order": "ascending"
},
            { "path": "/name", "order": "ascending" }
        ]
    ]
}
```

The order matters. The sequence of properties in the composite index definition must match the sequence in your `ORDER BY` clause. And the sort direction (ascending/descending) must match too. If your query sorts by `entityType ASC, name DESC`, you need a composite index with those exact directions.

Cost impact: Custom indexing policies can dramatically reduce RU costs. The default "index everything" policy writes an index entry for every property on every document, which means every write pays for all those index updates. If you only ever query on three properties, exclude the rest.

Cross-reference: Chapter 7 (indexing policy and RU impact).

Cross-Partition Query Detection

The problem: Your query is slow and expensive, and you suspect it's scanning across partitions but you're not sure.

How to tell: The `Benday.CosmosDb` library's `ICosmosQueryLogSink` includes an `isCrossPartition` flag in every diagnostic entry. If that's `true`, your query is fanning out across physical partitions.

Common causes:

16. **No partition key in the query.** If you don't specify the partition key in `QueryRequestOptions`, every query is cross-partition by definition.
17. **Incomplete hierarchical key.** If your hierarchical partition key is `/tenantId,/entityType` and you only specify `tenantId`, Cosmos still has to check across all entity types within that tenant.

18. **WHERE clause mismatch.** Even with a partition key in the request options, if your query's WHERE clause contradicts or omits the partition key columns, the engine may not be able to limit the scan.

The fix is almost always: Make sure your query specifies the full partition key. With hierarchical partition keys, that means all levels. In the cocktail app, a query for recipes specifies both `tenantId = 'COCKTAILS'` and `entityType = 'CocktailRecipe'` — which narrows to a single logical partition.

Cross-reference: Chapter 6 (partition key design), Chapter 7 (RU cost of cross-partition queries), Chapter 11 (diagnostic sink output).

Indexing Policies

The problem: You're burning RUs on writes and you haven't touched the default indexing policy.

The default: Cosmos DB indexes every property on every document with range indexes. That's convenient for getting started — any query works without configuration. But every write pays for all those index updates. On a container with documents that have 50 properties, every write updates 50 index entries even if you only ever query on 3 of them.

A targeted policy:

Start by excluding everything:

```
{
    "indexingMode": "consistent",
    "includedPaths": [],
    "excludedPaths": [{ "path": "/*" }]
}
```

Cosmos DB automatically indexes the partition key paths and `id`, so your basic operations still work. From there, add back only what you actually query on:

```
{
    "indexingMode": "consistent",
    "includedPaths": [
        { "path": "/name/?" },
        { "path": "/entityType/?" },
        { "path": "/tenantId/?" },
```

```
        { "path": "/ingredients/[]/name/?" }
    ],
    "excludedPaths": [{ "path": "/*" }]
}
```

The /? suffix means "index this specific property." The /ingredients/[]/name/? syntax indexes the name property inside each element of the ingredients array.

When to do this: After your schema and query patterns have stabilized. Don't optimize indexing policies during early development when you're still figuring out what queries you need. Do it before production, or when your RU costs on writes are higher than expected.

The embedding gotcha: If you're storing vector embeddings (Chapter 12), you absolutely want to exclude the embedding property from the regular index. A 1,536-dimension float[] is expensive to index with range operators and you never query it that way — that's what the vector index is for.

Cross-reference: Chapter 7 (cost impact), Chapter 12 (vector indexing policy).

VectorDistance Queries

The problem: You want to do semantic similarity search using vector embeddings stored on your documents.

The query:

```
SELECT TOP @maxResults
    c.id,
    c.name,
    c.description,
    VectorDistance(c.embedding, @queryVector)
          AS similarityScore
FROM c
WHERE c.entityType = 'CocktailRecipe'
AND c.tenantId = @tenantId
ORDER BY VectorDistance(c.embedding, @queryVector)
```

In C# with the SDK:

```
var queryText = @"
    SELECT TOP @maxResults
        c.id, c.name, c.description,
        VectorDistance(
            c.embedding, @embedding) AS similarityScore
    FROM c
    WHERE c.entityType = 'CocktailRecipe'
    AND c.tenantId = @tenantId
    ORDER BY VectorDistance(c.embedding, @embedding)";

var queryDef = new QueryDefinition(queryText)
    .WithParameter("@maxResults", maxResults)
    .WithParameter("@tenantId", tenantId)
    .WithParameter("@embedding", queryEmbedding);
```

The `@embedding` parameter is a `float[]` in C#. The SDK serializes it to a JSON array of numbers. You don't need to convert it to a string or do any special formatting.

Projecting out the embedding: Notice that the `SELECT` clause lists specific properties and does *not* include `c.embedding`. This is deliberate. The embedding array is 1,536 floats — about 12 KB of data per document. If you're returning 20 results, that's 240 KB of embedding data you don't need transferred across the wire. Project it out. Only select the properties you'll actually display or use.

No LINQ equivalent: `VectorDistance` is a Cosmos SQL function with no LINQ mapping. This is always a raw SQL query.

Vector indexing policy: The vector index must be configured at container creation time. You can't add it later. The container policy looks something like:

```
{
    "vectorIndexes": [
        {
            "path": "/embedding",
            "type": "diskANN"
        }
```

```
    ]
}
```

And the corresponding vector embedding policy on the container:

```
{
    "vectorEmbeddings": [
        {
            "path": "/embedding",
            "dataType": "float32",
            "distanceFunction": "cosine",
            "dimensions": 1536
        }
    ]
}
```

Plan ahead. If you think you *might* want vector search, configure the policy when you create the container. It's free if you don't use it. I learned this the hard way with the cocktail app — I had to recreate the container and re-import all the data when I decided to add vector search after the fact.

Cross-reference: Chapter 12 (full vector search implementation).

Data Explorer Quirks

The problem: Queries that work fine in your C# code behave strangely in the Azure portal's Data Explorer.

The pagination trap: Data Explorer shows results in pages and has a "Load more" button. But it doesn't show you the total result count upfront. If your query returns 500 documents, you'll see the first ~100 and have to click "Load more" repeatedly. This is fine for browsing but misleading if you're trying to validate result counts. Run a `SELECT VALUE COUNT(1)` separately if you need the actual count.

The timeout: Data Explorer has a query timeout that's shorter than what the SDK allows. Complex queries — especially cross-partition aggregates — may time out in the portal but succeed from your application. If a query fails in Data Explorer, try it from code before concluding it doesn't work.

Parameter support: Data Explorer doesn't support parameterized queries. You have to inline the values. This means you can't copy a parameterized query directly from your C# code into the portal — you need to substitute the parameter values manually first.

Partition key scope: Data Explorer lets you set the partition key for a query. With hierarchical partition keys, you need to provide all levels as a JSON array: `["COCKTAILS", "CocktailRecipe"]`. If you provide only the first level, you'll get cross-partition behavior and potentially different results (or higher RU costs) than your application sees.

SELECT * behavior: `SELECT * FROM c` in Data Explorer returns the documents with a `c` wrapper: `{ "c": { ... } }`. Use `SELECT VALUE c FROM c` to get the clean documents. Your SDK-based application code won't have this issue because the SDK handles the unwrapping, but it trips people up in the portal constantly.

That's the query cookbook. Bookmark it, come back when you need it, and when you find a query pattern that should be in here but isn't — well, I'm not that hard to find on the internet.

Next: *Appendix B: Cosmos DB Operations Reference*.

Appendix B — Operations Reference

This is Appendix B of Azure Cosmos DB for .NET Developers. Previous: Appendix A: Cosmos DB Query Cookbook.

Same format as the Query Cookbook. Problem first, practical answer, watch-out-for gotchas. This appendix is oriented around the Azure portal and the operational side of running Cosmos DB — the stuff that shows up after your code works and somebody asks "okay, but how do we run this thing?"

The Azure portal's resource blade for a Cosmos DB account is basically the table of contents for this appendix. If you see something in the left nav and wonder what it does, there's probably an entry for it here.

Throughput Management

The situation: You're setting up a new container and the portal is asking you to choose between Manual, Autoscale, and Serverless. You have no idea what to pick.

The three modes:

Serverless is the simplest. You don't configure throughput at all. You pay per-RU for every operation, no minimums, no commitments. If your container sits idle, you pay nothing. If it spikes, you pay for the spike. This is great for development, testing, low-traffic applications, and anything where the workload is unpredictable and bursty. The cocktail app ran on serverless for months during development. The downside: serverless has a 1,000 RU/s burst limit per partition, and a 1 TB storage limit per account. You also can't use serverless with multi-region writes or Fabric mirroring (continuous backup isn't supported on serverless accounts as of this writing).

Manual provisioned throughput is the traditional model. You set a specific RU/s number — say 400 RU/s — and that's what you get. Go over it and your requests get throttled (HTTP 429). The advantage is cost predictability. The disadvantage is that you have to guess your throughput needs. Set it too low and requests fail. Set it too high and you're paying for capacity you're not using. The minimum is 400 RU/s per container (or 100 RU/s per container if you're sharing throughput at the database level).

Autoscale is the sweet spot for production. You set a *maximum* RU/s, and Cosmos DB scales between 10% of that maximum and the full amount based on actual load. If you set a max of 4,000 RU/s, the system scales between 400 and 4,000 RU/s. You're billed for the highest throughput the system scaled to during each hour. Autoscale handles spikes without throttling, and costs less than manual during quiet periods because it scales down. For most production workloads, this is the right default.

The decision tree: Developing or experimenting? Serverless. Production workload with predictable, steady traffic? Manual, if you want to optimize cost. Production workload with variable traffic? Autoscale. Not sure? Start with autoscale — you can always switch to manual later if cost analysis shows your traffic is flat enough.

One more thing: You can provision throughput at the *database* level instead of the *container* level. Database-level throughput is shared across all containers in that database. This is useful if you have multiple containers with low individual throughput needs — instead of paying 400 RU/s minimum per container, you pay one pool that all containers share. The tradeoff is that a burst in one container can starve the others.

Cross-reference: Chapter 3 (Cosmos DB structure), Chapter 7 (RU costs).

Consistency Levels

The situation: The portal shows five consistency levels and the documentation reads like a distributed systems textbook. You just want to know which one to pick.

The five levels, in practical terms:

Strong — after a write, any subsequent read from any region sees that write immediately. This is what you're used to from a single-server SQL Server. The cost: writes are slower because Cosmos has to replicate to a majority of regions before acknowledging the write. For single-region accounts, this is effectively the same as Bounded Staleness without the latency penalty of multi-region replication.

Bounded Staleness — reads might be stale, but only by a bounded amount (you configure the window in seconds or operations). This is a compromise between consistency and performance in multi-region setups. For single-region accounts, it behaves identically to Strong.

Session — *this is the default and it's the right choice for most applications.* Within a single client session, you always see your own writes. If User A writes a recipe and then reads it back, they see the updated version. User B might see the old version for a brief moment. This is natural "I see my own changes" behavior and it matches how most web applications already work. The `Benday.CosmosDb` library tracks the session token automatically.

Consistent Prefix — reads might be stale, but you'll never see things out of order. If writes happen as A → B → C, a reader might see just A, or A → B, but never A → C (skipping B). Useful for event-stream scenarios where ordering matters more than immediacy.

Eventual — the cheapest option. Reads might be stale and might be out of order. This sounds scary but for read-heavy workloads where staleness is acceptable (caching layers, analytics, read replicas), it gives the best throughput and lowest RU cost. Reads cost roughly half the RUs compared to Strong.

What to pick: Session consistency, unless you have a specific reason to choose something else. It gives you "I see my own writes" semantics at a reasonable cost, and it's the default for a reason. The cocktail app uses Session consistency. I've never had a reason to change it.

Cross-reference: Chapter 3 (Cosmos DB fundamentals).

Backup and Restore

The situation: You want to know what happens if someone accidentally deletes a container or corrupts your data.

Two backup modes:

Periodic backup is the older model. Cosmos takes snapshots at intervals you configure (minimum every hour, maximum every 24 hours) and retains them for a configurable period (minimum 8 hours, maximum 720 hours / 30 days). To restore, you file a support ticket with Microsoft. They restore to a *new account*, not in-place. The restore is at the account level — you can't restore a single container. Recovery time depends on data size and support response time.

Continuous backup is the newer model and the one you probably want. It keeps a continuous log of changes and supports Point In Time Restore (PITR)

— you pick a timestamp within the retention window and Cosmos restores to that exact moment. Two retention tiers: 7-day (free) and 30-day (has a cost per GB/month). Continuous backup also supports granular restore — you can restore a single container or database to a new account rather than restoring the entire account.

Choosing between them: If you're setting up a new account, choose continuous backup. The 7-day tier is free. There is essentially no reason to pick periodic backup for new accounts. Continuous backup is also a prerequisite for Fabric mirroring (Chapter 14), so if you think you might ever want analytics, you'll need it anyway.

The migration catch: If your existing account uses periodic backup, you can migrate to continuous backup. But the migration is irreversible — once you switch to continuous, you can't go back to periodic. This is fine because continuous is strictly better, but know that it's a one-way door.

Point In Time Restore (PITR)

The situation: Someone deleted a batch of documents at 2:47 PM and you want them back.

How it works: With continuous backup enabled, you go to the Azure portal, select your Cosmos account, navigate to Point in Time Restore, pick a timestamp (any time within your retention window), and specify which databases/containers to restore. Cosmos creates a new account with the data as it existed at that timestamp. You then migrate the recovered data back into your production account.

The gotchas:

It restores to a new account, not in-place. You can't "undo" a deletion on the live account. You get a copy of the data at the point in time, in a separate account, and you have to move it yourself.

The restore granularity is per-container. You can restore a specific container without restoring the entire account. But you can't restore individual documents — you restore the whole container and then find the documents you need in the restored copy.

RPO (Recovery Point Objective) is essentially the timestamp you pick. If you know when the bad thing happened, you can restore to seconds before it. If you don't know when it happened, you'll need to poke around in the restored data to find a good timestamp.

Restore time depends on data size. Small containers restore in minutes. Large containers can take hours. Don't assume this is instantaneous for disaster recovery planning.

The practical advice: Think of PITR as insurance for "oh no" moments — accidental deletions, bad deployments that corrupt data, bulk operations gone wrong. For genuine disaster recovery with tight RPOs and RTOs, you'll want multi-region configuration as well.

TTL (Time To Live)

The situation: You have documents that should expire automatically — session data, temp files, event logs, cache entries — and you don't want to build a cleanup job.

How it works: TTL is the number of seconds a document should live after its last modification (based on `_ts`). You can set it at two levels:

Container-level default: Set a default TTL on the container. Every document in the container inherits this value unless it overrides it.

```
// Container setting: default TTL of 86400 seconds (24 hours)
{
    "defaultTtl": 86400
}
```

Document-level override: Set a `ttl` property on individual documents to override the container default.

```
{
    "id": "session-abc123",
    "ttl": 3600,
    "...": "..."
}
```

This document expires 3,600 seconds (1 hour) after its last modification, regardless of the container default.

Special values: A `ttl` of `-1` on a document means "never expire, even if the container has a default TTL." A container default of `-1` means "TTL is enabled on this container (documents *can* have individual TTLs), but documents don't expire by default."

Deletion behavior: Expired documents are deleted in the background by a system process. This process runs on leftover RUs — it doesn't consume your provisioned throughput. But "in the background" means there's a slight delay between when a document's TTL expires and when it actually gets removed. Don't write code that depends on documents being deleted at the exact second of expiration.

Common patterns: Session state with a 24-hour TTL. Event log entries with a 30-day TTL. Change feed processor lease documents with short TTLs for cleanup. Transient cache documents that auto-expire.

The RU benefit: Deleted documents stop costing you storage and stop being indexed. If you have a high-write container with transient data, TTL can significantly reduce your storage costs over time with zero maintenance code.

Monitoring

The situation: Something is slow or expensive and you need to figure out what's happening.

Where to look in the portal:

Metrics blade — the first stop. Shows RU consumption, request count, throttled requests (HTTP 429s), storage, and document count over time. The most useful view is "Total Request Units" broken down by operation type. This tells you whether your reads, writes, or queries are consuming the most throughput. If you see spikes in throttled requests, your provisioned throughput is too low (or you have a runaway query).

Insights blade — a curated set of dashboards built on top of the same data. More visual, less configurable. Good for a quick health check.

Diagnostic settings — for deeper analysis, you can send Cosmos metrics and logs to Log Analytics, Event Hub, or Storage. Once the data is in Log Analytics, you can write KQL queries to analyze query patterns, identify expensive operations, and track performance trends over time. This is where the serious operational analysis happens.

Alerts — set up alerts on the metrics that matter. The ones I'd start with: throttled requests greater than zero (you're exceeding throughput), normalized RU consumption above 80% (you're approaching throttling), and storage utilization approaching your limits. Don't set alerts on everything — alert fatigue is real and it makes people ignore the alerts that matter.

Application-level diagnostics: The `ICosmosQueryLogSink` from Chapter 11 gives you query-level detail that the portal metrics can't — individual query SQL, RU cost per operation, timing, cross-partition flags, and (when enabled) index utilization metrics that show which indexes your queries actually used and which ones Cosmos recommends adding. The portal tells you *how much* throughput you're using. The sink tells you *which queries* are responsible and whether they're hitting the right indexes.

The practical approach: Use the portal Metrics blade for "is anything on fire right now?" Use the `ICosmosQueryLogSink` for "which specific query is causing the fire?" Turn on `CaptureIndexMetrics` for "is the fire burning hotter than it needs to because I'm missing an index?" Use Log Analytics for "what's the trend over the last month and should I change my throughput configuration?"

Cross-reference: Chapter 7 (RU costs), Chapter 11 (ICosmosQueryLogSink).

Locks

The situation: You want to make sure nobody accidentally deletes your production Cosmos DB account or database.

How it works: Azure Resource Manager locks prevent accidental deletion or modification of resources. Two types:

Delete lock — prevents the resource from being deleted. You can still modify it (change settings, update throughput, etc.), but you can't delete it. This is the one you almost certainly want on your production Cosmos account.

ReadOnly lock — prevents both deletion and modification. This is too restrictive for most Cosmos accounts because you can't change throughput, update indexing policies, or make any configuration changes. Use this only if you have a very specific reason.

Where to set it: In the Azure portal, navigate to your Cosmos DB account → Settings → Locks. Add a lock at the account level. You can also set locks at the resource group level, which cascades to everything in the group.

The catch: Locks apply to management-plane operations, not data-plane operations. A Delete lock on the Cosmos account prevents someone from deleting the *account* in the portal or via ARM, but it doesn't prevent someone from deleting *documents* or *containers* via the SDK or Data Explorer. For data-level protection, use RBAC permissions (Chapter 9) to restrict who can perform destructive operations.

Best practice: Put a Delete lock on every production Cosmos DB account. It takes 30 seconds and prevents the "someone accidentally deleted the account" disaster. You can always remove the lock when you legitimately need to delete the resource.

Cross-reference: Chapter 9 (RBAC and permissions).

Networking

The situation: Your security team says the Cosmos DB account needs to be locked down, and you need to understand the networking options.

Public network access is the default. Your Cosmos DB account is accessible from the internet via its endpoint URL, authenticated by access keys or Azure AD tokens. For development and small projects, this is fine. For production, your security team will probably want more.

IP firewall rules restrict access to specific IP addresses or CIDR ranges. You configure them in the portal under Networking → Public Access → Selected Networks. Add your office IP, your build server's IP, your app's outbound IPs. Everything else gets rejected. This is the simplest security improvement and takes about two minutes.

Service endpoints allow Azure resources in a specific virtual network to reach your Cosmos DB account over the Azure backbone network (not the public internet). The traffic never leaves Microsoft's network. This is useful when your App Service or Azure Functions run in a VNet.

Private endpoints take it further — they assign a private IP address from your VNet to the Cosmos DB account. The public endpoint can be disabled entirely. All traffic goes through the private IP. This is the gold standard for production security and what most enterprise environments require. Fabric mirroring supports private endpoints as of March 2026.

The practical progression: Start with public access during development. Add IP firewall rules when you move to staging. Switch to private endpoints for production. Don't try to set up private endpoints on day one — it adds complexity that slows down development without adding value until you're running real workloads.

The Fabric mirroring note: If you're using Fabric mirroring (Chapter 14), you'll need either public access or a private endpoint that Fabric can reach. Service endpoints alone aren't sufficient for Fabric connectivity.

Cross-reference: Chapter 9 (security and permissions), Chapter 14 (Fabric mirroring prerequisites).

Dedicated Gateway and Integrated Cache

The situation: You have a read-heavy workload and you want to reduce RU costs by caching frequently-accessed documents.

What it is: The Dedicated Gateway is a compute layer that sits in front of your Cosmos DB account. It includes an integrated cache that stores the results of point reads and queries. Subsequent identical reads hit the cache instead of Cosmos, costing zero RUs.

How it works: You provision a Dedicated Gateway SKU (separate from your container throughput), change your application's connection string to use the gateway endpoint instead of the direct endpoint, and set `ConsistencyLevel` to `Eventual` on cached reads. The gateway transparently caches responses and serves them for requests with matching keys/queries.

When it makes sense: High read-to-write ratios where the same documents or query results are read repeatedly. Think of it like a managed cache specifically for Cosmos DB. If your app reads the same recipe detail page 1,000 times between updates, the cache saves 999 RUs worth of reads.

When it doesn't make sense: Write-heavy workloads, workloads where every read is unique, or workloads where strong consistency is required on every read (the cache introduces staleness by definition). Also not worth it if your total RU consumption on reads is already low — the Dedicated Gateway has its own cost, and it only saves money if the RU savings exceed the gateway cost.

The cost math: The smallest Dedicated Gateway SKU has a monthly cost. Compare that cost against the RUs you'd save by caching. If your read RU bill is significantly higher than the gateway cost, it pays for itself. If it's close or lower, stick with direct reads.

Container Copy

The situation: You need to move data between containers — maybe you're restructuring your partition key, changing your indexing policy in a way that requires a new container, or migrating between accounts.

Why you need it: Some container properties can't be changed after creation. Partition key paths and vector indexing policies are the big ones. If you need to change either of those, you create a new container with the correct settings and copy the data over.

The options:

Container Copy (preview as of this writing) is an Azure-managed job that copies data between containers within the same account or across accounts. You configure it in the portal or via CLI, and it runs as a background job. It handles large datasets, doesn't consume your container's RUs (it uses dedicated copy throughput), and supports transforms during copy.

Change Feed processor — write a small application that reads the change feed from the source container and writes to the target container. This gives you complete control over the copy process, including the ability to transform documents during migration. The change feed examples from Chapter 8 give you the pattern.

Data export/import CLI — for the cocktail app, I built CLI commands that export documents to JSON files on disk (one file per document, organized by entity type subfolder) and import them back into a container. This is the brute-force approach but it works reliably for datasets that fit on disk. It's also handy for seeding test environments.

Bulk executor — the Cosmos SDK's bulk execution mode lets you write large batches of documents efficiently. Combine a change feed reader (or a file-based export) with bulk writes for a fast migration pipeline. The `Benday.CosmosDb` library's bulk operations include automatic throttling and retry logic.

The practical advice: For one-time migrations with datasets under a few GB, export-to-disk-and-reimport is the simplest and most debuggable approach. For larger datasets or ongoing sync, Container Copy or a change feed processor is the way to go. Always test the migration on a non-production copy first. Always verify document counts before and after.

Cross-reference: Chapter 8 (change feed), Chapter 12 (vector indexing requires container recreation).

Bulk Operations

The situation: You need to write a large number of documents — initial data import, batch updates, embedding generation — and doing them one at a time is painfully slow.

Enabling bulk mode:

```
var clientOptions = new CosmosClientOptions
{
    AllowBulkExecution = true
};

var client = new CosmosClient(
     endpoint, credential, clientOptions);
```

That `AllowBulkExecution = true` tells the SDK to batch multiple operations into grouped requests. Instead of sending 5,000 individual write requests, the SDK groups them into efficient batches and sends them in parallel.

The pattern:

```
var tasks = new List<Task>();

foreach (var recipe in recipes)
{
    tasks.Add(container.UpsertItemAsync(
        recipe,
        new PartitionKey(recipe.TenantId)));
```

```
}

await Task.WhenAll(tasks);
```

You kick off all the tasks without awaiting each one individually, then wait for them all at once. The SDK handles the batching, parallelism, and connection management.

Throttling and retries: Even with bulk mode, you can exceed your provisioned throughput and get HTTP 429 throttle responses. The SDK's built-in retry logic handles transient throttles automatically. For heavy bulk operations, consider temporarily scaling up your throughput (autoscale helps here) and scaling back down afterward.

The `Benday.CosmosDb` library approach: The library includes bulk operation helpers that add structured logging (via `ICosmosQueryLogSink`), configurable parallelism, and throttle-aware batching. This is what the cocktail app's batch embedding process uses — it generates embeddings for thousands of recipes and writes them back with the embedding vectors.

When to use bulk: Initial data loads, batch transformations (adding a new property to every document), re-embedding after a model change, migrating data between containers. Any time you're touching more than a few hundred documents in a single operation.

Cross-reference: Chapter 12 (batch embedding process).

Multi-Region Setup

The situation: Your users are globally distributed and you want low-latency reads (or writes) from multiple regions.

Read replicas are the simplest multi-region configuration. Your Cosmos account has a single write region, and you add one or more read regions. Cosmos replicates data to the read regions automatically. Your application connects to the nearest region for reads, and writes go to the primary region. This reduces read latency for users far from your write region.

Multi-region writes are more complex. Multiple regions accept writes, and Cosmos handles conflict resolution (last-writer-wins by default, or custom conflict resolution policies). This gives you low-latency writes everywhere, but you need to design for potential write conflicts.

The cost math: Every additional region roughly doubles your RU cost (you pay for throughput in each region). Two regions = 2x cost. Three regions = 3x cost. This adds up fast. Make sure the latency improvement justifies the expense. For many applications, a single region with the Dedicated Gateway cache is more cost-effective than adding a second region.

Failover: With multiple regions, Cosmos provides automatic failover. If the primary write region goes down, Cosmos promotes a read region to the new write region. You configure the failover priority in the portal. For single-region accounts, if the region goes down, your data is unavailable until the region recovers — there's no automatic failover.

When it's worth it: Genuinely global applications with users on multiple continents where latency matters. SLA requirements that demand multi-region redundancy. Applications where regional outages are unacceptable.

When it's not worth it: Most applications, honestly. If your users are primarily in one geography and you can tolerate occasional regional outages (which are rare), single-region is fine. The cost difference is significant.

Fleet Management (Multi-Tenancy Patterns)

The situation: You're building a multi-tenant application and you need to decide how to organize your Cosmos resources across tenants.

Three levels of isolation:

Shared container — all tenants share a single container, separated by partition key. This is what the cocktail app does: `tenantId` is the first level of the hierarchical partition key. Tenant A's data lives at partition `["TenantA", "CocktailRecipe"]`, Tenant B's at `["TenantB", "CocktailRecipe"]`. Maximum cost efficiency, minimum isolation. One noisy tenant's query load can consume throughput that other tenants need.

Container per tenant — each tenant gets their own container within a shared database. Better isolation (each container can have independent throughput), but more management overhead. Useful when tenants have meaningfully different throughput needs or when regulatory requirements demand logical separation. If you've written logic into your app to track individual customer RU usage and want to bill for that, this might also be an interesting option.

Account per tenant — maximum isolation. Each tenant gets a separate Cosmos DB account. Completely independent throughput, networking, backup, and access control. The highest management overhead and the most expensive, but sometimes required for compliance reasons (data residency, for example).

The practical default: Start with shared containers and partition key separation. It's the simplest, cheapest, and most operationally lightweight approach. The `Benday.CosmosDb` library's `TenantItemBase` and hierarchical partition key pattern (`/tenantId,/entityType`) is designed for exactly this scenario. Move to container-per-tenant or account-per-tenant only when you have a specific isolation requirement that shared containers can't meet.

Cross-reference: Chapter 6 (partition keys and tenancy), Chapter 10 (multi-tenant cocktail app design).

Vector Embedding and Indexing Policies

The situation: You want to add vector search to a container and you need to know what to configure.

Two pieces to set up: Vector search requires both a *vector embedding policy* (which tells Cosmos the shape of your embedding data) and a *vector index* in your indexing policy (which tells Cosmos how to index it for similarity queries).

The configuration (for reference):

Vector embedding policy on the container:

```
{
    "vectorEmbeddingPolicy": {
        "vectorEmbeddings": [
            {
                "path": "/embedding",
                "dataType": "float32",
                "distanceFunction": "cosine",
                "dimensions": 1536
            }
        ]
```

```
    }
}
```

Vector index in the indexing policy:

```
{
    "vectorIndexes": [
        {
            "path": "/embedding",
            "type": "diskANN"
        }
    ]
}
```

Exclude the embedding path from your regular indexing policy. This one's easy to miss. A 1,536-float array indexed with range indexes wastes RUs on every write and provides zero query benefit — you never query embeddings with range operators. That's what the vector index is for.

Cross-reference: Chapter 12 (full vector search setup), Appendix A (VectorDistance queries).

Resource Visualizer

The situation: You're looking at the Azure portal and you want a quick picture of what's in your Cosmos DB account — how many databases, how many containers, what throughput is configured where.

Where to find it: In the portal, go to your Cosmos DB account → Resource Visualizer (under the Overview section in the left nav). It shows a tree view of your account hierarchy: account → databases → containers, with throughput information at each level.

Why it's useful: When you're working with an account that has multiple databases and containers — especially if some containers share database-level throughput and others have dedicated throughput — the Resource Visualizer gives you a single-screen overview. It's also useful for quickly confirming that a container you just created actually exists where you expected it.

What it doesn't do: It doesn't show document counts, storage utilization, or query performance. For those, use the Metrics blade or the individual container's Scale & Settings pane.

That's the operations reference. Between this and Appendix A, you've got a reference shelf you can come back to whenever Cosmos throws something at you that you haven't seen before — or that you've seen before and can't quite remember how you handled it last time.

These two appendices wrap up *Azure Cosmos DB for .NET Developers*. Thanks for reading. If any of this helped you ship something, I'd love to hear about it. Oh...and if you'd like to hire me to help you out on a project or to speak at an event or you just want to hang out, drop me a line at info@benday.com.

That's all, folks.

-Ben

www.ingramcontent.com/pod-product-compliance
Lightning Source LLC
LaVergne TN
LVHW060029210926
848481LV00013B/3819